Hidden Value

Hidden Value

*How Great Companies
Achieve Extraordinary Results
with Ordinary People*

Charles A. O'Reilly III
Jeffrey Pfeffer

HARVARD BUSINESS SCHOOL PRESS
BOSTON, MASSACHUSETTS

08   07   06   05   10   9   8   7

Library of Congress Cataloging-in-Publication Data

O'Reilly, Charles A.
  Hidden value : how great companies achieve extraordinary results with ordinary people / Charles A. O'Reilly III, Jeffrey Pfeffer.
    p. cm.
  Includes index.
  ISBN 0-87584-898-2 (alk. paper)
    1. Industrial management—United States—Case studies.
2. Human capital—United States—Case studies.   I. Pfeffer, Jeffrey.
II. Title.

HD70.U5 O69 2000
658—dc21   00-025016

Excerpts from Stanford University case studies reprinted with permission of Stanford University, Graduate School of Business, copyright © 1995, 1997, 1998, 1999 by the Board of Trustees of the Leland Stanford Junior University. Excerpts from "Organizing for Empowerment: An Interview with AES's Roger Sant and Dennis Bakke" by Suzy Wetlaufer, January–February 1999, are reprinted by permission of *Harvard Business Review.* Copyright © 1999 by the President and Fellows of Harvard College, all rights reserved.

Excerpts from *No Excuses Management* by T. J. Rodgers, William Taylor, and Rick Foreman, copyright © 1993 by T. J. Rodgers, William Taylor, and Rick Foreman, used by permission of Doubleday, a division of Random House, Inc.

Copies of *Nuts! Southwest Airlines' Crazy Recipe for Business and Personal Success,* © 1996 by Kevin and Jackie Freiberg, may be ordered by calling PSI Fulfillment at 1-800-945-3132.

Contents

Preface

THERE IS a story behind this book. For the past twenty-five years each of us has been trying to understand why some organizations invariably succeed at energizing their employees and are able to thereby enhance profitability and survival whereas others fail to tap the potential of their people, often to the detriment of the organization's long-term financial performance. Over time, we have seen many examples of companies that were better and worse in tapping the potential of their people. We have chosen to tell you the stories of eight remarkable companies that stand out in how they manage to engage the emotional and intellectual resources of their people. There are, of course, other companies that do similar things that could be included in a book such as this. We do not maintain that these eight companies are necessarily the "best" at unlocking the hidden value in their workforce, or that each will be successful forever. As with all organizations, circumstances can change: new technologies can emerge that make strategies and core capabilities less useful; financial markets can shift; managers can make mistakes; or competitors can improve. These changes can undermine any organization, no matter how successful. But, for the present, each of the firms we describe is a great exemplar whose practices illustrate how companies can realize the full potential of their people. Whether they are still successful ten years from now is, for us, not the issue. Today, these companies collectively offer a clear window into understanding how great companies achieve extraordinary results with ordinary people.

Another part of the story behind this book is how it was written and organized. Over the years as we have talked to people and taught them, both in degree programs and executive seminars, we noticed a curious fact about how managers learn—a fact that runs counter to how most management books are written. What we observed was that managers seem to learn best when they are provided with rich descriptions of how other managers and organizations operate, rather than the simplified, predigested "lessons" that are conveyed in most management books. Initially, this recognition seemed counter-intuitive because it didn't fit with traditional approaches to management education.

Think for a moment about the last few management books you've read or skimmed. Chances are that the book was structured in the following general format. First, the authors propose some "bold, new idea" that they assert can help you to be a better manager and your company to prevail against the competition. This idea—for instance, re-engineering, fast cycle time, the war for talent, continuous innovation, or the lessons of a leading corporate chieftain—is initially illustrated by several engaging vignettes, often contrasting how some manager or firm "got it" and others didn't. Having set up the new idea, most authors then walk the reader through a series of chapters illustrating the blueprint for how you as a reader can emulate the big idea in your organization. Each chapter, if it is well done, describes a set of easy-to-follow steps that can be taken to capture the benefits from the author's insights. Indeed, a common benchmark of success used by book publishers in deciding whether to publish a book formalizes this tactic: Does the book have a single good idea?

So, what's wrong with this approach? For conveying new knowledge, this can in fact be a highly efficient way of delivering material. It is the way we were taught in school, whether K–12, college, or most graduate business programs. The logic is impeccable. A "teacher" with special insight or knowledge predigests and summarizes complicated facts and concepts for passive "learners" who are then assumed to be able to apply these lessons in their own lives. Although this approach is reasonable in concept, it is frequently not useful in application. It is akin to providing a person with serious psychological problems the latest textbook on clinical psychology and assuming that reading the book will enable the person to understand and solve his or her problems. As individuals, and especially as managers, this is not how we learn best.

Research shows we learn best by watching and listening to others facing diverse situations and then trying to apply the insights to our own experience. We learn particularly well when we are given the opportunity to confront disconfirming evidence, problems, and challenges to our conventional way of thinking. Being given the "right" answer is helpful only insofar as it provides a benchmark against which we can calibrate our own efforts and insights. After trying out a new approach or technique, it is useful to be able to compare our results with those of someone more skilled or successful. But real learning results not from knowing how well the expert did but from our ability to compare what they did to our own actions and to use this information to guide our future behavior. In this sense, learning is enhanced by figuring things out for ourselves and by doing rather than by simply reading descriptions of how experts proceed or listening to them give us their distilled wisdom.

The recognition that most of us learn through a combination of watching those who are better than we are and figuring out how we can apply these lessons in our own environment was deepened when we thought about how most effective executive education occurs: not through lectures by professors or other experts but through engaged discussions of examples, typically in the form of a case, in which the interactions among the participants generates a variety of possibilities and perspectives. It is through the individual's engagement in this discussion that he or she is able to really gain useful insights that are relevant to his or her unique circumstances. Said differently, simply listening to an expert describe what you should do or how you should manage is unlikely to provide much of lasting benefit. Mark Twain, a great social scientist, observed that a man who chooses to carry a cat home by the tail learns at least ten times as much as someone who only watches.

How have these insights about learning guided the development and writing of this book? In several ways. First, rather than beginning by telling you our "answer," we invite you to help us solve a mystery we confronted as we went about our research attempting to understand why some firms did so well whereas others didn't. Specifically, we invite you to read about a set of remarkable firms that, in our view, have succeeded at tapping the potential of all of their employees. These firms have accomplished this, often in highly competitive industries, by violating conventional wisdom and doing things that, on the surface, seem to make little sense—at least according to much of current management theory.

Second, in describing these companies, we provide you with a rich, detailed portrait of how these firms actually operate as well as information about their industry and history. These descriptions give you sufficient information to decide for yourself what it is that these companies are doing, or not doing, that makes them successful. We believe that many books fail to enhance strategic thinking capabilities because they describe individual concepts or recommendations without providing a good picture of the context that gives each concept its real meaning and impact. We have tried to present material so you can see and learn for yourself what makes these companies work. Of course we have our own opinions and provide these at the end of each chapter, but what is most important is not whether you agree with us but what lessons you can abstract that you can use in your own organization. This is the real test of the usefulness of any learning: not whether you get the answer the authors put in the book, but whether you can apply the material yourself.

Each of the companies we describe operates in a different industry, but each is successful in a similar way. Therefore, in addition to any specific insights from each of these companies, there is a larger lesson we hope you will think about. We call this the *Anna Karenina* principle of management. Tolstoy's famous first sentence of this novel begins, "Happy families are all alike; every unhappy family is unhappy in its own way." Tolstoy's meaning was that in order to be happy, a marriage must succeed in many different respects, such as sexual attraction and agreement about money, child rearing, religion, in-laws, and other important issues that characterize long-term relationships. Failure in any respect can doom a marriage even if it has all of the other ingredients for happiness. So it is with organizations. To succeed, all organizations must have a combination of ingredients, all of which work together or are in alignment. To fail, only one of these ingredients needs to be missing or misaligned. We believe this is true of the organizations you will read about. All are different, yet all are also successful in the same way. We believe that this insight lies at the heart of the mystery of their successes.

We invite you to solve this mystery and to figure out how the companies we describe are similar even as they are different. To do this requires you to solve the puzzle for yourself. We think that in doing this, in reading about how each of these remarkable firms operates, you will engage the material in a way that will help you borrow ideas that you can actually use in your own organization. In this sense, whether you agree with our interpretation is largely irrelevant, for having carried the proverbial cat home by the tail, we have little doubt that you will have learned lessons far more useful than any we can convey.

ORGANIZATION OF THE BOOK

There are important and useful lessons to be learned from all of the companies we describe. There is also a logic to how we have organized these stories. We begin by briefly showing how much of conventional management wisdom is wrong or misleading—including why most of the excuses for not doing what we describe are also wrong. We then begin our set of mysteries by describing two very different firms that have successfully tapped the hidden value in their workforces: Southwest Airlines and Cisco Systems. Although worlds apart in terms of industries, each of these companies has found a unique way of linking its values, strategy, and practices in ways that provide for a competitive advantage that its competitors have been unable to replicate. These two chapters illustrate the importance of linking values to business strategy and management practices. These stories set the stage for a more careful exploration of the specific techniques used to align employee and company values.

The next three chapters offer you an in-depth look at how three companies have devised ways to tap into the energy and talents of their workforces. Each of these stories challenges the conventional wisdom about employee development, compensation, and control. These examples should make clear that not following the herd can be a path to success. Chapter 4 describes how The Men's Wearhouse has been able to grow in a declining market by investing in people. As you read this chapter, you might ask yourself why this company has been able to leverage its workforce whereas its competitors have not. The next chapter should challenge your beliefs about compensation and incentives in organizations. The SAS Institute breaks all of the rules for paying people in the software industry, such as the need for stock options and lots of individual incentive pay—and prospers. How can it get away with this? The sixth chapter recounts the growth of a company in the medical supply distribution business, PSS World Medical, to over a billion dollars in sales in only fifteen years. The founder and CEO, Pat Kelly, has accomplished this through acquisitions—an approach that for most firms seems fraught with difficulties and failure—and through a willingness to share all financial and operational information with all his employees. Why doesn't this give his competitors an easy way to attack him?

The next two chapters illustrate how two companies have put all of the pieces together to drive success in a way that most observers would say could never be done. Chapter 7 describes how AES, an independent producer of electric power, has learned how to operate power plants all around the world with basically no corporate staff and a total reliance on team-based management. Chapter 8 recounts the history of one of the most productive plants in the automobile industry, New United Motors Manufacturing, Inc. (NUMMI)—a plant that was once one of the worst plants in the General Motors system. How this plant was turned around and how it continues to operate successfully is one of the biggest mysteries that we challenge you to solve. Together, these two examples really show the power and promise of unleashing the hidden value in a company, even if these are the same employees who were mediocre performers under a traditional management system.

The final mystery, recounted in chapter 9, is the most challenging of all. Cypress Semiconductor is in its own way a success story. It has successfully competed against much larger competitors in the brutal business of semiconductor manufacturing. But Cypress is only a qualified success. Although it does many of the things described in the earlier accounts, it has not achieved the breakthrough success of the other companies featured in this book. Your challenge (sort of a final exam) is to figure out why this is so. Given that Cypress does so many of the right things, why isn't it as successful? What's missing? If you can understand this, you'll be ready to apply the lessons learned to tapping the hidden value in your own organization's workforce.

Having read about this remarkable set of companies, many readers may still remain skeptical. They will offer two fundamental objections for why the approaches used by the set of companies described in this book are either misleading or can never work in their own firms. We take these concerns seriously and in the last chapter offer a set of reasons why both these objections are likely to be wrong. We then invite you to compare your explanations to our own opinions for why these firms are successful. In doing this, we make no claim to have the ultimate answer, only a set of conclusions that we have reached after having studied these companies and talked to many smart managers about them.

We have a strong belief in what constitutes a "good idea" for a reader to have gleaned from reading books such as this one. For us, a "good idea" is not necessarily coming to the same conclusion as the author, or even being convinced that the author is correct. For us a "good idea" is more pragmatic: It is an idea that the reader can remember and actually apply in his or her own company. We hope you will apply this test as you read the following chapters. There are a large number of "good ideas" to be had in learning about these remarkable companies. So, put your detective hat on and see if you can solve the mysteries we have set out for you.

Acknowledgments

BEFORE ANY BOOK reaches a reader like yourself, three major things have to happen. First, the ideas expressed in the book have to be developed and refined until they are logical and useful. This means the authors must prevail upon their friends and colleagues, and sometimes even strangers, for their suggestions and feedback. Second, these ideas have to be written, clarified, critiqued, and rewritten until they become clear and understandable to the reader. Again, this means presuming on the help of friends and colleagues, many of whom may already be tired of the authors' obsessions. Finally, the manuscript has to be made into a book. A new set of people—editors and readers—once again give of their time and energy to help focus and polish the thinking and writing. In the end, the authors' names go on the final published product, but the book is really a collaborative effort reflecting the contributions of all the people who helped at each of the three stages. In this sense, the book that you are about to read (or skim, if you are like most of us) is really the product of many people who, although they are not listed as "authors," were an integral part of the creative process. They deserve credit for their contributions and we want to thank them.

The ideas for this book are less ours than those of a remarkable group of people who, rather than writing about management, actually went out and did it. Some of them founded and built the organizations we describe in the book. Others have continued the traditions of the founders and improved on the original concepts and designs. In doing this, these leaders often had to flaunt conventional wisdom and, instead, follow their own beliefs about what was right—even though experts from academia and Wall Street often claimed that they were wrong-headed or crazy. Although we tell their stories and explain why we believe what they are doing makes them successful, it is the people in these organizations who deserve the credit. We thank all of them, especially the founders and the senior managers of the organizations who carry on their values. We are particularly grateful to Herb Kelleher and Colleen Barrett at Southwest Airlines, John Chambers and John Morgridge at Cisco Systems, George Zimmer and Charlie Bresler at The Men's Wearhouse, Jim Goodnight and David Russo at SAS Institute, Pat Kelly and John Sasen at PSS World Medical, Dennis Bakke and Roger Sant at AES, Gary Convis and Jamie Hresko at NUMMI, and T. J. Rodgers at Cypress Semiconductor.

We also thank the many people in these organizations who shared their own experiences and taught us how these firms live their values. It is impossible to thank all the many people whose ideas found their way into the book, but several were especially generous with their insights and their time. We are particularly grateful to Ann Rhoades and Libby Sartain at Southwest; Beau Parnell, John Radford, and Barbara Beck at Cisco; Betty Fried, Barrett Joyner, and Gail Adcock at SAS Institute; Paul Burdick, Barry Sharp, Sarah Slusser, John Ruggirello, and the people at the Thames plant at AES; Eric Lane at The Men's Wearhouse; Charlie Alvarez, Susan Parker, Greg Griffing, and Eric Miller at PSS; and Joyce Sziebert at Cypress. It was largely through their efforts that this book happened.

In developing our ideas, we have also enjoyed the wisdom and feedback of many other people who participated in executive education programs and MBA classes at which we discussed early versions of the book. We thank all of them, particularly those in Stanford's Human Resources Executive Program and Human Resource MBA courses. Although they may not have always agreed with what we proposed, they always challenged us to think more deeply and make our arguments sharper. We also owe a debt of gratitude to our academic colleagues in the Human Resources Initiative at Stanford who have helped shape how we understand the companies we describe. Jim Baron, David Kreps, Bob Flanagan, and Eddie Lazear have enriched how we think about the importance of people in organizations. Dave Caldwell at Santa Clara University has been a long-term friend and coauthor and was instrumental in helping us study Cypress Semiconductor. Diane Burton at the Harvard Business School, who co-taught with Charles at HBS, also aided our understanding of how people-centered organizations work. Guido Spichty at Novartis has always been a champion of the ideas in this book. In our interactions with these friends and colleagues we always came away with greater clarity and insight than we began. They taught with us, but they also taught us. We thank them.

In writing the various drafts of the book, several people provided invaluable comments that made the chapters more useful and more readable. We thank the five almost anonymous reviewers for Harvard Business School Press who provided suggestions for how to improve both the content and style of the writing, including Mark Huselid and Diane Burton. Beth Benjamin provided detailed suggestions that helped us sharpen our presentation and focus the material. Finally, we thank Marjorie Williams, our editor at the Harvard Business School Press, who made the manuscript into a book.

As many of the companies we describe in the book illustrate, if work is to be fulfilling, it must also be fun. We have certainly had fun writing this book. We first met in 1973, and this book is just another collaboration between friends who like and respect each other. And, as some of the companies described here emphasize, work is not all there is to life—there is also family. This book is dedicated to the two people in our lives who make everything we do so enjoyable: Ulrike and Kathleen.

Dream...Create...Excel

Hibiscus Books
www.hibiscusbooks.com

Chapter 1

The "Right" People
or the "Right" Organization?

WHAT'S THE MOST important factor for success in today's knowledge-based economy—at least according to some in the media and many consultants? Attracting and retaining great people! McKinsey & Company, the large global consulting company, has dubbed this "the war for talent." The company maintains that "superior talent will be tomorrow's prime source of competitive advantage."[1] "In the new economy, competition is global, capital is abundant, ideas are developed quickly and cheaply, and people are willing to change jobs often. In that kind of environment all that matters is talent. Talent wins."[2] This realization has led to more emphasis on selection—there are now lots of books about hiring right[3]—more emphasis on effective recruiting, such as using the Internet to generate more applicants, and more emphasis on retention, for instance, through higher pay and better working conditions and benefits.

At first glance, the logic seems compelling. We do live in a world in which knowledge, rather than physical capital, is increasingly important. Therefore, we need smart people who can do great things—increase productivity, build new products and services—and do so ever more quickly. Consequently, we need great people. It all seems so sensible.

But we don't agree with the basic premise. Of course, companies that want to succeed need great people, and recruitment, selection, and retention are obviously important. But companies need something else that is even more important and often more difficult to obtain: cultures and systems in which these great people can actually *use* their talents, and, even better, management practices that produce extraordinary results from almost everybody. The unfortunate mathematical fact is that only 10 percent of the people are going to be in the top 10 percent. So, companies have a choice. They can all chase the same supposed talent. Or, they can do something even more useful and much more difficult to copy—build an organization that helps make it possible for regular folks to perform as if they were in the top 10 percent.

You don't think this is possible? Certainly you have worked at, or at least seen, companies that are filled with smart, motivated, hardworking, decent people who nevertheless don't perform very well because the company doesn't let them shine and doesn't really capitalize on their talent and motivation. Maybe you have even worked at such a place yourself and could describe, in agonizing detail, all the myriad things that happened that prevented you and your colleagues from doing your best for the business. What could those places accomplish if they just stopped undermining the performance of their people? And you have, we're sure, seen other places where somehow things just hum, even though the people don't, at first glance, seem to be particularly smarter, nicer, or harder working. Maybe you've even seen companies that have gone from being the first kind of place, where talent is wasted, to the second, where the potential of the company and its people is more fully realized. (You'll see such a company, NUMMI, later in this book.) Hiring and retaining talent is great. Building a company that *creates* and *uses* talent is even better.

This book is about building a high-performance company. But it is also a series of mystery stories—mysteries that we invite you to help us solve. In the chapters that follow, we describe some companies that have succeeded even though they have not followed conventional strategic wisdom for their industries and even though they have faced difficult, challenging, competitive conditions. Here's the mystery: They achieved this extraordinary level of success with people who really aren't that much different or smarter than those working for the competition. These companies have won the war for talent not just by being great places to work—although they are that—but by figuring out how to get the best out of all of their people, every day. In a sense, they haven't outrecruited other companies—they've left the competition in the dust by being better at unleashing the energy and talent of the people they have. And by the way, these places are also better at attracting and retaining people as a byproduct of how they operate. That is because great people want to work at places where they can actually use their talents, where they are treated with dignity, trust, and respect, and where they are engaged by the values and culture of the organization.

What makes this a particularly interesting mystery is *how* these companies have done this. As you will see, the secret to their success is at once both obvious and puzzling. Each of these companies has succeeded by engaging the knowledge, experience, skills, and energy of their people. In this sense, *what* they are doing is understandable. In a world in which there is a war for talent and in which knowledge work is increasingly important, being able to attract, retain, and energize people seems like an obvious recipe for success. But, like many mysteries, the issue isn't whodunit but uncovering *how* they did it. This is what we invite you to understand—how these firms have outwitted sometimes larger and more powerful competitors in ways that their competition has been unable to imitate. These firms have redefined the competitive landscape in their markets using methods that are as powerful as they are difficult for many managers to understand and use. We hope that in solving these mysteries, you will see and, more important, understand how it is possible to achieve extraordinary results with ordinary people—to unlock the value hidden in *all* organizations and in *all* people.

How unusual are these companies? Consider the following.

- **Southwest Airlines** is a well-known success story. The press is full of accounts about how Southwest has vanquished larger competitors such as United and Continental in short-haul markets and is currently fighting Delta and USAir's MetroJet division. In a cutthroat business in which all the competitors know their strategy and costs down to the penny, Southwest has succeeded not through clever strategic moves and sophisticated technology but by the painfully obvious method of leveraging the company's people for competitive advantage. CEO Herb Kelleher is characteristically blunt when he says:

What keeps me awake at night are the intangibles. It's the intangibles that are the hardest thing for a competitor to imitate, so my biggest concern is that . . . we lose the esprit de corps, the culture, the spirit. If we ever do lose that, we will have lost our most valuable competitive asset.[4]

- **Cisco Systems** is a $12 billion high-tech success story, achieving a market capitalization of more than $100 billion in twelve years, something that took Microsoft twenty years to reach. But its real success is not in the technology it uses, for it has no "technology religion," but in how it manages its 26,000 employees. Although the average Silicon Valley company has an employee turnover rate of close to 30 percent, Cisco is at 8 percent. In an industry in which the average product life cycle approximates that of the fruit fly, Cisco's abilities to retain people, control costs, manage hypergrowth, and change on a dime are key to its success. Cisco has kept up technologically by buying smaller companies with leading-edge ideas. But when you buy a company for its know-how, that intellectual capital can (and often does) walk out the door. In a world in which most acquisitions fail to provide any value, Cisco has mastered the art of not only doing deals but making the deals work after they close. How has the company accomplished this? CEO John Chambers credits a culture that values frugality, listening to the customer, teamwork, and embracing change:

    The key to success is having a culture with the discipline to accept change and not fight religious wars. . . . I did five layoffs totaling 5,000 people. It nearly killed me. I vowed never to do that again to employees or shareholders. . . . I learned a long time ago that in team sports or in business, a group working together can always defeat a team of individuals. Even if the individuals, by themselves, are each better than your team. . . . If you're going to empower people and you don't have teamwork, you're dead.[5]

- **The Men's Wearhouse** is the nation's leading retailer of off-price tailored men's clothing, with sales over a billion dollars in 1999. This is a tough, low-margin business in a slow-growth or even declining industry where increased sales come from taking market share away from competitors. George

Zimmer, the founder and CEO, has grown the company to more than 430 stores and 6,000 employees by emphasizing service, teamwork, empathy, and positive attitudes. Unlike its competitors in retailing, the company invests heavily in its people, offering extensive training, free substance-abuse programs, and sabbaticals. Zimmer, a child of the 1960s, believes:

> Most business practices repress our natural tendency to have fun and socialize. The idea seems to be that in order to succeed, you have to suffer. . . . I believe an organization that is authentically built on servant leadership, where people are not just trying to acquire for themselves and where they see cooperative effort that is all around them, ends up affecting things in very metaphysical ways. When people feel connected to something with a purpose greater than themselves, it inspires people to reach for levels they might otherwise not obtain. . . . Our business is based on human potential.[6]

- **SAS Institute** is a $1 billion privately held software company that has been described as "the world's sanest company."[7] In a business noted for long hours, little company loyalty, high turnover, and outrageous pay packages, SAS emphasizes thirty-five-hour work weeks, provides on-site day care and health care free of charge, has its own high school for children of the employees and from the community, and has a turnover rate of less than 4 percent. What SAS does not have is strategic planning, hierarchy, or even stock options. In founding the company, Jim Goodnight, the CEO, believed in treating employees the way he wants to be treated. Says David Russo, formerly vice president of human resources, who was with the company almost from the beginning:

> To some people, this looks like the Good Ship Lollipop, floating down a stream. It's not. It's part of a soundly designed strategy. . . . Jim's idea is that if you hire adults and treat them like adults, then they'll behave like adults.[8]

CEO Goodnight's financial strategy is "just to take in more money than we spend."[9]

- **PSS World Medical** is a distributor of medical supplies that in fifteen years has grown to almost $2 billion dollars in revenues and 4,500 employees. It has done this by explicitly avoiding policy manuals and memos, opening the books to all employees, and allowing employees to "fire" their bosses. CEO Patrick Kelly claims:

  > Business people don't like to talk about values. But without these, all business is about is making money. . . . To me, achieving business goals is great. But no business goal is worth sacrificing your values. If you have to treat people poorly, or cut corners in your dealings with customers, forget it. . . . You *can* build an organization based on mutual loyalty, even in today's economy. But you can't do it if you treat people as disposable.[10]

- **AES** is a radically decentralized power generation company operating more than 100 plants in nineteen countries. All plants, from Kazakhstan to Argentina to Pakistan, are run by teams. AES has more than 10,000 employees and operates with a headquarters staff of fewer than 30 people—all this in a highly regulated industry in which bureaucracy flourishes in most companies. With a view that shocks Wall Street and many business school faculty, CEO Dennis Bakke says:

  > My own choice for the reason corporations do and should exist—their ultimate purpose—is to steward resources to meet the needs of the world. . . . Don't get me wrong. Profits are an important aspect of a successful business. They provide compensation to shareholders for their equity capital, as well as provide an objective measurement of a company's ability to steward its resources. . . . This is an integral part of any successful business, but it is not the primary reason a business exists.[11]

- **New United Motor Manufacturing, Inc.** (NUMMI) is the Toyota–General Motors joint venture located in Fremont, California. In 1982, GM closed its assembly plant in Fremont. In 1984, the plant was reopened under Toyota leadership. More than 85 percent of the new GM consisted of the old GM employees, they used the same equipment, and the plant was still organized by the United Automobile Workers' Union. Today, NUMMI is one of the most efficient automotive assemblers in the United States and has won J.D. Power quality awards. Under the old system, absenteeism averaged almost 20 percent and the union filed more than 5,000 grievances per three-year labor contract. Today, with the same union, there is labor-management harmony and absenteeism is around 3 percent, even as the rest of GM struggles with high costs and sour union-management relations. This remarkable transformation was not one of technology but of values, culture, and the unleashing of the power of the workforce. Tatsuro Toyoda explains:

> The emphasis in Fremont is not on technology. Not on robots. Our emphasis is on people. People working together to accomplish common goals. That is the basis of New United Motors. . . . At NUMMI our success, or our failure, as a company will depend upon people, our team members.[12]

How these companies have achieved what they have is the mystery that needs to be solved by those who seek to emulate them. At a superficial level, the answer is easy: Each of these organizations is based on a set of values that energize their people and unleash the intellectual capital potentially available in all organizations. As Phil Jackson, the very successful basketball coach (at one point he coached the Chicago Bulls), has stated, "[T]he most effective way to forge a winning team is to call on the players' needs to connect with something larger than themselves."[13] But an answer at this level of detail is not particularly helpful. Telling a manager that he or she should tap the intellectual capital of the workforce by promulgating energizing values is akin to telling a parachutist whose chute has failed that birds fly by flapping their wings. Although true, it isn't helpful because it doesn't provide enough specifics to answer the question of *how*. The companies we describe in this book have figuratively learned to fly. This book gives you enough information about the management practices of each company so that you can answer the question of how and then use these insights in your own company.

The firms that we describe have turned the typical logic of strategic management on its head. Instead of beginning with a business strategy, aligning the organization with this strategy, and hiring people to fit the organization, they have begun by being absolutely clear about their values and how these values will define their organizations and determine how they run. As the quotes given earlier from these companies' leaders suggest, values come first. Only then do the companies ensure that the strategy is consistent with people's values. This logic violates the "business first" mentality so common in today's organizations. But by doing things this way, these companies have been able to align the company's purpose with the spirit of their employees, capturing their emotional as well as intellectual energies. This is a far cry from the "me generation" or "virtual organization" celebrated and lamented so often in the business press. These companies don't believe that loyalty is dead, that the war for talent has mostly losers, and that labor markets are essentially spot markets for economic transactions. These organizations offer their employees more than a job: They offer a sense of community, security, and mutual trust and respect.

As you will see, as out of favor as these concepts are, they are at the heart of what it means to unlock the value hidden in organizations. Moreover, this "hidden value" is not scarce or unique, but rather can be found in all companies. It resides in the intellectual and emotional capital of the firm and is in the power of the minds and hearts of its people. Although the organizations we describe have used this potential to achieve great success, most companies squander this resource even as they bemoan its scarcity.

WHY POPULAR MANAGEMENT FADS FAIL TO PROVIDE COMPETITIVE ADVANTAGE THAT LASTS

Why is there so much current interest in the war for talent? There seem to be several explanations. First, a number of observers, including the consulting firms McKinsey and Watson Wyatt, have noted that in the United States the coming demographic reality is that the relative size of the workforce in their so-called prime career years (aged thirty-five to forty-five) will be smaller: "In 15 years, there will be 15% fewer Americans in the 35- to 45-year-old range than there are now. That sets the stage for a talent war."[14] Although the demographic facts are unassailable, the implications that have been drawn for individual companies don't necessarily follow. Unless you are planning to employ a significant fraction of the U.S. labor force, labor market trends at the macro level may have relatively little impact on your company, just as sales growth trends at the industry level have little ability to predict an individual company's growth prospects.[15] There is already enormous variation in the ability of companies to attract, retain, and deploy talent. Companies need to be better at these tasks regardless of the size of the nation's workforce. Those companies that have developed positive and constructive, as opposed to toxic, workplaces won't ever notice a talent drought because they currently enjoy, and will continue to enjoy, a surfeit of applicants and loyal employees.

Second, there is so much attention to "talent" because of the striking obsession, particularly in the United States, with the importance of individual (as contrasted with organizational or collective) ability and motivation. The classic formulation in industrial psychology is that performance is a consequence of ability times motivation.[16] Not only is this inadequate to explain individual performance, it is much too simplistic for organizations, where performance is also a consequence of the environment in which individuals work and how they work together. Even in sports, this simple-minded dictum of the importance of individual talent fails. All-star teams often lose to teams of people who have played together and learned to work effectively *as a team*. Sports teams comprising the best individual talent do not always triumph over teams that have complementary skills and a system that brings out their collective best. This fact—that context and environment, not just individual attributes, matter—is even more relevant for companies, where performance is a consequence of the interdependent interactions of many individuals as they jointly produce products and services. In our view, the emphasis on hiring individual stars is another fad that will pass as companies realize that their success depends on what they do with and to their talent, not just on acquiring it.

Why is it that the history of business is one of fads and fashions, with the war for talent being just the latest? The past twenty years have been marked by a succession of miracle cures, beginning with *In Search of Excellence* and the famous eight characteristics claimed to describe the most successful U.S. companies and proceeding through Theory Z, Total Quality Management, empowerment and self-managed teams, re-engineering, globalization and boundaryless organizations, core competencies, customer intimacy, visionary management, open book management, EVA (economic value added), the balanced scorecard, and a host of other management concepts—including the occasional acknowledgment by a repentant author or consultant that the previous advice was wrong. A recent survey by a major consulting firm showed that the average big company had adopted over a dozen of twenty-five current management techniques. That's not to say that these various concepts were incorrect or that they didn't focus management attention on important issues. It's just that few of them provided the long-term, long-lasting benefits companies sought.

It would be wrong to blame managers for this pattern. As a group, leaders are not enamored of fads or easily sold on new fashions. What drives managers to grasp for new solutions is a deadly serious need on their part: the need to find ways that will enable their organizations to survive and prosper in an increasingly competitive world. Leaders understand too well how many organizations, even those that have been successful in the past, can eventually fail.[17] Their search is for ways to gain an edge over their competitors—preferably an edge that will last a while. Unfortunately, as readers of business books know, these new approaches, although well intentioned and occasionally helpful, almost always fail to provide organizations with a *sustainable* competitive advantage.

A moment's reflection will suggest why these "new" approaches seldom provide an enduring edge. If your competitors can readily adopt the same approaches, how can there be any long-term competitive advantage? Think about it. If the same consulting firm that helps one organization implement the hottest new approach then goes to a competitor and implements it there (except they may do it better because they learned a thing or two while helping the first client), how can this offer any real advantage? This leads to a predictable pattern: Each management technique, having been adopted by the competition, is simply replaced by a new one, with consulting firms and management gurus vying to be first with the new wave.

What makes these organizational innovations so easy to imitate? Ironically, the same things that make them so intellectually appealing. They are often based on readily understood conceptual frameworks that can be presented on a set of overheads or slides. They frequently have some catchy new terminology associated with them, such as re-engineering, the learning organization, the seven S framework, or the five forces. They often have checklists of things to do. They are, in a word, easily understood. If they weren't easily grasped, then they wouldn't generate consulting business. If they couldn't be graphically presented, they couldn't form the basis for the seminars and books that are the consultants' chief marketing tools. And most important, if they couldn't be readily taught and transmitted, the firms couldn't turn over the execution of those ideas to newly minted graduates, thereby leveraging the ideas into a revenue stream.

Another problem exists. The techniques are seldom presented in a way that makes doing them seem very difficult. Unfortunately, the key to success isn't in simply *knowing* something but in implementing it.[18] "When you think about it, most executives regard getting their workforces to carry out their plans as the most challenging part of enacting strategy. This is because they don't know how to do it."[19] Most fads ignore the boring, mundane details of implementation, but these are the key to actually doing something that others can't easily imitate. In today's world, executives "are more knowledgeable and confident spending money or cutting costs, adding technology or buying a new product line" than they are aligning management practices so that innovation, implementation, and the use of knowledge actually happen.[20] Anyone can learn the theory of golf and what a golf swing should be. Actually implementing a golf swing so that the ball travels a long distance in the desired direction is something much more difficult to accomplish and much more difficult to imitate.

Therefore, *what* the successful companies that we describe do is common sense and conceptually easy to comprehend. However, *how* they execute what they do is what makes these companies successful and is why so many firms fail when trying to copy them. This is why even managers who know what they should do seldom are able to do it. But when organizations are able to *implement*, not just discuss, these approaches, the results are simply amazing, as you will see.

So, what is the secret? The answer is not just in how these firms manage their people, but in the importance of their values and the *alignment* they achieve between their values, strategies, and their people. It sounds too simple. How can companies in industries as disparate as airlines, automobile manufacturing, medical supply distribution, power generation, retailing tailored men's clothing, and computers use the same approach to achieve sustainable competitive advantage? How can something as simple as alignment be the key to the success of businesses that range from high tech to no tech, and from products to services? One answer is that alignment isn't so simple. Aligning values, strategies, and management practices may be simple to understand and simple to talk about, but it is very difficult to actually implement. Another answer is found as we consider how an emphasis on values and alignment builds capabilities that permit companies to redefine the competitive dynamics in their industries.

A VALUES-BASED APPROACH TO DEVELOPING AND IMPLEMENTING STRATEGY

Step back for a moment and think about how strategy is approached in most organizations. The standard approach as adopted by most consulting firms and taught in business schools is based on the following logic (see figure 1-1). First, senior managers decide what business the firm is in, choosing the products, markets, and geographies in which the firm will operate. Second, this group decides how to position the company against the competition, determining how the firm will compete and develop a value proposition for the customer—first mover, low cost, service, quality, innovative technology, and so forth. Third, these decisions are employed to identify what competencies or capabilities the company will need. For example, if the company is going to compete on service, what does that imply for the specific competencies it needs? Next, these decisions are translated into specific functional plans and objectives that are delegated to accountable functional managers (e.g., marketing, finance, human resources) to implement and achieve. Finally, senior management monitors and oversees the operation of these plans, intervening when necessary.

In a somewhat more enlightened version of this process, senior management may also be encouraged to adopt an inspiring "vision" that motivates employees and to act as coaches and cheerleaders as well as directors in the execution of the strategy. Under this approach, senior managers are often cautioned to ensure that the "values" and

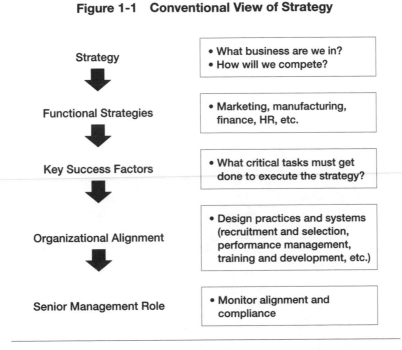

Figure 1-1   Conventional View of Strategy

Strategy	• What business are we in? • How will we compete?
Functional Strategies	• Marketing, manufacturing, finance, HR, etc.
Key Success Factors	• What critical tasks must get done to execute the strategy?
Organizational Alignment	• Design practices and systems (recruitment and selection, performance management, training and development, etc.)
Senior Management Role	• Monitor alignment and compliance

practices of the organization are aligned with the strategy. The message is to pick values that fit the strategy. Sometimes senior leadership is advised to involve some of the lower-level people in this process, so they will get "buy-in." This process is premised on the primacy of intellect and rationality, and it is assumed that those in leadership roles know more and are smarter than those who are actually doing the company's work—which is why they get to set the direction. In this rational world, strategy answers two fundamental questions that are critical for managers: What business are we in? and How shall we compete?

This logic should sound reasonable, familiar, and slightly boring. It answers the two basic strategic questions but does not engage anyone at an emotional level. It's an exciting intellectual exercise for those crafting the strategy—which is why strategy is such a popular course in business schools and strategy consulting such a desirable first job—but it is not engaging at all to those charged with implementing the strategy. Worse than that, it takes the competitive landscape as a given and devises maneuvers against a given set of competitors, presumed markets, customer tastes, and organizational capabilities.

Now consider how the companies we describe in this book approach the same set of issues. The process shown in figure 1-2 is almost the reverse of what we have just described. First, these companies begin with a set of fundamental values that are energizing and capable of unlocking the human potential of their people—values such as fun, fairness, challenge, trust, respect, community, and family. These values are then used to develop or at least evaluate management policies and practices that express the values in pragmatic ways on a day-to-day basis. For any management practice, be it the implementation of managed care at SAS (they wouldn't think of it because it conveys the idea that people can't be trusted to make decisions about their own health care) or surveillance cameras in a PSS World Medical warehouse (they wouldn't think of it, either, because it sends a message that the company doesn't trust its people), the question is, To what extent is this practice consistent with our core beliefs about people and organizations?

The management practices that are implemented have effects on people. Consequently, the management practices come to produce core competencies and capabilities at these companies, whether it is the teamwork, learning, and speed at AES, the service and personal development at The Men's Wearhouse, or the productivity and quality at NUMMI and Southwest Airlines. In turn, these capabilities and competencies can change the competitive dynamics of the industry. The Men's Wearhouse competes on a service proposition, not just on price. Southwest has productive employees who permit it to save on capital investment and labor costs and at the same time deliver a superior level of service. Cisco is able to change technology platforms and acquire and retain intellectual capital as the industry shifts around it. What these companies can do better than anyone else permits them to develop innovative strategies and approaches that outflank the competition. In this approach to management, strategy comes last, after the values and practices are aligned and after the company produces capabilities that set it apart.

Notice that we do not say that strategy is unimportant. Each of the firms we describe has a well-defined competitive strategy that helps it make decisions about how and where to compete. But these strategic decisions are secondary to living a set of values and creating the align-

Figure 1-2 A Values-Based View of Strategy

Fundamental Values or Beliefs	• What are our basic principles? • What do we believe in?
⬇	
Design Management Practices That Reflect and Embody These Values	• What policies and practices are consistent with these values?
⬇	
Use These to Build Core Capabilities	• What can we do for the customer better than our competitors?
⬇	
Invent a Strategy That Is Consistent with the Values and Uses the Capabilities to Compete in New and Unusual Ways	• Given our capabilities, how can we deliver value to customers in a way our competitors cannot easily imitate?
⬇	
Senior Management's Role	• Senior management "manages" the values and culture of the firm.

ment between values and people. We believe that many organizations miss this link and place too much emphasis on strategy and not enough on values and the management practices that produce implementation. Lew Platt, former CEO of Hewlett-Packard, said, "I [spent] a lot of time talking about values rather than trying to figure out business strategies. . . . Execution is what spells the difference between success and failure."[21] Larry Bossidy, CEO of Allied-Signal, echoes this view, claiming "The competitive difference is not in deciding what to do, but in how to do it. Execution becomes paramount."[22]

THE IMPORTANCE OF PHILOSOPHY AND ASSUMPTIONS ABOUT PEOPLE

The ability to execute strategy depends on a company's ability to attract and retain great people and, more important, to use their knowledge, wisdom, and insights. That is why unlocking the hidden value in your people is so crucial to success. One of the barriers to tapping the value in the workforce is the philosophy and assumptions about people that we bring to this crucial task. One's often unarticulated and possibly implicit assumptions about people, motivation, and individual and organizational performance have subtle but powerful effects. Depending on my initial assumptions about what motivates people, I am likely to design very different reward and control systems. These systems may then lead people to behave in very different ways. Once I "see" people behaving in response to the reward system, I may confirm my initial motivational assumptions—the well-known self-fulfilling prophecy effect.

To see how assumptions about people can affect organizations, consider the assumptions that underlie most economic theories of motivation. First, there is a presumption that people are unlikely to expend effort unless they are paid to do so or are supervised closely. A second common belief is that people, in the pursuit of their own interests, will often misrepresent their true preferences and engage in guile and deceit. A third widespread assumption is that the goals of managers and workers are not aligned; that is, employees and managers want different outcomes at work, which means that incentive systems need to be designed to ensure that people do what is right for the good of the organization.

Although each of these assumptions may be valid in a specific situation or for a particular individual, none is likely to be right in most settings with normal human beings. Worse, if you begin by designing systems to protect against the small minority, you end up by alienating the majority. Yet, under the economic logic, managers are encouraged to operate as though these implicit assumptions were always and everywhere true. Managers are encouraged to carefully design monitoring systems to check on people so that employees don't misbehave, to design jobs in ways that reduce individual autonomy and maximize standardization so that employees can be selected and monitored more efficiently, to craft incentive systems that rely on money (either current or deferred compensation) to ensure that employees put in a fair day's effort, and to otherwise ensure that management can check and control the behavior of subordinates.

When systems are designed to closely monitor and control people, those being controlled will soon begin to resent their lack of autonomy and the lack of trust. Thirty years of research in social psychology has documented how increased monitoring can undermine motivation and cause previously engaged people to reduce their effort.[23] It is only a short step from here to the economist's predicted outcomes of effort aversion and opportunism. This leads to a vicious cycle of tightened controls, more resistance, and greater tension. Seeing this, the economist will say, "See, I told you people can't be trusted!"

But what if there were another way, one that engages people in the business and leverages rather than destroys their energy, knowledge, and talent? In fact, such an alternative exists—a system that aligns the interests of employees, managers, and shareholders for the mutual benefit of all. And the best part of it is that it actually works. A wealth of empirical evidence shows the effectiveness of a people-centered approach that delivers value to the customer, the employee, the organization, and the shareholders. Consider the following examples from recent studies.

- Using multiple samples and employing multiple measures, research has found that a change of one standard deviation in an index of innovative human resource management practices produces increases of $20,000 to $40,000 in stock market value *per employee*.[24] One such study reported that companies that were one standard deviation higher in their use of high-performance work practices enjoyed more than $27,000 in increased sales per employee, $18,000 in increased market capitalization and $3,800 in profits, as well as a decrease in employee turnover.[25]

- A study of the five-year survival rate of 136 companies that made initial public offerings in 1988 revealed that those companies that emphasized the importance of their people and offered rewards to everyone, not just senior management, survived at a much higher rate than those that did not.[26]

- A worldwide study of the automobile assembly industry showed that lean production systems coupled with high-performance work practices such as training, contingent rewards, job rotation, and an egalitarian culture were associated with more than 40 percent better productivity and quality compared with conventional mass production techniques.[27]

- A longitudinal case study of a paper mill, which permits researchers to better assess causality, reported that a change to a system incorporating more high-performance management practices (working in teams, fewer job classifications, more training, employment security, and higher pay) resulted in higher productivity, higher sales, and an increase of more than 300 percent in profitability.[28]

- Similar studies in steel minimills and in the steel manufacturing, semiconductor fabrication, oil refining, and apparel manufacturing industries demonstrate that people-centered practices produce significant increases in quality, productivity, and profit margins along with decreases in costs and employee turnover.[29]

- The Gallup organization surveyed more than 2,500 business units in twenty-four organizations, using twelve questions that constitute the Gallup Workplace Audit (GWA). They reported that "every one of the twelve questions was linked to at least one of the four business outcomes: productivity, profitability, retention, and customer satisfaction. . . . [T]he twelve questions were . . . capturing those few, vital employee opinions that related to top performance."[30]

- These results are not unique to companies operating in the United States. For instance, a study of German companies found that companies that place employees at the core of their strategies produced higher shareholder returns than industry peers.[31] A study of Korean enterprises discovered that "dedicated positioning strategies appear to be executed more effectively where organizations exhibit a high level of commitment to their employees."[32]

If the evidence is so consistent about the importance of people to organizational success, why haven't organizations rushed to implement practices that are consistent with the large body of research evidence?[33] The reason is simultaneously simple and complex. The simple response is that for people-centered practices to work, a wide spectrum of management practices, ranging from selection to socialization to compensation, must be tightly aligned with each other. These management practices must then be focused on building and maintaining core capabilities and on devising a business strategy that capitalizes on the capabilities that have been developed. This is, as we will show, very easy to say and extraordinarily hard to do. Implementing this simple advice demands great consistency and relentless attention on the part of management in order to rigorously align values, strategy, and management practices. It requires sometimes rethinking competitive dynamics so that the company can capitalize on its capabilities by changing the rules of the game in the marketplace. Building capabilities that change the basis of competition requires courage to think and act outside the box, seizing the opportunities that unlock the hidden value in your people.

Now contrast the conventional assumptions discussed earlier with those of the organizations we profile in the following chapters. As you read these profiles, ask yourself, What are the assumptions the companies make about people and their motivations? What are the managers' beliefs that underpin how they organize and design the work environment? This is not an academic exercise, but rather is critical to solving the mysteries behind the success of these companies. Unless you are clear about these underlying assumptions, you are not likely to see how these firms operate or to understand why their competitors consistently fail in their attempts to imitate them.

SOLVING THE MYSTERY

To uncover the secrets of tapping the hidden value in all companies, we need to do what good detectives and scientists do: look carefully at the evidence and understand the patterns that point to the answer. The following chapters describe in detail how each company operates. We provide sufficient information for you to use your intuition and experience to develop and test your own hypotheses about why they are successful. Unlike many management books that offer you "the three things every manager needs to know," we don't begin with a list and illustrate how management practices across firms "prove" the wisdom of the list. The problem with that approach is that it belies what all of us know to be true about organizations—they are interrelated systems. By describing the numerous aspects of the management practices at each of our companies, you can see how they interrelate and the extent to which they are aligned. With this clinical detail, you can begin to think about implementing not piecemeal prescriptions but an integrated approach to management.

As you read about these companies, you should think about two questions: (1) Why, precisely, are these companies so successful? and (2) Why haven't their competitors been able to imitate them? If you have really understood how the alignment of people and values can lead to competitive advantage, you should be able to understand what has gone wrong with other companies you know about and to see what might have been done differently. To test your understanding, we have even included our version of a final examination—chapter 9. As you will see, this chapter profiles a company that does many of the things that the successful organizations do but is not as successful. This shows that getting extraordinary results from people is not as easy as it might appear. Chapter 9 asks you to figure out what the problem is. If you can understand this, you've succeeded—not just at discovering how companies can get extraordinary results from ordinary people, but, more important, at discovering how to use these insights in your own organization.

We, of course, have drawn our own conclusions and discuss these in the final chapter. Meanwhile, we invite you to reach your own judgments and to compare them with ours. In solving the mystery of hidden value, you will develop a template for managing your own organization—an approach that if applied may offer sustainable competitive advantage for your firm.

Chapter 2

Southwest Airlines:
If Success Is So Simple,
Why Is It So Hard to Imitate?

O ILLUSTRATE WHY the companies described in this book are "mysteries," we begin with a firm that everyone knows and many admire—Southwest Airlines. The basic facts about the company are well known: How it has grown in under thirty years from a four-plane regional carrier into the nation's fifth largest airline, a $4 billion company with over 29,000 employees serving fifty-two cities across twenty-six states. How it has consistently had the lowest costs and the best customer service as measured by on-time performance, lost bags, and customer complaints. How it was ranked by *Condé Nast Traveler* as the safest of the world's eighty-five major airlines.[1] How it is the only U.S. airline to have been profitable every year for the past twenty-six years. Most people also have a sense that part of its success is attributable to its unique, offbeat culture that emphasizes fun, family, and caring for employees and customers. This culture and the company's people-oriented leadership resulted in Southwest being rated as the top company in *Fortune* magazine's 1998 list of "The 100 Best Companies to Work for in America." Some of those who have experienced the strength of the Southwest culture have noted its cultish character, describing the company as "the Moonies" or "Branch Davidians without automatic weapons."[2]

Although Southwest's success is widely reported,[3] the reasons for that success are actually far less well understood. In fact, given the amount of interest and publicity the company has received, two significant questions remain unanswered. First, if the Southwest approach is so well known, *why hasn't the competition been able to copy the Southwest model?* As Tom Peters has noted, "the business model is understandable by any 3-year-old."[4] A host of competitors—small start-up airlines such as Vanguard, America West, Reno, and Kiwi Air—have attempted to replicate Southwest's approach and failed. For example, founded in 1981, America West became the nation's tenth largest airline in only four years and was considered "the highest flying young airline since People Express."[5] Yet, only two years later, the airline was in Chapter 11. As of 1999, America West continued to be at war with its employee unions, and its on-time performance, passenger service, and operating results have suffered as a consequence. Other start-up imitators (such as Vanguard Airlines, Kiwi, and Western Pacific) are either struggling or have already failed. Even better-established competitors such as Reno Air and Alaska Airlines have either been forced into mergers or are likely takeover candidates. Meanwhile, Southwest continues its uninterrupted growth.

Even more puzzling than the failure of small start-ups is the inability of some of the major airlines to successfully compete against Southwest. In 1993, Continental Airlines announced that it would challenge Southwest using an airline-within-an-airline, Continental Lite.[6] Two years later, having lost over $140 million, a defeated Continental gave up this attempt and closed Continental Lite. Why was a major airline with experienced management unable to copy Southwest?

It wasn't just Continental that has had trouble directly competing with Southwest. In September 1994, United Airlines announced the formation of Shuttle by United, which was unabashedly modeled after Southwest and designed to compete with Southwest in the lucrative West Coast market. With the invasion by Southwest, United's share in this market had fallen from 38 percent in 1991 to 30 percent in 1993 while Southwest's share had increased from 26 percent to 45 percent. Yet only a few years later, United had retreated from 40 percent of the routes where they competed with Southwest and was running the Shuttle at breakeven.[7] Recently, the union-management alliance at United has frayed to the point that union members of the board of directors vetoed the CEO's top choice for his successor. More than 19,000 nonunion customer service and reservation agents have approved a union certification effort. Meanwhile, Southwest has signed record-breaking ten-year labor agreements and continued to increase its market share, both nationally and in California.

As Southwest has continued its steady expansion into the South and Northeast, this same scenario has been played out with other major airlines; for example, USAir and Delta formed airlines-within-airlines (MetroJet and Delta Express) in an attempt to compete. These competitors have tried to adopt the Southwest model, emphasizing low fares and frequent no-frills service, typically without much success. This is a puzzle. On the face of it, there is nothing the competition does not know. They certainly understand the technology, cost structures, and route planning. They have the same equipment, locations, and marketing muscle. Yet, again and again, whether large or small, Southwest's competitors have been unable to replicate its success.

Southwest's long history of growth and expansion raises a second mystery for the discerning reader: *How has Southwest been able to grow to its current size without stumbling and how has the company been able to deliver consistent performance over such a long time?* For years, airline analysts have questioned how sustainable Southwest's advantage really is. Early on, skeptics claimed that the Southwest model would never work for a larger organization. Once the company achieved a reasonable size, skeptics then claimed that the model could not work outside the Southwest, as though there were something unique to that place or other regions that would affect Southwest's ability to grow. As the company prepared to enter the New York market, one commentator noted that "successful entry into the New York market is no sure thing."[8] Still others have argued that Southwest's culture and success were ephemeral and couldn't be sustained over time, and have waited for the company to stumble. More sophisticated critics noted how airlines with ostensibly similar strategies, such as People Express and America West, had ultimately failed, and used this as evidence that the model was self-defeating. Indeed, there is plenty of evidence suggesting that successful firms often become arrogant and victims of their own success.[9] So there is a related important mystery here: How has Southwest been able to maintain its success in the face of intense competition and its own history of success?

Understanding how Southwest Airlines has been able to achieve twenty-six consecutive years of profitability in a highly cyclical and competitive industry and has been able to achieve consistent performance is an important first step for understanding the success of all the companies we profile.

BACKGROUND

History

Southwest Airlines was founded by Rollin King, Lamar Muse, and Herbert Kelleher, who served as the company's attorney, in 1967. On February 20, 1968, the Texas Aeronautics Commission approved Southwest's petition to begin flying within Texas. The next day three competing airlines blocked the approval by obtaining a temporary restraining order.[10] It took three and a half years of legal struggle to get permission to actually begin offering passenger service. On June 18, 1971, Southwest Airlines, headquartered at Love Field in Dallas, began flying with three Boeing 737 aircraft serving the Texas cities of Dallas, Houston, and San Antonio. Southwest's competition was Texas International, Braniff, and, to a lesser extent, Continental.

Having used every political and regulatory means to ensure that Southwest would not get off the ground, competitors subsequently tried other legal and regulatory hurdles to hamper its operations. Such tactics included keeping Southwest from flying nonstop from Love Field to any except the four adjacent states. Southwest lost $3.7 million in its first year of flying and didn't turn a profit until the middle of 1973. In fact, Southwest was so short of cash when it began flying in 1971 that it had to sell one of its four planes. The company went to its employees and explained the situation—it could scale back its schedule, or fly the same schedule with just three planes. The employees agreed to operate the same schedule with fewer aircraft, but this required turning the planes around more quickly. This is how and why the company's vaunted quick turnaround originated.[11]

Herb Kelleher, CEO and formerly Southwest's corporate counsel, said, "You know, anger can be a great motivator. For me, this became a cause. I was a crusader freeing Jerusalem from the Saracens."[12] More recently, he was quoted as saying, "I have told people that I would retaliate if I became very angry, but now I think I would revise that. Let's just say that if I become peckish, I will attack."[13] This aggressive, underdog spirit still pervades the company, especially among longer-serving employees. Many see the goal of keeping this spirit alive as one of the firm's great challenges. One long-time employee noted, "In 1971, 198 people got together and did something that was impossible. Now we need to update the culture to today's problems."

In the early days, Southwest, with limited financial resources for marketing, gained attention by putting its flight attendants in hot pants and using its location at Love Field as the theme of an advertising campaign ("Make Love, Not War"), a theme that is still used today when Southwest refers to itself as the "Love" (LUV) airline. This designator is Southwest's stock ticker symbol. All aircraft have a small heart emblazoned on their sides, and hearts are used prominently on corporate communications and advertising. From its inception, Southwest encouraged its employees to identify with others at the company, deliver great customer service, and have fun.

In the mid-1980s, American Airlines and USAir, attempting to increase their share of the valuable California market, purchased Air California and Pacific Southwest Airlines (PSA) respectively, two successful regional carriers. However, American soon withdrew from some cities and routes when they could not be served profitably. USAir made a number of marketing and service mistakes and also cut back service in the region. Southwest seized the opportunity to expand in California. From basically a zero market share in California in 1989, Southwest moved to become the leading airline in passenger boardings in 1993.

Kelleher is not, however, focused on market share. "Market share has nothing to do with profitability. Market share says we just want to be big; we don't care if we make money doing it. That's what misled much of the industry for fifteen years, after deregulation. In order to get an additional 5 percent of the market, some companies increased their costs by 25 percent. That's really incongruous if profitability is your purpose."[14] And Southwest is clearly focused on profitability, even if it means forgoing revenue-producing opportunities that disproportionately increase its costs.

The Business Strategy

From the beginning to the present, Southwest has maintained the same strategy and operating style. It concentrates on flying to airports that are underutilized and close to a metropolitan area—for example, Love Field in Dallas, Hobby in Houston, San Jose and Oakland in the San Francisco Bay Area, Midway in Chicago—although it does fly to major airports such as Los Angeles International and San Francisco. The company also began by flying fuel-efficient 737s and now has over 300 of them, the only type of aircraft it flies. Southwest service involves frequent on-time departures as well as low-cost fares. The company emphasizes point-to-point routes, with no central hub and an average flight time of eighty minutes. Roughly 80 percent of Southwest's customers fly nonstop to their final destination. By avoiding a hub-and-spoke system, the company is able to avoid the systemwide delays often associated with connecting flights through hub airports that experience bad weather. This makes short-haul trips more attractive to travelers who might otherwise consider driving. It also pays off in shorter turnaround times (70 percent of their flights have a fifteen-minute ground time) and higher equipment utilization. For example, Southwest aircraft spend an average of eleven hours in the air daily compared with an industry average of eight, and they average 10.5 flights per gate versus 4.5 for the industry.

Following this basic strategy, Southwest has always seen itself as competing not so much with other airlines as with surface transportation, and as seeking to succeed by growing passenger volume in the markets it serves. For instance, in 1998 the average passenger fare for Southwest was roughly $75 for a trip of 597 miles. In 1984 the comparable numbers were $49 and 436 miles. In 1999, the round-trip undiscounted fare from San Jose to San Diego, a distance of over 500 miles, was $184 (or $128 with advance purchase). Since Southwest entered the Baltimore market in 1993, fares have fallen an average of 35 percent. In 1997, Southwest had the lowest fares among the nine largest U.S. airlines, with an average cost per mile of less than half that of its closest competitor.

Southwest uses these low fares and frequent flights to increase passenger volume two to three times. Gary Kelly, Southwest's CFO, emphasizes that the everyday low fares "are low by philosophy, not expediency." As an example, "on the 196-mile route between Tampa and Fort Lauderdale [Florida] . . . passenger traffic jumped to 487,210 last year [1996] from 196,530 in 1995."[15] In addition to dramatically low fares, Southwest has an increased frequency of flights. For instance, in August 1994 Southwest flew thirty-nine round-trips daily between Dallas and Houston, twenty-five between Phoenix and Los Angeles, and twenty between Sacramento and Los Angeles. When American abandoned their San Jose hub because they were losing money, Southwest moved in and was profitable from the first day of service. The company is typically the leading carrier in passenger boardings at airports served. Southwest has almost 70 percent of the intra-Texas market, about three-quarters of the intra-Florida market, and over 50 percent of the intra-California traffic.

Consistent with a strategy of low costs, low fares, and frequent flights, Southwest also keeps its fares simple. Unlike other airlines that rely heavily on computers and artificial intelligence programs to maximize flight revenue, Southwest typically offers only two fares on a route: a regular coach fare (there is no first or business class) and an off-peak fare. It also tries to price all fares the same within a state. Traditionally, Southwest did not sell interline connections with other carriers, and it only recently joined the Sabre reservation system. As a result, only 55 percent of Southwest's seats were booked by travel agents, compared with 90 percent of tickets for major airlines.

To further simplify their operations, Southwest has never offered meal service on its flights. Instead, passengers on Southwest are served beverages, peanuts (referred to as "frills"; in 1998 they distributed over 87 million bags of peanuts), and, on longer flights, crackers or other light snacks such as cookies. There is no assigned seating. Customers are served on a first-come, first-served basis. Upon arrival at a Southwest gate, which opens for check-in one hour before flight time, each passenger is given a reusable plastic boarding pass with a number from 1 to 137, the maximum load of the 737 aircraft. Passengers board in groups of thirty, with the lowest numbers first, and the boarding passes are collected for use on the next flight.

Although they are not affiliated with other frequent flyer programs, Southwest does have its own frequent flyer club ("Rapid Rewards"), also a model of simplicity. It is based on the number of trips flown, not the mileage. Members keep a card that is stamped every time they board a plane. After accumulating sixteen stamps, a free ticket is awarded and a Rapid Rewards card is issued. The card is then read into the computer system for each trip. This approach economizes on operating costs because it requires no effort to keep track of mileage. Prompted by some negative advertising by United about Southwest's frequent flyer program, Herb Kelleher sent a letter to all Rapid Reward members detailing how awards from Southwest took less mileage to obtain and were more widely available than those from other airlines. Kelleher argued that Southwest's program "is the greatest value because it gives you free travel faster, for much less money, without giving up great service." For instance, after fifty round-trips within a twelve-month period, a companion flies free, even if you're traveling on an award ticket.

Southwest Airlines has been profitable in every one of the last twenty-six years, a record achieved by no other U.S. airline. It was consistently profitable even during the 1991–1992 period, during which some 40 percent of the total capacity of the U.S. airline industry filed for bankruptcy protection or ceased operations completely. Table 2-1 presents selected financial and operating data for the last four years. According to *Money* magazine, for the twenty-year period from 1972 to 1992, Southwest's stock earned the highest returns of any publicly traded U.S. stock—a compounded return of over 21,000 percent.[16] Only Wal-Mart came close to being as good an investment over this period.

Competitive Advantage

Although the reasons for Southwest's success are many, one highly visible competitive advantage is its cost structure. Kelleher recognized that short-haul flying was inherently more costly than longer flights (the plane takes off and lands more often and has to be handled at

Table 2-1   Four-Year Financial Summary (in millions)

	1998	1997	1996	1995
Total operating revenues	4,164	3,817	3,406	2,873
Operating expenses	3,480	3,292	3,055	2,559
Operating income	684	524	351	314
Other expenses (income) net	(22)	7	9	8
Income before taxes	705	517	341	305
Provision for income taxes	272	199	134	123
Net income	433	318	207	183
Net income per share	$1.30	$0.97	$0.64	$0.56
Net income per share (diluted)	$1.23	$0.93	$0.61	$0.55
Cash dividends/Common share	$0.03	$0.02	$0.02	$0.02
Total assets	4,716	4,246	3,723	3,256
Long-term debt	623	628	650	661
Stockholder equity	2,398	2,009	1,648	1,427
Consolidated Financial Ratios				
Return on average total assets	9.7%	8.0%	5.9%	6.0%
Return on average stockholder equity	19.7%	17.4%	13.5%	13.7%
Operating Statistics				
Passenger load factor	66.1%	63.7%	66.5%	64.5%
Average length of trip	597	563	546	521
Average passenger fare	$75.38	$72.21	$65.88	$61.61
Size of fleet	280	261	243	224

Source: Southwest annual reports.

every gate). He understood that the lowest-cost provider could leverage that cost advantage most where costs are highest. Table 2-2 shows the costs per available seat mile for 1996 to 1998 for Southwest and a set of its competitors. Remarkably, Southwest's costs in 1994 averaged roughly 7.1 cents compared with 7.3 cents for 1998—a testament to the company's productivity improvement efforts and ability to control costs. In contrast, competitors' average costs are 15 percent to 40 percent higher. This achievement is even more striking when noting that Southwest's costs in 1984 were 5.86 cents. So, over a decade its costs had increased by only about 20 percent.[17]

Part of this cost advantage derives from the remarkable productivity Southwest gets from its workforce. For example, Southwest people

Table 2-2 Airline Costs per Available Seat Mile

	1998	1997	1996
Southwest	7.32	7.40	7.50
USAir	12.34	12.33	12.69
United	8.76	8.94	9.33
Continental	8.93	9.07	8.77
Delta	8.86	8.88	9.17

Source: U.S. Department of Transportation, Office of Aviation Enforcement and Proceedings, February 1999.

routinely turn around an aircraft in fifteen minutes from the time it arrives at the gate until it leaves (see figure 2-1). During this fifteen-minute period, Southwest people manage to change flight crews, unload 137 passengers and board another 137, unload almost a hundred bags and a thousand pounds of mail, load another hundred bags and 600 pounds of mail, and pump 4,500 pounds of fuel into the aircraft. Continental and United average thirty-five minutes for similar activities. Southwest's gates are typically staffed by a single agent and have a ground crew of six, rather than the three agents and twelve ground crew found at other airlines.

These low costs also come from other sources. Southwest pilots, for example, spend more time in the air than pilots at other airlines. Whereas some pilots at United, American, and Delta earn more than $200,000 a year for flying an average of fifty hours a month, Southwest's pilots average $100,000 a year flying seventy hours a month. These comparisons don't account for differences in the equipment flown (many of the other airlines' highest-paid pilots are flying 747s on international routes). Another cost advantage comes from having people who will do as many different tasks as required to get the flights out. Flight attendants and pilots will help clean the aircraft or check passengers in at the gate. Harold Sirkin, an airline specialist with The Boston Consulting Group (BCG), noted that "Southwest works because people pull together to do what they need to do to get a plane turned around. That is a part of the Southwest culture. And if it means the pilots need to load bags, they'll do it."[18]

Figure 2-1   Anatomy of a Fifteen-Minute Turnaround

2:45   Ground crew wait at gate position.

2:46   Aircraft sighted. Tug and belt loaders move into position.

2:47   Plane comes to a full stop at the gate. Baggage bins opened. Fueler arrives.

2:48   Pushback connected to the nose gear of the plane. Provisioning crew begins to stock ice, drinks, and snacks and empty trash. Passengers begin to deplane.

2:49   Freight coordinator checks to ensure freight is labeled.

2:50   First officer completes preflight check. Flight attendants move through the cabin and reposition seat belts and pick up trash.

2:51   All bags off-loaded and new bags begin to be loaded. Provisioning is complete. Current flight crew (pilots and flight attendants) is relieved and replaced by a new crew. Operations agent calls for preboarders. Fueler unhooks hose from wing.

2:52   Boarding in groups of thirty begins. Most of the ground crew leave to prepare for the arrival of another aircraft.

3:00   Passenger loading is complete. Operations agent gives weight and balance sheet to the pilot. Pilot trims the aircraft. Ramp agent connects the communication gear to talk to the pilots from the tarmac.

3:01   Jetway pulls back. Pushback maneuvers the plane away from the gate and plane begins to taxi toward the runway.

Source: *Nuts: Southwest Airlines' Crazy Recipe for Business and Personal Success*, © 1996 by Kevin and Jackie Freiberg.

Hard-working, motivated people give Southwest a tremendous advantage in workforce productivity. In 1998, for example, Southwest had an average of 94 employees per aircraft whereas United and American had almost 160. The industry average was in excess of 130. Southwest served an average of over 2,500 passengers per employee whereas United and American served less than 1,000, about the industry average. Southwest thus needs a much lower load factor to break even. Rapid turnaround of aircraft and use of less congested airports means that planes are in the air more, actually earning revenue. Finally, by using a single type of aircraft, Southwest is able to save on maintenance and training costs.

But Southwest is not just a low-fare, low-cost carrier. It also emphasizes customer service. In fact, the word "Customer" is always capitalized in Southwest corporate communications, whether it is the annual report or an internal newsletter. Colleen Barrett, the Chief Operating Officer and highest-ranking woman executive in the airline industry, insists on this. She is also adamant about treating employees as internal customers and tries to make sure that Southwest is a comfortable and fun place to work. "If you're comfortable, you're smiling more and you give better service," Barrett says. "It doesn't take a rocket scientist to figure that out."[19] The results are undeniable. In 1992, the Department of Transportation began giving an annual Triple Crown to the airline having the best on-time performance, fewest lost bags, and fewest number of customer complaints for the year. Southwest has won the Triple Crown for five years in a row.

Southwest's employees routinely volunteer to help customers in need. Once a customer arrived at the airport for a vacation trip with his dog in tow, only to learn that he couldn't bring the dog with him. Rather than have him cancel the trip, the gate agent took care of the dog for two weeks so the fellow could enjoy his holiday. Another employee accompanied an elderly passenger to the next stop to ensure that she was able to change planes. Still another employee took the initiative to arrange for an earlier flight for a customer flying home to visit a sick relative—only to learn later that because of this effort the customer was able to get home before the relative died. Stories of this sort abound. No wonder that the Department of Transportation statistics show Southwest with the fewest customer complaints by a factor of three compared with its closest rival and a factor of almost twelve compared with the worst.

SOUTHWEST'S VALUES, PHILOSOPHY, AND SPIRIT

There are three basic values or philosophical pillars at Southwest Airlines:

Value 1: Work should be fun . . . it can be play . . . enjoy it.

Value 2: Work is important . . . don't spoil it with seriousness.

Value 3: People are important . . . each one makes a difference.[20]

Southwest's fundamental business proposition is that its people come first. Commenting at the time of the company's twenty-fifth anniversary in 1996, Kelleher said:

> It used to be a business conundrum: "Who comes first? The employees, customers, or shareholders?" That's never been an issue to me. The employees come first. If they're happy, satisfied, dedicated, and energetic, they'll take real good care of the customers. When the customers are happy, they come back. And that makes the shareholders happy.[21]

Southwest Airlines' mission statement reflects its concern with employees. After the statement "The mission of Southwest Airlines is dedicated to the highest quality of Customer service delivered with a sense of warmth, friendliness, individual pride, and company spirit," there is a section headed "To Our Employees":

> We are committed to provide our employees a stable work environment with equal opportunity for learning and personal growth. Creativity and innovation are encouraged for improving the effectiveness of Southwest Airlines. Above all, employees will be provided the same concern, respect, and caring attitude within the organization that they are expected to share externally with every Southwest Customer.

Lots of companies say their people are important. Southwest actually acts as if this statement is true. That includes being with people through tough times. The company has a catastrophe fund, which raises voluntary contributions for distribution to people who have experienced serious problems. When a former employee developed a drug problem, the company arranged to pay for his medical care so long as he stayed in the rehabilitation program. Kelleher stated, "I feel that you have to be with your employees through all their difficulties, that you have to be interested in them personally."[22]

Southwest consistently tries to convey that all people are important and that everyone should be treated with dignity and respect, even those not currently part of the company. For instance, when Midway Airlines ceased operations some years ago, Southwest assembled a team of more than thirty people to fly to Chicago and interview Midway employees who might work at Southwest. The team spent nine days interviewing 2,400 people, hiring 800. During the interviewing process, everyone on the Southwest team wore a flight attendant's uniform. The group set up a training program for Midway employees on how to interview and to write a resume, trying to help everyone, even those who would not be hired at Southwest. Every Midway employee was offered a personal interview, scheduled at a specific time so that they would not have to wait. At United Airlines, by contrast, Midway employees had to stand in line up to two hours just to fill out a job application.[23]

Part of taking care of employees at Southwest entails emphasizing having fun at work. Humor is a core value and part of the Southwest style and spirit. Kelleher commented that after he became chairman of the company in 1978, he "charged our personnel department with the responsibility of hiring people with a sense of humor."[24] Southwest Airlines' pilots and flight attendants are encouraged to make safety and other announcements fun and funny, and to be creative in the process. Flight attendants have been known to pop out of the overhead bins, to organize "who has the biggest hole in their sock" contests, and to get the passengers to sing happy birthday to someone on board celebrating a birthday. Elizabeth Sartain, now head of the People Department, commented: "We feel this fun atmosphere builds a strong sense of community. It also counterbalances the stress of hard work and competition."[25]

This philosophy of fun pervades the entire company. Serious attention is paid to parties and celebrations. Every year, for instance, each station (city) is given a budget for parties for the employees and their families. Most stations supplement this by doing their own fundraising. Up until several years ago, all Southwest employees used to fly to Dallas for the annual company party. Now that the company has grown too large for that, they hold a rolling party in several cities, with Herb and the senior managers moving from one location to another. Celebrations and contests occur continually. The Love Field corporate headquarters in Dallas is filled with banners and with pictures of Southwest employees at parties, awards, trips, and celebrations. In fact, there is no corporate art in the headquarters. All paintings and sculptures, and there are many, are those donated by employees.

This people-oriented atmosphere is extremely informal and egalitarian. Everyone is called by his or her first name. Individuals' home telephone numbers are published in the company directory, and employees will call officers at home at night. Dress, for both flight crews and people at headquarters, is casual. This is not a place where people stand on ceremony. Instead, there is a feeling of an egalitarian culture in which people work together to accomplish what needs to be done.

Colleen Barrett, who has been Herb's right-hand person for years, understands the importance of the Southwest spirit and culture and has done numerous things to maintain and build the atmosphere. For instance, in 1990 she became concerned with the size and geographic dispersion of the company and set up a culture committee consisting of sixty-five people from all levels and regions of the company, not just headquarters, to perpetuate the Southwest spirit. These people are zealots about the culture and work behind the scenes to foster commitment to values such as profitability, low cost, family, love, and fun. It is one of the very few standing committees at the airline. One of its accomplishments has been to encourage groups of employees to express their appreciation to others for their contributions. So, for instance, the pilots held a 3:00 A.M. barbecue for mechanics working the night shift. In 1995, the committee encouraged a program known as "Walk a Mile in My Shoes," in which over 75 percent of employees voluntarily spent a minimum of six hours working in another job. A group of pilots decided to thank the reservation agents by coming in and spending a shift with them. Even the officers and directors of the company have a program that requires that they spend one day per quarter working in a frontline job. Colleen is adamant that this means real work, not standing around and drinking coffee.

Treating people with respect and dignity also entails driving out fear. Not only has the company never had a layoff or furlough—quite unusual in its industry—but it also doesn't punish honest mistakes. The company's official policy states: "No employee will ever be punished for using good judgment and good old common sense when trying to accommodate a customer—no matter what our other rules are."[26]

THE SOUTHWEST SYSTEM

The Southwest culture is built and maintained by a set of operating practices that are largely the responsibility of the People Department. About ten years ago the human resources function at Southwest was renamed "The People Department." This reflected a concern that the old human resources group was, in the words of John Turnipseed, manager of People Services, "a police department." To counteract this, Ann Rhoades, then the vice president of the group, first threw away the 300-page corporate handbook and then brought in new people with marketing backgrounds. Commenting on why she did this, she claimed that, "Most HR people have no courage. They never take a chance. No guts. No capability of making a decision. They're so afraid of being fired. . . . We need to have confidence in people doing the right thing."[27] To operate this way, she believes that it is imperative that you get the right people into HR to begin with. Therefore, to join the department, an employee must first have line experience.

Libby Sartain, the current vice president, sees the role of the People Department as saying "yes" rather than "no" and encourages them to do what it takes to make their Customers, the 29,000 Southwest employees, happy. To accomplish this, however, the People Department has a staff of only approximately 100. All members of the department sign the department's mission statement, which is prominently displayed on a very large poster on the wall of their headquarters office. It reads:

> Recognizing that our people are the competitive advantage, we deliver the resources and services to prepare our people to be winners, to support the growth and profitability of the company, while preserving the values and special culture of Southwest Airlines.

The people in this department take this charge seriously and emphasize the two C's: compassion and common sense. Libby Sartain worries about maintaining the culture and tells people to break the rules if they need to. Although in many companies human resources is considered a backwater, the People Department at Southwest is "like the keeper of the flame."[28]

What Southwest Airlines *does* creates what it *is* and how it feels to work at the company. There is much to be learned by examining the company's specific practices for managing people.

Recruiting

To ensure that the company hires the right people, Southwest is extraordinarily selective in recruiting. Because of the company's outstanding reputation as a great place to work, it does not need to rely on headhunters or employment agencies. The company receives a lot of resumes over the transom, and its employees also encourage their friends and family to apply. In 1998, Southwest had almost 200,000 job applicants. Of these, roughly 35,000 were interviewed and over 4,000 hired. To make it through this screen, aspiring employees have submitted resumes on the icing of a large sheet cake, cereal boxes, the top of a pizza, and the labels of bottles of Wild Turkey bourbon (Herb's favorite), demonstrating the creative spirit that Southwest looks for. The company recruits primarily for attitude, believing that skills can be learned. In explaining why they emphasize hiring for spirit, vice president of ground operations Dave Ridley noted that "It's hard to take bad people and make them into good people. We hire happy people. We don't hire fruitcakes."[29]

To ensure fit, there is an emphasis on peer recruiting. For example, pilots hire other pilots, baggage handlers hire baggage handlers, and so on—even if this means coming in on their day off to do background checks. Describing how pilots hire other pilots, Libby Sartain explained, "They can get far more information in a phone call to the chief pilot of another airline than anyone else."[30] They turned down a top pilot who worked for another major airline and did stunt work for movie studios. Even though he was a great pilot, he made the mistake of being rude to a Southwest receptionist. Teamwork is critical. If applicants say "I" too much in the interview, they don't get hired. Sartain described how one group of eight applicant pilots were being kidded about how seriously they were dressed (dark suits and black shoes and socks). They were encouraged to loosen up. Six of them accepted the invitation to wear the standard Southwest Bermuda shorts and interviewed for the rest of the day in suit coats, ties, Bermuda shorts, and dress shoes and socks. They were the six hired.

The hiring process consists of an application, a phone screening interview, a group interview, three additional interviews (two with line employees), and a consensus assessment and a vote. During the interview process, the applicant will come into contact with other Southwest employees. These people are also invited to give their assessments of whether the person would fit in at the company. To further screen for the Southwest spirit, Southwest will let its best customers become involved in the interviewing process for new flight attendants. The entire process focuses on a positive attitude and teamwork. For example, applicants are given crayons to draw a picture that tells the story of their life. They look for people who are willing to draw outside the lines. Even their advertisements emphasize the Southwest spirit. One ad for people with computer skills showed a picture of a techno-nerd, with tape holding his glasses together, and emphasized that "We're not looking for the typical computer geek."

As befits a company where selection is important, Southwest has spent a lot of time identifying the key components comprising effective performance and behavior. It uses a hiring approach developed by Development Dimensions International, Inc. (DDI):

- Use past behavior to predict future behavior
- Identify the critical job requirements (target dimensions) for the position
- Organize selection elements into a comprehensive system
- Apply effective interviewing skills and techniques
- Involve several interviewers in organized data-exchange discussions
- Augment interview with observations from behavioral simulations[31]

For instance, the People Department identified their top thirty-five pilots and systematically interviewed them to identify common characteristics. One key trait identified was the ability to work as a part of the team. This is now used as a part of the pilot selection process. The company does not use personality tests, but instead emphasizes previous actual behaviors. Southwest believes that most skills can be learned and doesn't screen heavily for these except for certain specialist jobs, such as pilots and mechanics. Attitudes are what count. Kelleher says, "We draft great attitudes. If you don't have a good attitude, we don't want you, no matter how skilled you are. We can change skill levels through training. We can't change attitude."[32]

An important awareness on the part of the People Department is that the company rejects literally tens of thousands of applicants each year. These are all potential customers. Therefore, the recruiting process is designed to not make any applicants feel inferior or rejected. Some applicants who were turned down have claimed that they had a better experience being rejected by Southwest than they did being hired by other companies. Rita Bailey, head of corporate employment, always tries to call any internal or managerial applicants who were turned down. She uses this as a chance to counsel them, trying to be honest but not damaging their self-esteem. She invites them to call again if they want to talk more. She is concerned not only about how well a person will do at the job for which they are applying, but also how they'll do in the next job. She says, "It's important to do it this way or you're setting people up to fail when they get promoted."[33]

The company hires very few people with MBAs, and even those that do get hired are selected for their fit, not for their credentials. In fact, Southwest prefers people without extensive industry experience. For example, 40 percent of their pilots come directly from the military, 20 percent to 30 percent from small commuter airlines, and the rest from the major airlines. To encourage employees to help in the recruitment effort, Southwest offers a free space-available pass (which permits a person to travel free when the plane isn't full) to any employee who recommends someone who is hired to fill a position that is difficult to fill, such as in finance or information systems. For instance, in a creative recruitment effort for information systems openings, they recently had a contest among Rapid Reward club members that offered vacations for those who submitted resumes. Libby reported that they received over 1,500 responses, 200 of which looked really good.

Southwest also actively encourages nepotism and has 820 couples who work for the company. One woman described how she had gotten her son a job with the airline, but then described how he had been fired. "He didn't deserve to work here," she said. Thus, when these people describe the company as "family," a common reference throughout the airline, they really mean it.

Training

Given the emphasis on selecting for attitudes and fit and the importance of culture, it follows that training is an important part of Southwest. At Southwest's University for People, 25,000 people are trained each year. The emphasis is on doing things better, faster, and cheaper; understanding other people's jobs; delivering outstanding customer service; and keeping the culture alive and well. For instance, all new employees begin by attending a program entitled "You, Southwest, and Success." This gives all newcomers, from pilots to ramp agents, a crash course in Southwest's history, reputation for impeccable service, culture, and how they can contribute. From the beginning, the emphasis is on getting employees enthused and excited. A continual concern is to help employees avoid complacency. One trainer observed that "Our level of external service is only as good as our internal service." She also worried that positive press accounts don't help and may lull employees into believing that they are better than they actually are.

New flight attendants go through six weeks of classes, typically with less than 5 percent attrition. Much of this training is oriented toward customer service—"the care and feeding of customers." Customer expectations about service are quite high, and these are communicated to both new and experienced employees. All new hires are exposed to the history, principles, values, mission, and culture of the company. They are also told how the company views leadership and management. All training emphasizes teamwork and team building, all in good humor. For instance, new hires often do a celebratory skit at the conclusion of their training. One new pilot class donned dark sunglasses and white canes and stumbled into Kelleher's office.

For managers, there is a three-and-a-half-day course on leadership, pricing, revenue management, and how the business works. A member of senior management always attends a two-hour session and talks openly with the participants. Training is virtually 100 percent internal. "If it ain't born and bred here, they don't want any part of it," says one trainer.[34] Frontline leadership gets a specially designed two-day course each year. These programs are designed to address particular needs, such as cross-functional teamwork, and are heavily experiential. They involve managers from different levels and different parts of the organization, but never have a superior and a subordinate in the same session. Each year as the new program begins, members of the senior team are always in the first class. In addition to this special program, supervisors receive eighty hours of training per year. Courses include the usual offerings of communication, time management, and career planning, as well as others emphasizing the employee's role in creating legendary customer service and more interpersonal explorations on topics such as accepting responsibility and developing trust.

Another highlighted training program is "The Front-Line Forum," in which twelve to fifteen individuals with ten to fifteen years' experience in the company are brought together to discuss how the company is doing and how it has changed. They meet with top line officers and explore questions such as, "We promised you something around the culture and spirit of the company. Have we delivered?" Although the selection is done randomly, the idea is to assemble people who may be a bit beaten down to see what needs to be done to keep the culture alive.

Southwest does not have a tuition reimbursement program for taking outside courses. It also tends not to sponsor people to attend outside training. However, it is clear that Southwest's training is an important form of two-way communication. Not only are the values of hard work, fun, and cost consciousness inculcated, but the training is used to get internal customer feedback. In the words of one trainer, the issue is "To figure out how we can get better everyday, not worry about American Airlines or Delta."

Labor Relations

People are often surprised to find that Southwest, with its low costs and great service, is the most unionized airline in the United States. The company is 84 percent unionized but has had only one six-day walkout by the machinists over fifteen years ago. Recently both the pilots' and dispatchers' unions overwhelmingly ratified ten- and twelve-year labor agreements emphasizing gains in stock rather than wage increases. A senior executive noted that "Herb really is an extremely gifted labor-relations talent, especially when you consider he has somehow managed to get union people to identify personally with this company."[35] One of the keys to accomplishing this identification is the egalitarian, nonhierarchical, personal culture of trust that has been created over time. A transportation analyst with the firm Gruntal and Company noted, "He'll go out with a couple of mechanics and have a few drinks until 5 A.M., listen to what needs to be changed and go out the next day and fix it."[36] This culture of trust, built through personal contact, is nicely illustrated by the following anecdote:

> A Wall Street analyst recalls having lunch one day in the company cafeteria when Kelleher, seated at a table across the room with several female employees, suddenly leapt to his feet, kissed one of the women with gusto, and began leading the entire crowd in a series of cheers. When the analyst asked what was going on, one of the executives at his table explained that Kelleher had at that moment negotiated a new contract with Southwest's flight attendants.[37]

Another thing the company does to maintain cooperative labor relations is to encourage "union members and negotiators to research their pressing issues and to conduct employee surveys before each contract negotiation."[38] This process of involving people from both sides in identifying issues and developing information in advance of the actual negotiations is something observed at many companies that have been able to build less adversarial labor relations.

Obviously, those employees covered by a union contract are paid on the basis of seniority. Kelleher insists that there be no work rules in the union contract, which accounts for people's willingness and ability to help each other out. There is a system whereby employees can bid for shift and work hours. Almost every job class contains people earning between $40,000 and $60,000 a year. Everyone receives a raise on the anniversary of his or her employment.

Southwest uses few part-timers and does not contract out as much as many other airlines. This has helped to maintain labor peace. More important, it gives the company more control over critical elements of its operations that deliver the basic value proposition.

How Pay Helps Build the Culture

Southwest's compensation practices entail several simple elements: comparatively heavy use of collective, as contrasted with individual, rewards—for instance, profit sharing and stock ownership compared with individual pay for performance; relatively low executive pay; and consistent treatment—no giving executives big raises as employees are being asked to accept wage freezes or layoffs.

Libby Sartain notes, "There's no miracle compensation program here. The story is low pay at the beginning and high pay after you get seniority."[39] Below-market wages are offered to both clerical and management positions. Most people take a salary cut to join Southwest, and many have turned down large raises to leave. One former manager at EDS who left to join Southwest was offered two and a half times his starting salary to stay with EDS. An article in *Incentive* magazine explored what motivates Southwest's top performers. The answer was not money, but "Happiness."[40]

At Southwest, pilots and flight attendants are paid by the trip. Kelleher often emphasizes that airplanes don't make any money while they're sitting on the ground. While comparisons are tricky, *Fortune* reported that for 1992 the average wage at Southwest was $44,305, compared with $45,801 at American and $54,380 at United.[41] Derek Deck of the Air Conference (a trade group that gathers comparable wage data across airlines) believes that Southwest employees may earn less per hour than they could at other airlines, although they do have the flexibility to work more hours and earn more. Deck believes that Southwest personnel can, and often do, fly more trips, giving them ten to fifteen hours more per month. Consistent with this, a recent comparison of flight attendant salaries placed Southwest as the second highest paid group behind only those at Delta Airlines.[42]

There is also little or no pay for performance in the executive ranks, where compensation is modest by most standards. CEO Kelleher is routinely listed as one of the five lowest-paid CEOs in Dallas, and the lowest paid on a performance-adjusted basis—a distinction of which he is particularly proud. Of course, he does hold stock, but its worth pales besides that of the likes of Larry Ellison at Oracle or Bill Gates at Microsoft. In fact, there was no executive stock option plan until a few years ago. When Southwest sought a salary freeze from its pilots in 1996, Kelleher voluntarily agreed to a wage freeze for four years and only a modest raise in 2000.[43] There are no country club memberships or company cars, and officers stay in the same modest hotels as the flight crews.

Profit sharing covers all employees who have been with the firm for over a year, and they are required to invest 25 percent of their profit-sharing money in Southwest stock in a retirement account. Recently, those eligible received 8 percent of their salary as a bonus. Employees can also take advantage of a discounted stock purchase program. This has produced several millionaires. Approximately 85 percent to 90 percent of the employees own stock in the company, with about 10 percent of Southwest's outstanding shares owned by employees. However, Libby Sartain notes that she tries to encourage employees to diversify and not hold too much of the company's stock. Southwest has a relatively low level of employee ownership compared with the 55 percent of stock owned by employees at United after the buy-out and the 30 percent held by TWA employees.

Providing Information So That People Can Be Involved

As the previously discussed differences suggest, by itself, employee ownership is not a panacea. Southwest employees act like owners of the airline—even though they own a fraction of the stock compared with employees at United—because they are treated like owners. They are encouraged to take responsibility and make decisions. Management seeks out their opinions and listens carefully to what they say.

People at Southwest are also provided with the information needed to think and act like owners. For instance, in 1995 all employees were provided with the following information:

> How important is every Customer to our future? Our finance department reports that our break-even Customers per flight in 1994 was 74.5, which means that, on average, only when Customer #75 came on board did a flight become profitable!

The report went on to show that dividing the 1994 annual profit by total flights flown resulted in a profit per flight of $287. If this was divided by the average one-way fare, it showed that just five customers per flight meant the difference between profit and loss for the company. Further, the report went on to describe how studies have shown that for every customer who is "wronged" and complains, there are twenty-five others who remain silent. Each of these unhappy customers tells an average of twelve people about their bad experience. Data from 1994 showed that there were about 60,000 customer complaints at Southwest, translating to over 1.5 million possible dissatisfied customers who may have communicated their dissatisfaction to 18 million others. The report concluded by wondering if 18 million un-happy customers were enough to put Southwest out of business.

To keep employees focused, information is provided to all employees recapping the company's monthly statistics on costs, operations, and financial data. Particular attention is paid to how Southwest compares with its competitors. All this information is presented in creative and engaging ways, so employees are constantly aware of how the company is doing. In addition to providing focus, John Turnipseed said that sharing information builds trust, and trust is an important part of the Southwest story. "The level of trust has never been broken. In many organizations, everybody's against someone—union versus management, head office versus the field, etc. Not here."[44]

LESSONS FROM SOUTHWEST AIRLINES

So how do we answer the two questions posed at the beginning of the chapter: Why hasn't the competition been able to copy the Southwest model? and How has Southwest been able to continue to grow and to be successful over such a long time? Before giving you our analysis, it is important to emphasize what does *not* answer these questions. First, Southwest's success and its competitors' failures are not due to some unique strategy, intellectual property rights, technology that can't be imitated (anyone can fly the same planes with the same avionics), sophisticated management information systems, smarter managers, or secret policies and procedures. Everything that Southwest does is known to its competition and presumably can be imitated by them.

Second, we don't think the company's success is just because of its CEO. We acknowledge that many observers have argued that the company's success comes from its charismatic CEO, Herb Kelleher. A *Fortune* article asked, "Is Herb Kelleher America's Best CEO?"[45] His antics are legendary: appearing one Halloween at a Southwest maintenance hangar dressed in drag with a feathered boa, imitating Corporal Klinger from the television program *M*A*S*H*; appearing in print advertisements dressed as Elvis Presley; arm wrestling another company's CEO for the rights to the slogan "Just Plane Smart" (the other company had already registered Plane Smart; Kelleher lost, but got to keep using the slogan anyway); confounding Wall Street types "by claiming his two greatest achievements were a talent for projectile vomiting and never having had a really serious venereal disease";[46] rushing to catch a plane and, after stopping at the curb to talk to a Southwest employee, going off to the plane leaving his car idling at the curb. More recently, more credit has gone to Colleen Barrett, an executive vice president who provides discipline and consistency and has taken a large role in preserving the culture of Southwest.[47] There is no question that Southwest has some very effective leadership.

But it would be a mistake to overemphasize Kelleher's behavior and his personal charisma. If this were the sole source of the company's success, growth would have been a bigger problem because as the company grew, fewer and fewer people could be directly touched by Herb. Colleen Barrett has said "she is offended people make such a big deal out of his inevitable departure. It's ludicrous to think a single person could motivate Southwest's . . . employees and ensure the operation runs properly every day."[48] Kelleher's and Barrett's brilliance is not just in their leadership *behaviors,* but in building a strong management team and culture as well as putting into place myriad things to ensure the consistency and perseverance of that culture. Like other great leaders we will see throughout this book, Kelleher and his colleagues are *architects,* designers of sets of practices that ensure that the company's operations remain focused and effective. There have been other great leaders in the airline industry. Indeed, some have commented that there have been too many strong egos in this industry. What Kelleher and his senior management team have done is to transform personal leadership into an *organizational system* in which everyone has the opportunity to develop his or her leadership skills and to exercise leadership.

Thus, the Southwest "secret recipe" lies in the alignment between the values of Southwest, what it stands for, and the systems and practices it uses to implement its strategy and values. As Kelleher has stated, "They can imitate the airplanes. They can imitate our ticket counters and all the other hardware. . . . But they can't duplicate the people of Southwest and their attitudes."[49] Success comes from the consistency with which management has articulated and implemented its vision and from the relentless attention to detail in ensuring that all policies and practices support the company's values. In that sense, Southwest's success comes from its myriad management practices (e.g., recruiting, selection, training, rewards). But competitors can copy these, can't they? Conceptually, the answer is probably yes, but the empirical evidence suggests otherwise. Firms such as United, America West, and USAir have tried to emulate these policies without much success. The reason for this lack of success can be found in how they have attempted to do this.

Most fundamentally, the imitators often don't have the same values as Southwest. Instead, they pretend to copy the Southwest model, only to have their people see that they don't truly value employees and their contributions. They say employees matter, but their actions aren't consistent with this avowal. Second, competitors frequently imitate only some of the most visible practices and fail to capture the full alignment needed to release the hidden value in their organizations. Southwest is more than flying 737s and putting flight attendants in shorts. It has a reward system that shares success, and senior executive compensation that creates a sense of truly shared fate. It shares detailed operational information and tries to take care of its people. The Southwest system isn't one thing, it's many. Finally, the competition often doesn't have the stomach and stamina to stay the course. Other airlines implement some of the practices and get bored and impatient when immediate results aren't forthcoming. What senior managers really want are short-term financial results, not empowered, involved employees.

So, what are the lessons to be learned? We think there are three important conclusions to be drawn from Southwest and to be kept in mind as you read about the other successful companies profiled in the coming chapters. First, Southwest isn't a charitable institution. It is in business to make money, and, in their business (or any high fixed-asset operation) the key to success is asset utilization and low variable costs. Southwest does this through their fifteen-minute turnarounds and incredible worker productivity. This productivity and quick turnaround translate directly into Southwest's ability to effectively get one extra flight per plane per day—a significant increase in asset utilization and something their competitors cannot equal. How much of an advantage this gives Southwest can be seen in the stark contrast in the costs per seat mile shown in table 2-2. Southwest's average cost per mile in 1998 was 7.32 cents, an average of 20 percent lower than Delta, United, and Continental and over 60 percent lower than USAir. Imagine trying to compete in almost any market with a competitor that had this cost advantage.

How they achieve this advantage stems from the second lesson to be learned from Southwest. Their success comes not from some secret but from the exquisite attention they and the other firms we describe pay to aligning their values with systems, structure, and strategy. This requires a relentless attention and consistency on the part of managers at all levels to live these values. The third lesson to keep in mind has positive and negative aspects. The good news for those who would like to learn from companies like Southwest is that there is a real, sustainable competitive advantage to be had in unleashing the potential in a company's workforce—an advantage that competitors cannot easily imitate even when they "understand" exactly what you are doing. The bad news is that it is hard to do. Aligning values, systems, structure, and strategy is not for the insincere or the faint-hearted. It requires real belief and commitment and a willingness to persevere.

Armed with these insights, we will now consider how other managers and firms in disparate industries have implemented similar, value-based management approaches—and by so doing transformed their industries in the same manner that Southwest has transformed the airline industry.

Chapter 3

Cisco Systems: Acquiring and Retaining Talent in Hypercompetitive Markets

AS REMARKABLE as Southwest Airlines is, some people will remain cynical about a company's ability to get extraordinary performance from ordinary people. After all, they will say, this is the age of the Internet, of high technology, of blinding speed and revolutionary change. In this world, the argument goes, only organizations with extraordinary talent are likely to prosper—and these people don't come cheap. As described by the magazine *Fast Company,* this new marketplace is also a "free agent nation," with workers pursuing their own careers and owing loyalty only to "the brand of you."[1] While not trivializing the success of Southwest, the newer, hipper manager would note that running an airline is not exactly high tech. Sure, there are technical aspects to it, but fundamentally running an airline today is pretty much like it was thirty years ago. And whatever changes have occurred (for instance, the use of yield management software to help maximize revenues per flight or the ability to make reservations over the Web) have occurred comparatively slowly, giving management plenty of time to adjust. So, the fact that Southwest achieves its competitive success through clear values and tight alignment and consistency between its strategy and its people practices is interesting, but possibly not relevant for today's fast-paced world of high technology.

A more forceful version of this argument might even claim that Southwest's quaint ideas about leveraging people could be a disadvantage in today's hypercompetitive market. "Get real," the new paradigm manager might say, "we're competing on Internet time!" Worrying about soft issues like values and putting people first can divert attention from the marketplace and technology. Thinking about people and not business results can easily result in a firm missing the next technological wave or, worse, being stuck with people who don't have what it takes—the losers who aren't able to find a great new job elsewhere. What matters are results—and this means doing whatever it takes to attract and retain the brightest minds for as long as the project lasts, even if it's as long as a year or two.[2]

For this reason, we offer you another mystery: Cisco Systems, a company that has succeeded in this new high-tech world by doing things that are reminiscent of Southwest's practices, even as they are different in some of the specifics. A reporter from the *Wall Street Journal* noted that "Cisco is among the rarest of Wall Street birds: an internet-driven company with a proven business plan, actual products and ample profits."[3] To many people, Cisco is a $12 billion high-technology stealth company: the fastest-growing company of its size in history, faster even than Microsoft, with a market capitalization of over $200 billion. Cisco competes in markets where hardware is obsolete in eighteen months and software in six. It operates in the heart of Silicon Valley, where employee turnover averages almost 30 percent, and yet the turnover at Cisco is less than 10 percent. Its CEO, John Chambers, gets less attention than that paid to bigger stars of the high-tech world such as Bill Gates, Andy Grove, Larry Ellison, or even Lew Platt of Hewlett-Packard. But Cisco's success has dazzled Wall Street. If you had the prescience to invest $1,000 in Cisco stock in 1990, you'd now be walking around with roughly $100,000. Put another way, Cisco's stock has risen roughly 50,000 percent during the decade (adjusted for nine stock splits).[4]

How did this company, with its unglamorous origin in making routers for computer networks, become the worldwide leader in networking for the Internet—a company referred to in a recent article as "the Godzilla of datacom"?[5] This is a company that has repeatedly reinvented itself by focusing on different technologies, products, and markets. The first mystery is figuring out what Cisco has that others don't, how it has been able to be so flexible and fast, and what the company's sustainable competitive advantage is and where it comes from.

Managing rapid growth is invariably difficult. It is hard to find people. It is hard to get the people you find acculturated and productive quickly. It is hard to grow systems and processes—the organizational infrastructure—so that growth doesn't overwhelm the company. So, we offer you a second thing to think about. How has Cisco managed this startling growth in an industry where technology is constantly changing, intellectual capital is scarce, financial capital for new start-ups is abundant, and the competition from players such as Lucent and 3Com is brutal?

Finally, there is an even bigger puzzle to consider as you learn about Cisco. Cisco has frequently used acquisitions to obtain new technology. It has completed more than 40 mergers since 1993 and spent more than $18 billion acquiring nine companies in 1998 and fourteen in 1999, an average of more than one acquisition per quarter over a five-year period. The evidence is clear that most mergers are failures, not only failing to achieve their intended objectives but, in many cases, actually destroying economic value as companies struggle to combine cultures, systems, and products. One study found that in two-thirds of 100 large deals made between 1994 and 1997, the merged companies underperformed in the stock market for more than a year afterward.[6] Moreover, "mergers of technology companies are notoriously difficult."[7] In the networking industry, Wellfleet Communications and SynOptics were strong competitors of Cisco until they merged in 1994 to form Bay Networks. The problems with the merged firm left Bay, a $1 billion business almost as large as Cisco at the time of the merger, in the dust. Although the merger made strategic sense, combining companies in the router and the hub businesses, the difficulties in combining two different cultures located on two separate coasts resulted in product line gaps and time-to-market problems. Eric Benhamou, CEO of competitor 3Com, commented, "We have all benefitted from Bay's mistakes."[8]

Mergers are difficult, and, in theory, Cisco should have even more trouble. Cisco's acquisitions are not just to acquire customers, branches, or plants—its mergers are specifically designed to acquire technology and know-how embodied in people, frequently including the founders of the acquired companies. If people leave, the merger fails. And people can leave—there is no slavery in the United States, and alternative opportunities abound. So perhaps the biggest mystery of all is how Cisco has been able to enhance its technology base through mergers. If you can learn how Cisco does it, perhaps you will be able to more effectively manage your own merger and acquisition process.

As you will see, the answer to these questions is to be found in an approach to managing people that is eerily similar to Southwest's approach. For a technology business, it is a unique approach because it is based on people, frugality, and attention to customers. It is an approach to managing intellectual capital that adds real value to the business.

BACKGROUND

Cisco was founded in 1984 by Leonard Bosack and Sandy Lerner, a husband and wife team working in computer operations at Stanford University. They invented a technology to link the separate computer systems at Stanford together. With venture funding from Don Valentine at Sequoia Capital and a new CEO in John Morgridge, Cisco went public in 1990 and today is one of America's great success stories, with revenue growth nearly a hundredfold in seven years (see table 3-1 for financial information). Consistent with our emphasis on people management, the company was ranked twenty-fourth on *Fortune's* list of the "100 Best Companies to Work for in America" in 1999, and was ranked fourth on *Fortune's* list of America's most admired companies in 2000.[9] Cisco has a voluntary attrition rate among employees of about 8 percent—low by most standards but extraordinary in the Silicon Valley. In 1999, it had more than 26,000 employees operating in over fifty-four countries around the world. Its products enable computers to communicate with each other, offering customers end-to-end scalable network solutions.[10]

Networks are one of the least sexy businesses in the world. They consist mainly of routers, switches, servers, and software that compose local area networks (LANs), wide area networks (WANs), and the remote access network. Cisco began by offering high-end routers pri-

Table 3-1 Financial Data (1995–1999)

	1999	1998	1997	1996	1995
Revenue (in billions)	12.2	8.5	6.4	4.1	2.2
Assets (in billions)	14.7	9.0	5.4	3.6	2.0
Net income (in billions)	2.1	1.4	1	0.913	0.456
Return on assets (%)	14	15	19	25	23
Return on equity (%)	18	19	24	32	29
Earnings per share	0.62	0.42	0.34	0.30	0.16
Employees (approx.)	26,000	15,000	12,000	9,000	4,000

marily for the LAN market. Routers are the stand-alone boxes that can network traffic and send it along to the proper address. However, in 1993 Cisco changed its strategy and began to diversify into other network markets and technologies. Its competitors have done the same, building companies that could offer one-stop networking solutions. Figure 3-1 provides a simplified schematic of this market.

The industry consolidation has been driven by customers who have come to rely more heavily on networks and who demand not only product innovation and quality but also service and reliability— something smaller competitors were unable to provide on a consistent basis. For instance, a recent survey of 1,000 companies revealed that 40 percent of respondents preferred a single supplier to provide all their networking hardware.

Ongoing developments in products and technology highlight the need for Cisco to be flexible in its strategy and technology. Commenting on this, one industry analyst observed that "Three years ago, switching was the biggest threat to Cisco. Now they're the leader" in this market segment. CEO Chambers has a simple response to criticisms about a lack of clarity in Cisco's strategy: "We let our customers decide."[11]

Cisco's Strategy

In contrast to many technology companies, Cisco does not have a technology religion. That is, Cisco refuses to take a rigid approach

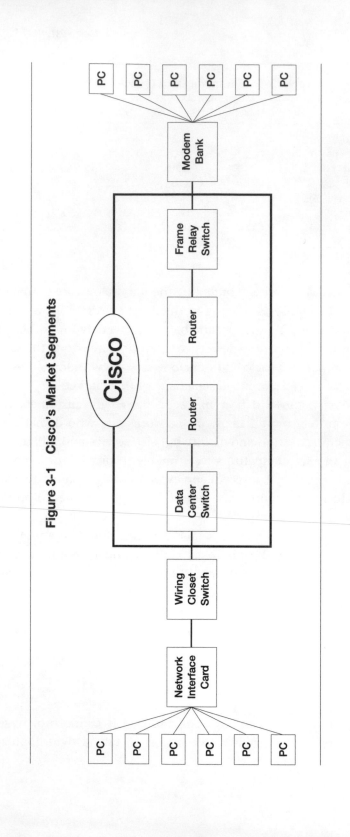

Figure 3-1   Cisco's Market Segments

that favors one technology and imposes it on customers as the only answer. Cisco's philosophy is to listen carefully to customer requests, monitor all technological advancements, and offer customers a *range* of options from which to choose. To do this, Cisco attempts to develop products using widely accepted industry standards. In some instances, technologies developed by Cisco have become the industry standard, but their starting position with regard to customers is to espouse no technology religion. Chambers is adamant about this, claiming "We have no technology bias. We are going to be the leader in every major segment of technology. Number one or number two, or not competing."[12]

Cisco defines the company mission as follows: "Be the supplier of choice by leading all competitors in customer satisfaction, product leadership, market share, and profitability." Their business purpose is "To shape the future of global networking by creating unprecedented opportunities and value for our customers, employees, partners, and investors." In their view, a global networked business is an enterprise of any size that strategically uses information and communications to build a network of strong, interactive relationships with all its key constituencies. This business model opens the corporate information infrastructure to all major constituencies rather than relying on the information gatekeepers common in other approaches to information management. In applying this model to itself, Cisco does over $30 million a day in electronic commerce—three times the average daily Internet sales of Dell Computer.

Unlike some industries in which product life cycles are measured in years, in the computer network business the average product life cycle is estimated to be six to eighteen months. Worse, an industry rule of thumb is that each new product solution should offer twice the speed at the same or less cost. In this environment, Cisco recognizes that if the company does not have the internal resources to develop a new product within six months, it must buy its way into the market or miss the window of opportunity. But to do this and avoid the usual pitfalls of most mergers and acquisitions is not easy. How can Cisco simultaneously adapt to short-cycle, rapid change, grow to offer the scale and scope customers demand, and effectively integrate new acquisitions without losing critical intellectual capital—all without losing control or adopting the micromanagement that would kill the entrepreneurial culture they have developed? This seemingly impossible task is what Cisco has perfected.

COMPETING ON INTERNET TIME: IDENTIFYING AND MAKING ACQUISITIONS OF KNOW-HOW

In 1993, Chambers and his senior team realized that although they had grown quickly up to that point, they had missed important opportunities. They concluded that their earlier conservatism had cost them at least 20 percent in growth that they could have had if they had been more aggressive. There was also a concern with the increasing pace of change—from calendar years to Internet years, where each calendar year is equivalent to seven Internet years. Based on this realization, Chambers says that "instead of looking at a one-year plan, we began looking at every quarter and adjusting our plan up or down." He went on to note that "we made the conscious decision, for example, that we were going to attempt to shape the future of the entire industry. We decided to play very aggressively and truly attempt in the networking industry what Microsoft did with PCs and IBM did with mainframes."[13] Doing this required leaving behind their "religious" mind-set regarding technnology for a nonreligious view that acknowledged that customers were the arbiters of choice. This quickly led them to the decision to acquire new technologies. Since 1993, Cisco has acquired over forty companies (see table 3-2).

Their initial approach to acquisitions began with an acknowledgment that most mergers and acquisitions are beset with problems. In reflecting on the decision not to seek out a merger of equals, Chambers noted:

> If you merge two companies that are growing at 80 percent rates, you stand a very good chance of stalling both of them out. That's a fact. When you combine companies, for a period of time, no matter how smoothly they operate, you lose business momentum. Our industry is not like the banking industry, where you are acquiring branch banks and customers. In our industry, you are acquiring people. And if you don't keep those people, you have made a terrible, terrible investment. . . . So we focus first on the people and how we incorporate them into our company, and then we focus on how to drive the business.[14]

Table 3-2   Cisco Acquisitions

Company	Date
1. Crescendo Communications	September 1993
2. Newport Systems	August 1994
3. Kaplana, Inc.	October 1994
4. LightStream Corp.	December 1994
5. Combinet, Inc.	August 1995
6. Internet Junction	September 1995
7. Grand Junction	September 1995
8. Network Translation	October 1995
9. TGV Software, Inc.	January 1996
10. StrataCom, Inc.	April 1996
11. Telebit-MICA Technologies	July 1996
12. Nashoba Networks, Inc.	August 1996
13. Granite Systems, Inc.	September 1996
14. Netsys Technologies	October 1996
15. Telesend	March 1997
16. Skystone Systems, Inc.	June 1997
17. Global Internet Software	June 1997
18. Ardent Communications	June 1997
19. Dagaz Technologies	July 1997
20. LightSpeed International	December 1997
21. WheelGroup Corporation	February 1998
22. NetSpeed, Inc.	March 1998
23. Precept Software	March 1998
24. CLASS Data Systems	May 1998
25. Summa Four, Inc.	July 1998
26. American Internet Corp.	August 1998
27. Clarity Wireless Corp.	September 1998
28. Selsius Systems	October 1998
29. PipeLinks, Inc.	December 1998
30. Sentient Networks	April 1999
31. Fibex Systems	April 1999
32. Amteva Technologies, Inc.	April 1999
33. GeoTel Communications Group	April 1999
34. TransMedia Communications	June 1999
35. StratumOne Communications	June 1999
36. Calista, Inc.	August 1999
37. MaxComm Technologies, Inc.	August 1999
38. Monterey Networks, Inc.	August 1999
39. Cerent Corporation	August 1999
40. Cocom A/S	September 1999
41. WebLine Communications Corp.	September 1999
42. Tasmania Network Systems, Inc.	October 1999
43. Aironet Wireless Communication	November 1999
44. V-Bits, Inc.	November 1999

Barbara Beck, vice president of human resources, is direct in saying, "One of Cisco's core strategies for growth is acquisitions, and one of the primary purposes for acquisitions is for the engineering talent."[15] Chambers reinforces this, noting that "When we acquire a company, we aren't simply acquiring its current products, we're acquiring the next generation of products through its people. . . . In the average acquisition, 40 to 80 percent of the top management and key engineers are gone in two years. By those metrics, most acquisitions fail."[16]

An awareness of the frequent failure of mergers and acquisitions has prompted Cisco to devise an approach to help maximize success. Drawing a lesson from Hewlett-Packard, Chambers and his team adopted a philosophy of breaking up markets into segments. Using the General Electric mentality of being either the number 1 or number 2 player in each segment led them to a set of strategic guidelines for Cisco:

- The use of business units to target specific market segments

- The importance of being either number 1 or number 2 in each segment in which they compete

- The definition of a set of criteria that could be used to determine the suitability of an acquisition

- The reliance on empowered teams and programs to increase the speed of assimilation of the acquired company

- The notion that the acquisition of technology is the acquisition of people

The Planning Matrix

Because the market moves too quickly for all innovation to come from within Cisco, early feasibility studies lead to decisions about whether a product is to be developed in-house or the technology is to be acquired through acquisition. If the decision is to develop in-house, product planning moves to the next phase and a well-specified development process is followed. If the decision is to acquire a technology, the next step is to involve business development to determine the most appropriate acquisition target. One of the key tools resulting from these rules was a planning matrix to analyze emerging markets.

This matrix uses a grid of markets by source of innovation (internal development, acquisition, partnering, or original equipment manufacturer) for each line of business to permit the identification of opportunities for market leadership—with market leadership defined by Chambers as an initial 20 percent share leading to an eventual 50 percent share. Currently this matrix is used to assess more than sixteen separate markets. The team then determines the product, services, and distribution needs for each market segment and a way of getting these products developed and sold—whether internally, through joint development, or acquisition. These decisions are then used to fill in the matrix, including those areas where Cisco is currently not playing or is trailing the market.

The recognition is never lost that the acquisition is not of technology but of people—and that all efforts must be made to retain this pool of talent if the acquisition is to be successful. Selby Wellman, senior vice president of business units, says that although 70 percent to 80 percent of Cisco's products are developed in-house, these are often created by engineers who started with smaller firms acquired by Cisco. "From this perspective, Cisco will never engage in a 'hostile' takeover. To assure this, the entire acquisition process must be characterized by honesty and trust—both before the acquisition and after. This means all people must be fully informed throughout the acquisition in order to avoid negative surprises and maximize retention."[17]

Identifying Acquisition Targets

Charles Giancarlo, vice president for business development, heads up Cisco's merger and acquisition unit. The group is composed of finance and human resource personnel, supplemented by business unit leaders and technology specialists. This team of fifty to sixty people continually analyzes new markets and technologies for their fit with Cisco's strategic plans. Any target candidate must have the requisite "great" technology that can be turned into a definitive product within six months, must have a shared vision, and must be culturally compatible (e.g., aggressive, focused, entrepreneurial). Lack of this fit, or a lack of honesty, results in a decision on Cisco's part to seek other candidates. Giancarlo always insists on having leaders from the various business units involved in the negotiations because an acquired company must be embraced by an internal group or it will flounder and die.

Typically this process results in the identification of a small technology-driven firm with between 60 and 100 employees whose product has not yet hit the market. The team shies away from old-line, slow-moving firms or from turnaround candidates. In many respects, the ideal candidates look like an early-stage Cisco and are referred to within the company as "Cisco-kids." Their employees are more motivated by developing "cool" technology than by monetary gain. For instance, Howard Charney, cofounder of both 3Com and Grand Junction Networks, left 3Com because of the politics but stayed at Cisco when Grand Junction was acquired and is now a senior vice president. He says that although he misses some of the control he enjoyed before the acquisition, "What they've given me instead is the chance to kick our products through the roof." He notes, "I'm still running an operation whose mission is managing lives and technology, but I don't worry about cash flow. I don't worry about having enough R&D money to keep up with the big boys. We *are* the big boys."[18]

Adhering to this approach for identifying and accomplishing acquisitions helps guarantee a quick win for both the acquired company and Cisco and further cements the embryonic relationship. This early success also sets the stage for the long-term wins. For example, Cisco's first acquisition, Crescendo, cost $89 million in 1993 for a company with only $10 million in revenue. Chambers said that at the time, they "caught unbelievable heat in the press" for making this purchase. But this unit now provides over $500 million in annual revenues and is worth more than $4 billion to the shareholders, a four-year return of 430 percent. Studies have shown that Cisco acquisition returns range from 10 percent to over 400 percent.

Throughout the acquisition process, the Cisco team constantly screens the target against the following five principles:

1. The presence of a shared vision

2. The likelihood of a short-term win for both the acquired company and Cisco

3. A long-term win for all parties

4. The right chemistry or cultural compatibility

5. Reasonable geographic proximity

Cisco also prefers to acquire companies that are much smaller than it is. Beau Parnell, director of human resource development and a key player in the integration of new acquisitions, stressed that you cannot overemphasize the importance of chemistry in determining the suitability of an acquisition.

The process of due diligence begins with informal conversations between senior Cisco managers and the CEO and senior team of the target firm. This is typically followed by an exchange of documents on technology and human resources. Part of this assessment process is based on what information the target is prepared to share. In the Cisco experience, excessive secrecy may signal a lack of openness and honesty. They also look for how flexible the target firm's managers are in the conversation and how widely they share their equity within the company. Again, an unwillingness to share the equity may signal a misfit for Cisco's values. Similarly, "we won't do a deal if the candidate company has accelerated vesting" of stock options, says Giancarlo. With these "golden parachute" provisions, "The minute you buy the company, they all get rich. We prefer 'golden handcuffs,'" he says.[19] Typically, these consist of two-year noncompete agreements with key executives and technical personnel and the provision of Cisco stock options that vest over time. Mike Volpi, vice president of business development, notes that this approach is also an effective way for Cisco to retain people.

Once a decision is made to continue negotiations, Selby Wellman is direct in saying, "When we acquire a company, we don't tell them, 'We'll leave you alone.' We say, 'We'll change everything.'"[20] But Ed Kozel, Cisco's chief technical officer, adds that "we try to establish an environment where we are attractive to small, innovative companies."[21] Chambers says that "We've learned that to make it [the acquisition] successful, you have to tell employees up front what you are going to do, because trust is everything in this business. You have got to tell them early so you don't betray their trust later."[22] This direct approach seems to work well enough that venture capitalists and entrepreneurs now often seek out Cisco as a primary exit strategy.

Adhering to these guidelines, Cisco has made a number of decisions not to go ahead with an acquisition because of a lack of cultural fit. Chambers volunteered that "We've killed nearly as many acquisitions as we've made . . . even when they were very tempting. I believe it takes courage to walk away from a deal. It really does. You can get caught up in winning the acquisition and lose sight of what will make it successful. That's why we take such a disciplined approach."[23] For instance, once Cisco had a chance to acquire a company on great financial terms. But even though the price was right and there was even a fit on chemistry, Chambers passed on the deal because he knew that they would not need the employees after the initial product was absorbed into the Cisco line. Chambers wouldn't acquire the company knowing that they would have to lay off the employees. While at Wang "I did five layoffs totaling 5,000 people. It nearly killed me. I vowed I would never do that again to employees or shareholders."[24]

The Human Resources Screen

Mimi Gigoux is a director in the corporate acquisitions group who is responsible for due diligence on the human resources side. Her activities begin before a decision is made to acquire a company, with a careful scrutiny of management styles, organizational structure, and cultural fit issues. She notes that these topics are highly visible in the early stages of discussion because the key personnel at the target company are often far more concerned about their own future than they are about the actual acquisition price of the firm. This offers her a window into their style and the operating basis of the company.

In one acquisition, her due diligence uncovered $60 million in uncovered pension liabilities—more than the actual price of the company. In another instance, an acquisition discussion was well underway with seemingly good fit regarding the technology and product when she discovered that because of the stock distribution arrangements, it would be very difficult for Cisco to retain key engineers. This arrangement was changed and the acquisition was completed—and the engineering talent stayed.

Chambers instructs the business development group to take all possible actions to retain *all* personnel, although the senior management and key technologists are the most important. Gigoux periodically follows up on Cisco's retention rates. Part of the success of the human resources screen can be seen in these retention figures. In her latest calculation, the turnover rate for acquired personnel is identical with that of the Cisco population as a whole. Over 70 percent of the senior managers from acquired firms are still with Cisco. These are people who often have multiple start-ups under their belts and have substantial personal wealth. But her follow-up studies show that they stay because they now have the corporate resources and backing to pursue their dream projects.

Integrating New Acquisitions

Once the deal is approved, the final details and formal arrangements (such as price) are worked out. In most acquisitions, the formal deal is closed quickly because of the amount of honest communication and mutual sizing up that has already occurred. The subtext for this process is captured in a Cisco saying about acquisitions and product development: "Early if not elegant," meaning that time to market is more important than getting things completely right. This makes good sense in a world of short product life cycles, where if you're late, the market might not exist anymore. The goal is to ship the acquired company's product under the Cisco label by the time the deal is closed, usually within three to six months. Chambers underscores the importance of this emphasis on speed: "Make no mistake about it, the fast will beat the slow."[25]

With a final agreement in place, the focus shifts immediately to integrating the new company into Cisco as quickly as possible. Integration teams (e.g., MIS, product, logistics) act immediately to see that new employees are up on the intranet, have office space and free soft drinks, and get immediate training in the Cisco way. This is made easier since more than half of Cisco's employees have been hired within the past four years and have a culture of welcoming new members with little "insider versus outsider" attitudes.

Mimi Gigoux welcomes new employees with an acknowledgment that change is painful and that—like taking off a Band-Aid—Cisco will do it fast. Her goal is complete honesty. She pulls no punches, informing people that this was an acquisition, not a merger of equals. She also offers a first lesson, noting to the new employees that "The more flexible and positive you are, the better it will be for you." But she also points out the plentiful good news, such as retention plans, compensation, benefits, increased vacation days, tuition reimbursement, and career opportunities.

In a typical acquisition, the engineering, marketing, and sales units will be integrated into the sponsoring business unit, while human resources, service, manufacturing, and distribution are merged into the Cisco infrastructure. This integration takes place at two levels, structural and cultural. The structural part includes the organizational rearrangements needed to ensure operation of the business functions and rationalization of functions such as payroll, information systems, and other services. This process has been refined to the point that it usually takes only two to three months, with smaller acquisitions being completed in as few as ten days and the largest, with 1,200 employees, taking only four months.

Cultural integration includes the use of integration teams who explain and model Cisco's values, the holding of orientation sessions, and the assignment of "buddies." The integration teams are composed of Cisco employees and members of the new unit who are chartered to perform specific tasks. This arrangement serves both to ensure the accomplishment of specific tasks and to begin the process of bonding between old and new Cisco employees. Special orientation sessions involve employees from previously acquired companies who offer their insights, as well as change management sessions to assist the people within the acquired firm in supporting the transition. The buddy system involves pairing each new employee with a seasoned Cisco veteran of equal stature and similar job responsibility. The buddy offers personalized attention better suited to conveying the Cisco values and culture.

In the early stages of the transition all integration processes are monitored and controlled by project management. This group is composed of employees who have come from an acquired company and have experienced the process themselves. They also act as a source of institutional knowledge and learning, ensuring that new insights and refinements are added to the acquisition process. There is also a careful effort to assess and track 30-, 60-, 90-, and 120-day milestones so that there is no loss of productivity. During this phase Gigoux acts as a conduit, ensuring that the new company isn't overrun by hundreds of Cisco employees who are fascinated with the new company and want to "help." At the conclusion of this process, there is a "lessons-learned" review designed to improve the acquisition process for the next iteration.

Not all employees of acquisitions stay with Cisco. As one member of the business development team observed, "Cisco isn't for everybody. Some people don't fit."[26] Chambers likens the process to marriage. "If you are selecting a partner for life, your ability to select the partner after one date isn't very good." That is why this selection process is crucial for successful acquisitions. "If you don't spend a fair amount of time on the evaluation of what are the key ingredients for that, your probability of having a successful marriage after one date is pretty small. We spend a lot of time on the up-front."[27]

Because the purpose of any acquisition is to retain people and their intellectual capital, the processes are designed to empower and retain people. Giancarlo notes that retaining the leaders of the acquired firm is critical because "If you don't retain executive management, you don't retain the rank and file." Giancarlo, who came to Cisco as part of a 1994 deal and had previously founded several other companies, says, "Cisco is able to hold onto people like me because they gave me a chance to play a major role."[28] Others, like Andy Bechtolsheim, who was a founder of Sun Microsystems, came to Cisco when his start-up Granite Systems was acquired in 1996. He stays because of a desire to build breakthrough products that, with Cisco's marketing, sales, and distribution, can change the world. He also stays because "Most people at Cisco came from start-ups, so the place has a small-company mentality."[29]

Mike Volpi points out that acquisitions not only bring in the obvious technical talent but also are an important way to bring in scarce managerial talent, a critical element in a fast-growing company. He is optimistic. "We have the process down. We have a generic process. Sometimes in all this speed we end up paying too much. But the acquisitions are not financial—we don't do them because we can swing a good deal—they are strategic. We do them to grow the company in the right direction."[30]

Why Cisco Succeeds with Its Mergers

Upon reflection, several elements of Cisco's experience with acquisitions are important. First, the focus of any acquisition is a clear identification of specific technology or product needs as determined in their strategic matrix. So, Cisco knows why it is doing what it is doing; it is not doing deals just for the sake of making investment bankers money. Second, the vision of the leader of the company being acquired and the direction the company is headed must be compatible with Cisco's. Says Chambers, "If your visions are not the same—about where the industry is going, what role each company wants to play—you are constantly going to be at war. . . . So you have to look at the visions of both companies and if they are dramatically different, you should back away."[31] Third, Cisco's acquisition identification process emphasizes cultural compatibility. For example, one senior Cisco executive observed that in addition to having complementary technologies and a shared vision, Cisco acquisitions are typically entrepreneurial, fast-growing Silicon Valley companies that thrive in dynamic markets, with an excellent fit of cultures, values, and chemistry. The fact that Cisco is a player in all the hot network technology areas makes it attractive to the employees of acquired firms.

Fourth, Cisco sets very clear expectations as to how the merged entity will function. For instance, specifying who the leader of the combined operation will be and to whom this person will report. Fifth, Cisco manages the change process that accompanies an acquisition quickly. Leaving acquisitions alone doesn't work. Finally, Cisco ensures that there are short- and long-term wins for the stakeholders in both companies. The short term is typically defined in financial terms. In the long term all constituencies, shareholders, employees, customers, and business partners must also benefit. Part of the benefit is ensuring that employees in the acquired company can have a future at Cisco. Almost embarrassed, Chambers says, "I know that sounds corny, but it is true." Since Cisco pays between $500,000 and $2 million per employee, the economic rationale for retaining these assets is clear.

CISCO'S VALUES, CULTURE, AND LEADERSHIP

John Chambers

John Chambers, Cisco's CEO, has an energetic, self-effacing manner that has been described as being less CEO-style bravado than the cheerful, earnest energy of a country doctor—something both his parents were. A *Fortune* writer, noting Chambers's West Virginia accent, once described him as talking "like Mister Rogers on speed."[32] With both business and law degrees, Chambers joined Cisco in 1991 after stints at Wang Labs, where he had been senior vice president of U.S. operations, and IBM. Noting his experience at Wang, one admirer observed that this "taught him how a high-tech company ought not to be run," especially as "a textbook example of the vertically integrated company that didn't change with the times." He is a charismatic but modest leader who carefully watches the bottom line, always flies coach class, and has been known to double up in hotel rooms to save money. In fact, when asked why the senior management of Cisco was becoming more high profile, Chambers acknowledged that after studying Microsoft "[w]e realized that it gets most of its marketing for free. Since we're a frugal company, that really appealed to us. As a result, we made the decision as a team that we wanted to become much more visible."[33]

Chambers says, "My definition of leadership is, Don't ask someone else to do something you wouldn't do."[34] He admires Hewlett-Packard as a company that has transformed itself over the years. "They adjusted their vision to what the market required, and they flourished," he said. "They are fine people. They make agreements on a handshake. They're what we'd like to be when we grow up."[35] He has also learned important lessons from his time at IBM and Wang. "I learned at both companies that in high tech, if you don't stay ahead of trends, they'll destroy everything you work for and tragically disrupt the lives of your employees. I don't ever want to go through that again."[36] He also claims that he bases his strategy on what his father taught him as they played competitive bridge when he was a teenager: "I learned early in life there might be people smarter than you, but if you have a combination of skills and strategy, you can beat them."[37]

Employees don't mistake John Chamber's kindness for weakness. Three things can get you fired at Cisco: not producing business results, not recruiting and developing the right people, or not being a team player. One executive seconded this view, noting that "He's probably the most polite person in the world to fire you. But boy, he doesn't hold back." Another Cisco executive, a 17-year veteran of DEC, reinforces this view:

One thing that keeps Cisco healthy as we get larger is the fact that a lot of people on the executive staff have come from places that caused their own downfall. My back arches and my fur goes up when I see us going down one of those tracks, like setting up a committee to make a decision. Or making it difficult for people to get recognition, because some manager wants to grab it. Or focusing on internal competition rather than the real competition. Or not being sensitive to people who are fast trackers but don't quite fit.[38]

Values and Philosophy

Cisco espouses five core values: a dedication to customer success; innovation and learning; partnerships; teamwork; and doing more with less. Each of these values is continually articulated and reinforced in the mission statement, current initiatives, policies and practices, and culture of the company. Customer satisfaction, for example, drives the entire organization. CEO Chambers constantly reinforces this view. "There is a one-to-one relationship between customer satisfaction and profitability. A lot of companies lose sight of that," he says.[39] Underscoring the importance of customer satisfaction as a core value, he personally reviews as many as fifteen critical accounts each day, often calling on customers himself to straighten out problems. "I'm probably the only CEO in the world in a company this size who does this," says Chambers. "But the fact that I pay attention to these issues at this level means that the whole company has to." Further, Chambers asks employees on critical accounts (defined less by size than the fact that someone associated with the account is concerned about its instability) to leave a voice mail for him every evening. "Sure, e-mail would be more efficient," he says, "But I want to hear the emotion, I want to hear the frustration, I want to hear that person's level of comfort with the strategy we're employing. And you can't get that through e-mail."[40] In the mid-1990s, roughly two-thirds of Cisco's customers called themselves "satisfied." Now 85 percent of customers are satisfied. The jump in ratings occurred the first year all employees' bonuses were tied to how well the company was doing as a whole.

Innovation and learning are other values that permeate the company. There is constant pressure from Chambers and senior staff to "make it happen," whatever it takes. Individuals are encouraged to think and respond in ways they consider appropriate and consistent with the company's values. They are encouraged to take risks and think outside the box—to look for new ways of doing things to achieve Cisco's strategic objectives. A "not invented here" attitude is not tolerated. As Chambers says, "You must take risks to succeed—if you do the same thing that everyone else has done in the same situation, you will get exactly the same result. If you take a risk and don't succeed, learn from that failure. But make no mistake about it, if you take a risk and fail, don't ever plan on making that same mistake twice. There is no room in this organization for people who cannot learn from failure. It's more important to do and make mistakes than to sit back and wait to get permission."[41]

Openness is also the rule, with people encouraged to challenge the status quo. For instance, Chambers holds a monthly "birthday breakfast" meeting open to anyone with a recent birthday and answers every question put to him—no matter how tough the question. To ensure that the questions and criticisms will be honest, he strongly discourages directors and vice presidents from attending these meetings. At the same time, "doing more with less" is deeply ingrained. Nobody flies first class. There is no executive dining room, and executives brag about how much less their buildings cost than others in the Valley. "We're very cheap," boasts Ed Kozel, the chief technology officer. Teamwork is another of Chambers's important themes and one of three things that can get a person fired at Cisco for disregarding. Says Chambers, "If people aren't team players, they're off my team."[42]

These values do not stand alone but are put in the context of executing the business strategy. To reinforce this, every employee at Cisco is expected to be able to recite what the top initiatives are for the year. Managers are expected to provide frequent updates on the status of initiatives, and there is tremendous peer pressure to know what these initiatives are.

Organizational Design

At the time of the 1993 shift in strategy, senior management decided to follow Hewlett-Packard's lead and organize by business units. At that time, Cisco was organized by product lines. However, because they believed that time to market was the key to successful domination of the market, they realized that Cisco needed to act like a small company from a product development point of view while retaining big-company strengths in manufacturing, distribution, and finance. This led them to an independent market-focused organizational design based on lines of business (LOBs) in three domains: enterprises (large corporations such as Intel and local governments), service providers (such as telephone companies), and small to medium-sized businesses (such as universities). There is also a direct sales force with LOB market focus, and a centralized R&D function funded at the rate of approximately 12 percent of sales, about the same percentage as rival 3Com. All component manufacturing is outsourced, but there is a centralized final assembly and test manufacturing organization. Frequent reorganizations respond to changing markets.

To ensure decentralization, Cisco has adopted a policy of setting stretch goals—goals that people would never have thought possible—and making these a part of the culture. Chambers described how "[r]ather than trying to do the impossible just by working harder—we asked: What are we going to do uniquely to accomplish our stretch goals? The first thing is to empower teams. We went through an evolution from a very tight central management group with four or five people making all the decisions to the empowerment of groups. Our aim was to drive our strategy down through the company."[43] The overarching intent is to develop high value added products that offer high margins. Achieving high margins and profitability growth is key to Cisco's continual investment in technology.

HOW CISCO MANAGES ITS PEOPLE

An illustration of how Cisco manages its people can be seen in the experience of a journalist from *Wired* magazine who made the trek to Cisco to report on the experience of the employees, whom he referred to as "Ciscoids." After spending some time there, he wrote that Cisco employees were "basically very, very good mechanics of a type that is peculiar to our age: they build the plumbing of the Internet. And all they do is smile, smile, smile."[44] His attempt to find something bad about working at Cisco met with comments from employees such as

"It's addictive. It can take over your life if you let it. It's electronic heroin!" Another employee enthused, "You get amazed at your own productivity. You can work any 60 hours a week you want!" Some managers have even complained that a big problem is to convince employees to go home at night. The journalist's ultimate answer to the question of why these people were smiling was that they all believe that it's a great place to work—and they're all getting rich from stock options. They take the stock price personally. Said one employee, "If I do my job right it will support the stock. If I screw up and the stock goes down, people will come around and beat on me with hammers." So how does Cisco develop this sense of ownership and loyalty? Management policies and practices are the key, and it all begins with recruiting.

Recruitment and Selection

For the past several years Cisco has hired an average of over 1,000 new employees every three months—and it has done this in Silicon Valley, one of the tightest job markets in the country. The simple logistics of identifying and processing the applications necessary to accomplish this feat are daunting. But the Cisco staff is up to the challenge. First, the recruiting team identified exactly the kind of people they needed to hire. Next, by holding focus groups with ideal recruitment targets, they figured out where these types of people spent their time and how they did their job hunting. Then the team got innovative in designing the hiring process, including infiltrating art fairs, microbrewery festivals, and other places frequented by potential recruits. Rather than listing specific job openings, Cisco's ads feature their Web site address. As Barbara Beck, vice president of human resources, notes, Cisco is a high-tech company and "If you don't leverage the technology, you won't be able to leverage HR's capabilities." Besides, Beck notes, "The top 10 percent are not typically found in the first round of layoffs from other companies, and they usually aren't cruising through the want ads."[45] This means that the strategy for recruiting relies heavily on the Internet.

By monitoring the Cisco Web site, the recruitment team realized that their jobs page recorded over 500,000 hits per month, with the heaviest load occurring between 10 A.M. and 2 P.M. Silicon Valley time. This meant that people were trolling for jobs on company time. To help facilitate this practice, Cisco is developing software to make life easy for stealthy job seekers. It will let users click on pull-down menus and profile themselves in ten minutes. If the boss walks by, users can hit a button that activates a screen disguise, changing it to "Gift List for Boss and Workmates" or "Seven Successful Habits of a Great Employee." The real power of this Web site, however, is that it actively targets passive job seekers by making it fun and easy to match personal skills and interests to job openings. For instance, to attract applicants, Cisco's site is linked to the Dilbert Web page, the darling of disenfranchised programmers. Importantly, Cisco's site allows visitors to pair up with a volunteer "friend" from within the company. Focus group results had shown that referrals from friends were a powerful factor in the job search process. As a result of the Web site, from 30 percent to 50 percent of all resumes are submitted electronically and automatically routed into a database that can be accessed immediately.

But the technology isn't the full story. To really involve potential recruits, the Friends Program is key. Michael McNeal, Cisco's director of employment, designed this effort to "put some grace into the hiring process."[46] For example, when Dawn Wilson, a printed-circuit board designer at Tandem Computers, was surfing the Cisco Web site, she clicked on the "make friends @ Cisco" button and was swept into the recruiting pipeline.[47] The day after she did this, a printed circuit board designer at Cisco called her at home and talked about life at Cisco. He referred her to his boss and a few days later she had a relaxed visit to Cisco. After a minimum of five interviews, she accepted a job—even though she had been at Tandem for eleven years and was not really looking to leave. Having a "friend" made the difference. Chambers claims that about 60 percent of the people who join Cisco join because they have a friend there. And every time a referral is hired, the Cisco employee gets from $500 to $1,000. The day they make the referral they also become eligible for prizes such as stainless steel commuter mugs, athletic bags, and trips to Hawaii. Small wonder that referral rates at Cisco are twice the industry norm.

Clearly, if all Cisco did was pay employees for referrals, the ultimate success rate for retaining employees would suffer. To rapidly turn new employees into motivated and productive employees requires the same sophistication in the orientation and indoctrination process, and Cisco has done this. Beau Parnell, director of human resource development, calls a new employee's first day "the most important eight hours in the world."[48] His personal mission is to help Cisco achieve "the fastest time to productivity for new hires in the country." To do this he created the Fast Start program, a collection of employee-orientation initiatives that alerts facilities teams before the new recruit arrives so that the employee begins with a fully functional work space, has been assigned a "buddy" (a peer in the company) who can answer questions about how Cisco works, and has been enrolled in a two-day course called "Cisco Business Essentials" that begins the indoctrination. Two weeks after they've begun, the new hire's boss receives an e-mail reminding him or her to review departmental initiatives and personal goals with the new employee.

Managing the Culture

Given the importance of Cisco's values for continued success, the human resources group also ensures that the culture is aligned with the business strategy and continually reinforced. A variety of mechanisms are used to repeatedly communicate the company's values. Quarterly "all hands" meetings are held to communicate the big picture and to make sure everyone feels included. This is more important as growth and the inevitable compartmentalization occur. The culture and values are also emphasized in communications through the company intranet, with Webcasts of important events delivered to desktop computers. Attempts are made to create an exciting environment through high levels of motivation, empowerment, and recognition and by removing barriers to creativity. Like any good Silicon Valley company, Cisco has parties—including a Christmas bash with 100 food stations and entertainment ranging from Elvis imitators to psychics. They also provide the usual complement of other employee-friendly services, such as on-site stores, dry cleaning services, fitness centers, ATMs, and automobile oil changes and mobile dental clinics with appointments made via e-mail. As one employee said, "I have a very Cisco-centric view of the world. It would be difficult for me to go to [a competitor] at this point because I feel a part of Cisco . . . it's become a part of my life, especially the people I work with."[49]

The culture and values are also reinforced through the way jobs are structured and managed. Micromanagement is rare and decentralization is encouraged. "I don't have to get permission on every little thing. There's no time for it," says one employee. Another adds that "when there's a problem, it's put more as a question to the team—a challenge, rather than dictating the task." At Cisco, unlike Dilbertland, senior management gets cubicles in the center of the fluorescent-lit space while employees get the windows—but all offices are the same 12 feet by 12 feet. For Cisco employees in sales offices there aren't even assigned spaces: It's all "hot desks" or "nonterritorial" office space.

Aligning the Reward System

The reward system is also carefully aligned with the strategy and values of the company. Stock options are distributed generously, with a full 40 percent of all Cisco stock options in the hands of individual employees without managerial rank. The average employee who has been with Cisco for over a year has over $125,000 in profit on unexercised options. That's on top of an average starting salary of about $70,000. The fact that most acquisitions involve the replacement of local stock options with Cisco options is a big selling point, given that Cisco shares have split five times since 1990 and doubled in value in 1996 alone. But executive salaries are only about 25 percent of the industry average. Chambers is paid $250,000, and former CEO John Morgridge earns a mere $50,000 as chairman. Management-level salaries are about 65 percent of the industry average. Chambers is adamant about rewards being tied to customer satisfaction. He ties the compensation of all managers to measures of customer satisfaction—really listening to the customer. "We are the only company of anywhere near this size that does it."[50]

Individual contributions are widely celebrated around the company. Mimi Gigoux said, "Never in my life have I seen such consistency in recognition."[51] For example, with the approval of the boss, anybody can give anybody else an on-the-spot bonus ranging from a free dinner to as much as $5,000 for going the extra mile—and these can be approved within twenty-four hours. To encourage the use of these rewards, the annual performance review includes an evaluation of whether supervisors have spent their reward budget.

LESSONS FROM CISCO

What is your explanation for Cisco's success? It isn't their strategy, for their competitors are trying to do roughly the same things. It isn't their ability to internally generate leading-edge technology either, for Cisco is more of an applied technology company than one dedicated to research. After all, it frequently acquires the technology that it needs. Leadership perhaps? Possibly, but Chambers was a part of two "failures" before arriving at Cisco, and many of Cisco's executives came from smaller companies—just like those sometimes acquired by their competitors. How about their people management practices? Certainly these are an important ingredient in Cisco's success, but they have been well described in the press and are available for any would-be imitators. How about plain old luck? Certainly there is some of this. Cisco entered an industry whose time had come. Had they been founded based on making VCRs in 1984 instead of the plumbing for the Internet, they would not be the success story they are today. But, although partly true, good fortune doesn't provide an explanation for their continued succcss. After all, in 1994 Bay Networks, one of their competitors, was about as large as Cisco. Today, however, Cisco dwarfs Bay Networks and is growing faster. So the question remains, What accounts for Cisco's competitive advantage?

Think about this deductively. First, the evidence is that Cisco has been more adept than its competitors at providing customers with the technology and equipment that they want. Why has Cisco been better able to meet these needs than the competition? It probably is not because Cisco engineers are smarter. The Silicon Valley labor market works well, and if a firm is willing to pay top dollar, great technology talent can be had. Cisco has smart, motivated people, but so does the competition. So, why has Cisco been better able to meet customers' needs? A more sophisticated explanation for Cisco's continued success has to do with two of their core values: the strong belief in having no technology religion, and listening carefully to the customer.

Sound too simplistic? Think again about why Cisco has been able to ride several different technology waves, and how they have been able to adapt in spite of disruptive technological changes. They have been able to do this, and to avoid being trapped by an existing technology, only because of their willingness to provide their customers with what they want, even if this means killing technologies that have been developed by the company and even when engineers are convinced that their technology is better than what the customer wants. "Understand one thing about Cisco," says Chambers, "we are technology agnostics. We really don't care."[52] These values have enabled Cisco both to really understand what customers need and to be willing to provide them with the technology they ask for, even if it means going out and acquiring it. "One of our strengths," Chambers says, "is the ability to eat our own when the market grows fast."[53]

This point is easily overlooked. In many technology firms, the engineers understand the capabilities of the technology better than the customers. Armed with this insight, the technical experts then "know" what's best for the customers and tend to force this solution on them. Besides, for the technologist it's more challenging to work on cutting-edge technologies than deliver old solutions. At Cisco, however, they truly listen to the customer and offer solutions that the customer wants—even if it means delivering older technology or technology that the engineers understand will not stand the test of time. A commitment to this belief, constantly reiterated by management and reinforced by the measurement and reward systems, has enabled Cisco to go in whatever direction the market and customers dictate.

But simply listening to the customer and not becoming wedded to a particular technology are not sufficient to guarantee the success that Cisco has enjoyed. How, for example, has Cisco been able to deliver this technology given the speed with which Internet solutions change? The answer to this, and to the mystery of Cisco's ability to grow rapidly, has to do with several other complementary values that also permeate the company: the importance of cultural fit and a shared vision, speed, frugality, and the need to continually change. Cisco understands that obtaining technology is fundamentally about acquiring people—the intellectual capital that is the source of the technology. Unlike many other companies, Cisco really understands the difficulties of mergers and the importance of keeping talent after the merger has occurred. For this reason, they are absolutely rigorous in screening potential acquisitions and quickly integrating new acquisitions into the Cisco culture. People, not technology, are the key to winning this game.

Cisco works hard to ensure a fit before an acquisition takes place, then rapidly assimilates the new company and works to ensure that the new employees are satisfied and want to stay with Cisco, not go off and create another start-up. To think about this in terms of intellectual capital, consider the following thought experiment. For any company, consider the number of employees who have left and started up their own firms. Sum the revenue of these spin-offs and you have an estimate of the lost intellectual capital from a firm that is unable to retain its people.

Cisco's success comes from more than *having* these values. Success derives from the company's ability to *implement* the values and cultural norms that differentiate it from the competition. In this sense, they have a comprehensive system of policies, practices, and leader behaviors that are aligned and internally consistent. For example, they are absolutely clear in signaling their values in the ways in which they recruit people and make acquisitions. If a person or small company does not fit their vision and values, they won't be asked to join. Once the person or company joins the Cisco world, intense efforts are made to socialize the newcomer to the Cisco way. Senior management is consistent about signaling their unwavering commitment to these values. There is no uncertainty or ambiguity about the importance of teamwork, customers, cost control, or flexibility. Says Chambers, "If you're going to empower people and you haven't got teamwork, you're dead."[54] All Cisco employees understand this, and any who don't behave accordingly are quickly socialized or ejected.

Both Cisco and Southwest Airlines have built their organizations on a set of fundamental values that the competition has been unable or unwilling to imitate. The long-term success of both rests on these fundamental values and on the alignment that the organizations have achieved in expressing these values through their treatment of people. The result in both cases is a remarkable success that comes from capturing the value of the entire workforce, not just a few superstars.

Chapter 4

The Men's Wearhouse:
Growth in a Declining Market

AN IDEA EXISTS, propagated by the literature on business strategy, that a company must be in a "good" industry in order to achieve outstanding business results. A good industry is one with substantial barriers to entry, perhaps provided by some technological advantage, trademark, or brand; market power with respect to suppliers and customers; and limited rivalry.[1] However, the existing evidence shows that industry growth rates are largely unrelated to a specific company's ability to produce outstanding shareholder returns and even to the company's own growth rate. These aggregate statistical results are nicely illustrated by the example of The Men's Wearhouse. The company, one of the largest off-price retailers of men's tailored business attire, achieved a five-year compounded annual growth rate of 26 percent in revenues and 29 percent in net income during the period from 1995 to 1999.

The Men's Wearhouse achieved these outstanding financial results in an industry that, to put it mildly, presents some substantial business challenges. It is an industry facing little or no growth and intense rivalry. In a report in 1995, Needham & Company noted:

> The men's tailored clothing market has been consolidating. Men have been spending less on tailored clothing. . . . The decline in the men's tailored clothing market has squeezed independent operators and has caused department stores to shrink the space dedicated to this merchandise category.[2]

In April 1996, Robertson Stephens published a report on the industry that included a table listing "some of the chains that have closed or consolidated their stores or are in financial distress."[3] The list included C & R Clothiers, Today's Man, Barney's, Kuppenheimer's, Hart, Shaffner and Marx, Hastings, Gentry's, Anderson Little, and several others. The first mystery for us to consider, therefore, is how this company has succeeded in a declining industry beset with intense rivalry, one in which many of its competitors have been forced into bankruptcy.

There is another mystery, perhaps even more intriguing. It's one thing to talk about achieving success through people and leveraging a company's human assets in businesses where intellectual capital is critical and the workforce is highly educated and skilled. For instance, many high-technology companies, recognizing the importance of their people, have added all sorts of amenities (such as health clubs, concierge services to run errands, and fancy food) in an effort to attract and retain the people essential to business success. But The Men's Wearhouse has achieved competitive advantage by leveraging a workforce that many managers would characterize as less than desirable. Charlie Bresler, one of the top four executives in the company and the person responsible for overseeing the human resources function, commented, "The retail worker in the United States is somebody who often came from a dysfunctional home, like a lot of us . . . somebody who didn't do well in school, who basically told their teachers in one way or another to go to hell."[4]

Most people don't start out with the goal of working and remaining in retailing, simply because it is not a very desirable employment destination. So those who work in the industry are often young people, immigrants, or those who for whatever reason have difficulty obtaining better work.

Retailing in the United States is the largest industry in terms of employment. About 16 percent of the workforce, more than 20 million people, work in retailing. In 1995, some 66 percent of the retailing workforce was female, compared with 46 percent for the economy as a whole.[5] It is a very low wage and, for the most part, low skilled industry. "Real wages for retail trade declined from 91 percent to 62 percent of the national average between 1948 and 1992. Turnover is endemic and the percent of part-time workers is extremely high. . . . Health care coverage tends to be minimal and ratio of skilled to non-skilled workers dismal."[6] The Men's Wearhouse has succeeded in this industry by breaking all of these rules of low pay, little training, and lots of part-time work and actually treating its people as well as, if not better than, some professional service firms treat theirs. The second mystery is how and why the company has done this, and why this strategy, which would seem to *raise* labor costs, has worked.

If we can understand the mysteries of how The Men's Wearhouse has succeeded in such a hostile competitive environment and how it has built a culture and workforce that provides it an advantage even though it operates in a difficult labor market, we will gain some important insight into how great companies achieve truly extraordinary results from ordinary people. If this company can succeed given the challenges it faces, think of what you can do by applying its lessons in more favorable environments.

BACKGROUND

George Zimmer, the founder of The Men's Wearhouse, opened the first store in Houston, Texas, in 1973 when he was twenty-four years old, with an initial investment of $7,000. Zimmer's father had been in the retailing business and had subsequently manufactured raincoats. George's first full-time sales experience was living in Dallas and selling his father's raincoats to stores as a manufacturer's representative in several western states. In the early 1980s, Zimmer opened his first stores in the San Francisco Bay Area. At that time, the firm's offices were in his house. The company developed a headquarters in an office park in Fremont, California, and currently has part of its head-quarters functions (mostly finance, information systems, warehous-ing, and distribution) in Houston and the rest (focusing on employee relations, store operations, merchandising and advertising, purchas-ing, and training) in Fremont.

The company initially grew slowly, opening stores mostly in Texas and California. When the company went public in 1991, it had 85 stores. Since that time, the pace of expansion has increased dramatically. By October 1999, the company operated more than 600 stores in about thirty-five states and Canada. This included 437 stores in its flagship chain, 52 stores that were part of a newer, Value Priced Clothing business that offered clothing at lower prices with much less service and restricted hours of operation, and 113 stores, mostly in Canada, that it had recently acquired when it purchased Moores Retail Group. Table 4-1 presents selected financial information on The Men's Wearhouse.

Table 4-1   Selected Financial Information for
The Men's Wearhouse

	1995	1996	1997	1998	1999
Net sales (in millions)	317.1	406.3	483.6	631.1	767.9
Net earnings (in millions)	12.1	16.5	21.1	28.9	40.9
Total assets (in millions)	160.5	204.1	295.5	379.4	403.7
Shareholders' equity (in millions)	84.9	137.0	159.1	220.0	298.2
Earnings per share ($)	0.43	0.55	0.67	0.89	1.21
Number of stores	231	278	345	396	431
Sales per square foot ($)	406	416	413	420	437

Strategy

"The Men's Wearhouse stores target middle to upper middle-income men, and offer designer brand name and private label merchandise at prices . . . [that] are typically 20% to 30% below the regular retail prices of traditional department and specialty stores. . . . [M]erchandise . . . includes suits, sport coats, slacks, business casual, sportswear, outerwear, dress shirts, shoes, and accessories."[7]

The company believes that men do not like to shop and structures its approach on that assumption. So, for instance, there is only one sale each year, in January. Consequently, the customers don't have to pay attention to when a sale or special is running—they can shop when they need something and not worry that they are paying too much. Zimmer calls this an "every day low pricing strategy." It is an approach that also helps build profits and margins, because you don't train the customer to wait for sales. Zimmer explained:

> The notion of driving customers through your door by lowering your prices is almost like committing suicide in a very slow way, because eventually the only way you can do business is to give it away so there are no gross profit dollars even when there is volume. . . . By using our strategy of running only one promotional event a year and the rest of the year selling everything at the ticketed price and relying on our people to drive the traffic creates a much different margin story.[8]

In the 1998 fiscal year, The Men's Wearhouse generated about $100 million cash on about $800 million sales, and had a pretax operating income of about 10 percent, at least double the historical industry average.

The stores are typically small, 4,000 to 7,000 square feet, and are located in shopping centers or in storefronts rather than regional malls. This permits the customer to drive right to the store and not have to walk through a big mall for access. The locations also typically offer lower rents than large regional malls. Because the stores are relatively small, when customers enter they are immediately seen, thus allowing someone to approach and wait on them. Pressing and tailoring can be and are done on the premises, and free pressing is offered for any garment purchased at any Men's Wearhouse store. The store price for a garment does not include any tailoring, including finishing the cuffs on pants, so all alterations cost extra, though once the seam has been touched, subsequent alterations are free.

The company uses almost no print advertising, instead relying on radio and television. Zimmer believes that there are several problems with print advertising. First, people can easily ignore it. Second, the only thing you can really display in a print advertisement is the item, perhaps with a picture and description, and its price. However, The Men's Wearhouse differentiates itself not on price but on the basis of a shopping experience that affords outstanding customer care. In order to describe that experience (for instance, using customer testimonials), you need an approach that permits more of a story line, such as you can get with a radio or television spot. In the fiscal year ending

January 1998, the company spent $38 million on its advertising. Part of its growth strategy is to target larger metropolitan areas, where the company can locate a greater number of stores (there are thirty-five, for instance, in the San Francisco area) and thereby leverage its media purchases over a larger number of locations.

The core of the company's strategy is to offer superior customer service, delivered by knowledgeable, caring salespeople, called wardrobe consultants. George Zimmer's trademark phrase, "I guarantee it," represents the company's position that it stands behind what it sells and will, for instance, provide free some alterations and pressing for the life of a garment and will take back merchandise if there is a problem of any kind. The Men's Wearhouse seeks to build a long-term relationship with its customers—customer loyalty is considered to be very important—and to become the preferred place for them to shop for all of their clothing needs for items that it carries.

The phrase "wardrobe consultant" was chosen intentionally. Charlie Bresler, executive vice president for human development, commented:

> We talk about a clerk, a consultant, and a slammer. A clerk is somebody who will meet your initial request but doesn't expand off your initial request. A slammer is somebody who'll sell anything they can get you into or sell you regardless of what your interests are, for their benefit. And a consultant is like a physician or an attorney, a professional.[9]

Unlike most other retailers, where merchandising is the center of power, The Men's Wearhouse emphasizes store operations and the sales process. George Zimmer explained:

> When you get down to what really happens in the retail world, it's a customer who wanders into the store and there's an employee there. And as they walk up to greet the customer, the question is: what type of energy, what type of feeling, does that employee have as they begin to engage the customer? . . . [I]s it a genuine feeling or is it something that has been hammered into them through fear and intimidation?[10]

VALUES AND PHILOSOPHY

George Zimmer believes strongly that the company's strategy and how it operates come from a philosophy or world view:

> I think where this really emanates from . . . is your world view. The way your parents and your community and your extended family informed you about how the world operates. . . . It all comes down to whether you believe that the world is basically, as we teach in economics, the allocation of scarce resources, or is the world filled with infinite love and compassion.[11]

Zimmer has said, "We're in the people business, not the suit business."[12] Charlie Bresler says that this means the company's job is to help people understand others, listen better, and develop excitement about helping themselves and their teammates reach their potential as persons. Realizing their potential is not just about selling men's clothing, but also about becoming a better spouse, a better parent, and personally more self-fulfilled.

George Zimmer believes in the power of untapped human potential, in creating abundance rather than allocating scarce resources, and in a win-win-win philosophy, where the customer, the wardrobe consultant, and the company all do well. Considering the idea of untapped human potential, Zimmer has remarked:

> What creates longevity in a company is whether you look at the assets of your company as the untapped human potential that is dormant within thousands of employees, or is it the plant and equipment? Or the trademarks? And I'll tell you the last thing most . . . MBAs probably think is of value is the untapped human potential. . . . The culture says, "It's got to be quantifiable . . . don't talk about human potential. How do I measure human potential?"[13]

The company's mission statement reflects Zimmer's humanistic philosophy, developed in part because he came of age and attended college during the Vietnam War and developed a countercultural perspective:

> Our mission at The Men's Wearhouse is to maximize sales, provide value to our customers, and give quality customer service while still

having fun and maintaining our values. These values include nurturing creativity, growing together, admitting to our mistakes, promoting a happy, healthy, lifestyle, enhancing our sense of community and striving to become self-actualized people.[14]

Zimmer has stated that the company has five stakeholder groups; ranked in order of importance, they are employees, customers, vendors, the community, and shareholders. "We create a quality relationship with our people, and since we're in the retail business, hopefully they will create a quality relationship with the customer. . . . The best way to maximize shareholder value is to put that at the bottom of the hierarchy. By taking care of your employees, your customers, your vendors, and your communities, you will maximize long-term shareholder value."[15]

Zimmer has recognized the connection between customer loyalty—important for building profits—and employee loyalty, which is why he puts the employees first. As Frederick Reichheld wrote, "Employees who are not loyal are unlikely to build an inventory of customers who are."[16] Focusing on the customer makes good business sense, because "raising customer retention rates by five percentage points [can] increase the value of an average customer by 25 to 100 percent."[17] Providing outstanding customer service and building loyal customers is enhanced by great vendor relations. Employees can more easily offer quality service to the extent they can remedy problems. They will feel freer to accept customer returns if the vendor, in turn, is more willing to take back defective or unwanted merchandise. Therefore, great relations with vendors and strong bonds between the company and its employees are both part and parcel of a value-added service strategy.

Because The Men's Wearhouse draws on a labor pool that is not always the best, recruiting people who have had problems and difficulties in their lives and jobs, and because the company believes that its job is to develop untapped human potential, the firm will not necessarily fire people for the first instance of stealing from the company. The company also loans money at no interest to employees who are having financial difficulties—for instance, so an employee can get his or her car repaired. This philosophy about people and the need—indeed the obligation—to develop them to be the best they can be is very much at odds with the prevailing view of employees in most other retailers. For that matter, The Men's Wearhouse's philosophy about people differs from that found in most other industries and companies. These values and the perspective on people they reflect make The Men's Wearhouse's operations difficult to copy. Charlie Bresler, executive vice president for human development and store operations, said:

> Most people who are executives or managers in retail . . . look at human beings who work with them—and they perceive it as *for* them—and see people who are supposed to do tasks and don't do them very well. . . . [W]hat the typical retailer sees are a bunch of people who are stuck there and if they could get a better job, they would. And I think what George has seen . . . are people who have never been treated particularly well, and that when you treat them well and give them a second and sometimes a third chance, even when they've ripped off a pair of socks, even when they've taken a deposit and put it in their pocket and not returned it for several days . . . you try to re-educate the person. . . . We've looked at how to help ourselves and other people get better than most of the world thought we could ever be.[18]

An important part of the company's philosophy is the idea of interdependence and the consequent importance of teamwork and helping others. The company emphasizes "team selling" and a person's responsibility to others. As part of the training at Suits University provided to wardrobe consultants, Bresler told the group that "[a]s a wardrobe consultant, you are expected to define your success in part as only achieved when your teammates . . . are also successful . . . and that you will, over time, define your success not only in terms of your own goals, but also the goals and aspirations of the other people in your store. And that you will really come to care about them as human beings."[19]

HOW THE COMPANY OPERATES

Much of what the company does has been learned through trial and error over time. The management practices of The Men's Wearhouse have evolved intuitively over the past twenty-five years as Zimmer and his management team have gained experience in doing things that operationalize the company's philosophy and values.

Staffing

The Men's Wearhouse has somewhat more staff per square foot than the typical men's clothing retailer, as a way of executing its customer service strategy. In a typical store of about 4,500 square feet, there are two tailors, two managers (a manager and an assistant manager), three wardrobe consultants, and two to three sales associates. To encourage employee retention and good service, virtually all the positions are full-time. Overall, including tailors, only 12 percent of the positions in the company are part-time.

Except for sales associates, who are the people who ring up sales and encourage customers to purchase additional accessories, hiring is centralized at the regional manager level. The company encourages regional and district managers to develop a reserve of people who are interested in joining the company, so that when an opening occurs, it can be filled quickly. The company trains people how to interview. Charlie Bresler described what the company is looking for: "We're looking for people who are potentially consultants, not clerks. We're looking for people who have energy, have a sense of excitement, seem like they care about people, and we don't care about how much clothing background they have."[20]

Although the company emphasizes hiring for fit, basic ability, and personality rather than for experience, this policy is not always followed. Under pressure to fill positions quickly, and deluged with applications from other retailers, there is a tendency to hire experienced salespeople. Working to improve the quality of the people in the company is an ongoing challenge and focus of attention.

The Men's Wearhouse uses relatively few outside consultants and contracts out comparatively little, preferring to use its own people, even for specialized tasks such as information systems development. George Zimmer noted that "if it's important enough that you would consider hiring some consultant, then it's probably important enough to do it internally."[21] He believes that one of the reasons companies use outside consultants is from a fear of making a mistake:

If every time you were a kid and you made a mistake, either your parents or the teacher said something that made an emotional impact on you, then you can grow up with a fear of making a mistake, which will bring you to the world of consultants quicker than anything else. It's a way to theoretically avoid making a mistake. I take the position that the best way to grow a business is to encourage people to make mistakes and learn from their mistakes. In fact, our corporate mission statement says that we're a company that wants people to admit to their mistakes.[22]

Compensation

Wardrobe consultants are paid a base salary and a commission. The base salary in 1997 was about $5 per hour. The commission system has two tiers: 3 percent for sales under $500 and 7 percent for sales over $500. The commission structure is designed to encourage wardrobe consultants to not just fill the customer's initial request—what a clerk would do—but to see what other clothing needs the person has and help implement a plan to develop the individual's wardrobe. Including both base salary and commission, wardrobe consultants receive between 8 to 9 percent of the revenues they produce. Most consultants earn between $25,000 and $30,000 per year. In a typical small store in a mall such as those where The Men's Wearhouse is located, an assistant manager makes about $18,000 per year. So, the wardrobe consultants earn somewhat more than standard for the industry.

Sales associates earn about $12,000 to $14,000 per year and share a pooled commission based on their sales of accessories such as belts, socks, and ties. Store managers receive a base salary and a commission on their own sales, since all managers in the store are expected to sell. They also receive bonuses based on the sales volume and shrink (inventory losses) in their store. Each person in a store, except the managers, receives $20 if the store meets its "good" sales target for the month and $40 if it meets the "excellent" target level. Managers receive a $1,500 bonus if the inventory shrink is less than 1 percent and $3,000 if it is less than 0.5 percent. About 15 percent to 20 percent of the typical store manager's salary is based on store performance. The rest is based on the manager's individual sales.

The $20 and $40 monthly storewide awards, paid in cash, seem quite nominal, and one might wonder what their effect is on people. George Zimmer and his colleagues, however, have over the years developed a very sophisticated view of the use of incentives:

> [I]ncentives can sometimes be so large financially that it becomes
> very important in the actual day-to-day life of the recipient. And in
> that case it can overwhelm the intended spirit, if you will, because it's
> too much money. It can also be too small, in which case, it may be
> meaningless. . . . And believe it or not, it's [the $20 and $40 monthly
> bonus opportunity] the perfect situation. It creates so much excite-
> ment, even though the money is not material. It allows the team
> spirit to become the focal point, and not the money.[23]

Managers throughout the company are eligible for a bonus plan based
on the company's profits. Almost 100 percent of the company's people own stock in The Men's Wearhouse because there is an employee
stock ownership plan and the company actively promotes participation in its 401(k) retirement program. Senior executive salaries are
low compared with similar companies, given the firm's performance.

One important issue is how to build a team-oriented, collective
feeling in a company that pays people essentially on their *individual*
sales achievements. The Men's Wearhouse has addressed this problem
in several ways. First, in much of its training, the company notes that
if you help a colleague in his or her sales efforts, that person will, in
turn, help you. The idea of reciprocity is emphasized. Second, the
company tracks the number of "tickets" written by each salesperson
in a month. If someone writes a lot more than the others in the store,
this suggests hogging the walk-in traffic, and the person will be coun-
seled. If the behavior persists, the individual will probably be terminated. In fact, the company fired one of its top-producing salespeople
because he stole other people's sales and didn't buy into the company's values and philosophy. Although no one in that store subsequently sold as much as the person who had been fired, total store
sales went up almost 30 percent. That one individual brought the others down, and when he was gone, they could also do their best.

Perhaps the most important answer comes from the values, philosophy, and culture that is built and maintained through the various
training activities and other management practices—all of which emphasize the responsibility of every person to help his or her peers develop their potential. George Zimmer commented:

> When I hand out certain awards at those [Christmas] parties, I always
> say the same thing: "I love the fact that we have a company in which

somebody writes a thousand dollar sale and somebody else comes over and gives them a 'high five,' that we celebrate each other's successes" . . . I like to live in a world in which I can celebrate my colleague's success without feeling inadequate, or jealous, or envious. . . . We have to walk that thin line between having highly motivated, incented people trying to really do the best they can and also being part of the overall team.[24]

Training and Career Development

The Men's Wearhouse believes in promotion from within, and almost all of the senior executives have been with the company a long time and worked their way up. Four members of the senior management team have been with the company since it started, and several others have tenures of ten to fifteen years. Ted Biele, the senior vice president of store operations, started as a wardrobe consultant. Julie Aguirre, the director of employee relations, is under thirty and started as a cashier. Because of the company's rapid growth, there have been many opportunities for wardrobe consultants to move into store management positions.

Development and training are important to The Men's Wearhouse. This emphasis is even reflected in the company's organizational structure. Charlie Bresler has commented that most retail companies have only one layer of multiunit managers, but they have two. "One of the reasons is that our district managers are sales trainers on an on-going basis for our wardrobe consultants. . . . [T]hey're also management trainers."[25] The extra multiunit managers help provide training and coaching. Management development occurs mostly by observing others and being coached by more senior managers.

Training and off-site meetings are important ways for building and transmitting the culture that provides The Men's Wearhouse with its competitive advantage. The company uses virtually no outside training or outsiders to do its training, and has very little specialized training staff internally. Instead, the training is done almost exclusively by line managers and senior executives. The model is one of cascading down the hierarchy, with the people at each level having responsibility for the development of those below them.

The company has a number of formal meetings throughout the

year, often at Pajaro Dunes, a resort on Monterey Bay near San Francisco, which many senior leaders consider to be the spiritual home of The Men's Wearhouse. In February, there is a meeting of all the multiunit managers in store operations, regional managers of tailoring, the managers of the sales associates, all of the managers in merchandising, and all of the buyers, as well as the senior executives in store operations. "We have a three day combination of training, spiritual renewal, parties, lots of sports, lots of drinking, lots of dancing. It's kind of a wild three days with a lot of training thrown in," Charlie Bresler explained.[26]

Bresler described the other components of the training and meeting schedule:

> Shortly after February, our Suits University calendar starts up and we bring wardrobe consultants from all over the country to Fremont [California]. The primary emphasis is on sales training and a socialization experience into our culture. A lot of key executives . . . address that group.
>
> Then, in the markets, we have two other meetings that go on throughout the year. One is called Suits High, which is preparation to come to Fremont and Suits University. It is an introduction to selling. And the other is called Sales Associate University, which is basically a training session for our cashiers. They get training in the store but they also get training in this group meeting.
>
> And then every summer, we have manager meetings. These are meetings that take place in the markets. This coming year we'll have five different locations. And we fly people to the nearest location. About two years ago, George came up with the idea of adding all the wardrobe consultants to the meetings. So we now have every manager, every assistant manager, and every wardrobe consultant in the company going to a summer meeting. . . .
>
> In September, we have another multi-unit manager meeting where all of our district and regional managers and store operations executives get together again at Pajaro Dunes. . . . And we have another meeting to get ready for the fourth quarter, with more training. . . . A major part of our training program takes place with our district managers who are the primary sales trainers. These people have between six to 12 stores.[27]

The company almost doesn't have a training budget—it spends whatever senior leaders think is necessary to keep the culture vital and people energized. There is, of course, ongoing pressure to justify and to cut training expenditures, but Zimmer has stood firm on this issue. He described one example:

> Every year my closest friends, Charlie and the rest of the senior people in our company, say to me, "George, this business of flying the managers and the *assistant managers* . . . to Monterey Bay for three nights in this Pajaro Dunes resort environment" . . . I think it actually cost in the vicinity of three-quarters of a million dollars. And so the president of our company who's a good friend of mine and a former partner at Deloitte and Touche and even [Charlie Bresler] said, "I don't know why we continue to do this."
>
> And my response, and this is where you have to sort of be strong as the CEO, is: "I'm not really sure what we're going to talk about either. That's your job, to make sure it's quality. . . . I'm going to tell you that this is the best money we spend." . . . I know it's very expensive and hard to create a cost-benefit analysis.[28]

In addition to imparting selling skills and a lot of product and market knowledge, all of these meetings and training do one other important thing: They signal to people that the company takes them seriously. If The Men's Wearhouse invests in you, under the norm of reciprocity, you will feel some obligation to the company—to stay, to work hard, and to be loyal. Moreover, for people who have typically been treated poorly in the retail environment, all of this training raises their self-esteem and self-image. Feeling better about themselves, with higher expectations and beliefs about their own potential and capabilities and with the title of "consultant," employees leave the training energized and committed to doing a great job.

Performance Management

The Men's Wearhouse emphasizes providing constructive feedback as part of the coaching and development effort and as a way of building an individual's self-esteem. On the first day at Suits University, Charlie Bresler tells the wardrobe consultants that one of the company's expectations is that they will be open to feedback from others who are helping the individual become more skilled at implementing the sales philosophy and techniques. The company encourages people to provide praise when they see someone doing something right. But constructive criticism is also important in building self-esteem. Bresler said:

> You know why constructive criticism is one of the best ways to build up self-esteem? It's because ultimately the single best way to feel good about yourself is to do a better job. And the best way to do a better job is to get good coaching and criticism so that you know not only what *not* to do, but also what *to* do.[29]

The Men's Wearhouse emphasizes feedback that is behaviorally specific, focused on actions and behaviors that can be changed. This is, of course, a sensible approach because it makes the feedback actionable. It is, however, frequently violated in many other companies' performance appraisal and performance management systems in which *characteristics*—such as conscientiousness, intelligence, and being personable—rather than specific *behaviors and actions* become the focus of attention and evaluation. Figure 4-1 presents some elements of The Men's Wearhouse's performance review form for both wardrobe consultants and store managers. We present this material in some detail not because most readers are managing retail stores, but because it is a wonderful example of one company's ability to develop a list of specific actions necessary for success and to implement and continually refine a performance management process that is focused on those specific behaviors.

Leadership and Communication

Zimmer and his colleagues believe in the importance of energy and the company culture. Maintaining cultural consistency and core values in the face of rapid growth and geographically dispersed operations is obviously a big challenge. The company uses some formal media, such as a monthly newsletter called *Clotheslines*. The newsletter contains news about the company, new markets, and employees; tips about selling and becoming a more successful salesperson; and a list of outstanding sales achievements. There is a focus on the largest sin-

Figure 4-1 Performance Review Form

Questions for Wardrobe Consultant

- Greets, interviews, and tapes all customers properly.
- Participates in team selling.
- Is familiar with merchandise carried at local competitors.
- Ensures proper alteration revenue collection.
- Treats customers in a warm and caring manner.
- Utilizes tailoring staff for fittings whenever possible.
- Involves management in all customer problems.
- Waits on all customers, without prejudging based on attire, age, or gender.
- Contributes to store maintenance and stock work.
- Arrives at work at the appointed time and is ready to begin immediately.
- Dresses and grooms to the standards set by TMW.

Questions for Manager and Assistant Manager Positions

- Engages in quality sales coaching.
- Uses multiple selling techniques.
- Maintains and coaches floor awareness.
- Ensures proper alteration revenue collection. Audits alteration tickets.
- Greets and welcomes customers.
- Participates in 15-day customer service calls.
- Conducts exit interviews.
- Ensures that customer policies relative to pressings, fittings, realterations, alteration appointments, charges, and specials are communicated consistently.
- Responds to employee concerns on a timely basis.
- Provides timely and effective feedback concerning performance.
- Conducts weekly Saturday morning meetings that have positive formats.
- Helps resolve personnel problems.
- Communicates clear expectations to staff. Helps each individual set, monitor, and achieve their personal behavioral goals.

These and other behaviors on the performance review form that we have not listed are graded as: above standard, meets standard, below standard, and unsatisfactory.

gle sales, consistent with the company's goal of increasing the amount of merchandise sold to each customer.

The Men's Wearhouse also sends videos to its stores about six times a year. The videos, produced in-house and shown at store meetings, contain a combination of inspiration and information. The goal is to create entertaining presentations that emphasize specific merchandise and effective selling behaviors.

There is also great emphasis on personal contact. District and regional managers are expected to be in the stores regularly, helping to mentor and train store managers and wardrobe consultants. Senior leaders also travel to the stores regularly and meet employees at off-site training activities. George Zimmer goes to about thirty Christmas parties during the months of November and December. There is incredible loyalty in the company to Zimmer and strong identification with him. Until quite recently, he knew every manager and virtually all the assistant managers by name.

One of the other ways the culture is built and maintained is through informal social contact outside work. In addition to the off-site training and meetings and the Christmas parties, the company encourages people in the stores to associate with each other informally outside work. Eric Lane, a senior executive, said:

> We pay for a lot of things. Baseball teams, bowling teams, softball teams. We have an ice hockey team. . . . But in fact I think the whole relationship thing really starts at the most basic level, which is, the people in the stores can be friends with their manager. The managers can be friends with the district manager. They . . . socialize together. If the manager wanted to have a meeting at his house . . . we would pay for that.[30]

The company expects leaders to help develop their people, not be bosses who order others around. There is an emphasis on democratizing the management process and on having leaders serve the organization and the people in it. In the training materials for Suits University, The Men's Wearhouse defines what it means by this concept of servant leadership:

> Servant Leadership forces a change of perspective from the traditional Boss/Employee relationship to the Service Provider/Customer relationship. Servant Leadership says that as Men's Wearhouse Managers, your customers are Sales Associates, Wardrobe Consultants, Tailors, Store manager/assistant manager. The people you manage and work with are YOUR customers, as well as Clients of the Store.[31]

LESSONS FROM THE MEN'S WEARHOUSE

On close inspection, the mysteries we posed at the beginning of this chapter turn out to be not so mysterious once we realize that doing things differently is the only way a company can earn returns that are also different from its industry. The Men's Wearhouse's strategy entails differentiating itself on the basis of service, not price, in a price-sensitive, competitive market. Its ability to be successful doing so suggests that simply competing on the basis of price may not be the only viable strategy even in supposedly "commodity-like" markets.

The company understands that talking about customer service, as so many companies do today, and actually delivering service that can provide real differentiation are two different things. What is unique about The Men's Wearhouse is its willingness and ability to turn its theoretical knowledge about how to obtain higher margins into action. The actions the company takes, particularly its extensive investment in training, its use of a mostly full-time workforce, and its building of a culture in which people help each other sell and help each other learn and get better, all contribute to achieving its success. The mystery then becomes not why this company has done these things, but why so few have learned from its example.

As Eric Lane noted, "If you look at department stores and . . . the chain retailers, the emphasis isn't on the stores or on the people. It's more on the merchandising and the marketing."[32] George Zimmer's insight that you only make money when you *sell* the merchandise, not when you *buy* it—which has led to his emphasis on people and store operations—seems incredibly obvious once stated. But it requires a shift in mind-set that apparently few other retailers have been willing or able to make.

The second mystery is also less of a puzzle once we think it through. The apparent paradox is how and why The Men's Wearhouse has succeeded by focusing on and doing things for a workforce that many companies would view as not very highly skilled and, in fact, not very high quality. But that is the point. If you are a computer engineer in today's market, you expect to be wined, dined, courted, and pampered. If you are in retail, you expect to be treated badly. By exceeding people's expectations concerning the chances they will be given, the dignity and respect with which they will be treated, and the opportunities they will have, the company builds an incredible sense of loyalty and commitment. Doing the unexpected—doing more than is expected—earns the company extraordinary performance from its people. If there is a lesson here, it is the power of treating everyone as if they are important and matter.

The Men's Wearhouse also illustrates a theme we have seen in Southwest Airlines and Cisco: Values come first. This is an organization that seems genuinely interested in helping people be better than anyone thought possible. It really is in the people development business. The emphasis on people development has had the salutary effect of building organizational competence and capability that has permitted the company to execute a very demanding service differentiation strategy. There is no question that the business results from implementing The Men's Wearhouse's values—lower shrink, achieved without expenditures on tagging and other security measures, lower turnover, and a higher level of motivation and energy—have included lowering costs as well as providing a service edge. But there is also no question that the values are sincere and are not promulgated as means to ends but as ends in themselves. In fact, George Zimmer speaks openly about doing things to retain his commitment to a set of ideals, to avoid becoming too materialistic and not spiritual enough.

Most of The Men's Wearhouse's wardrobe consultants have worked for other retailers. Many came from competitors that went bankrupt. In fact, bankruptcy in retailing, particularly in the early 1990s, was quite common. What the company has demonstrated is that it is possible to redefine the basis for competition within an industry, and to do so by building a set of competencies that come from how it has chosen to manage its people—management practices that are premised on its values and philosophy.

Chapter 5

The SAS Institute: Succeeding with Old-Fashioned Values in a New Industry

TREATING PEOPLE DIFFERENTLY (and better) than they expect to be treated, and differently than other companies in the industry treat them, is not something that only works in retailing. Even in the world of high technology and software development, there is a case to be made for being different. And few companies in this industry are as different as the one described in this chapter, SAS Institute.

SAS Institute, the largest privately owned software company in the world, is an anachronism. "In an era of relentless pressure, this place is an oasis of calm. In an age of frantic competition, this place is methodical and clearheaded. In a world of free agency, signing bonuses, and stock options, this is a place where loyalty matters more than money."[1] In a world of outsourcing and contracting out, SAS Institute outsources and contracts out almost nothing. Day care workers, on-site health professionals, food service workers, and even most security guards are all SAS Institute employees. In an era of managed care, SAS offers a full indemnity health plan with low deductibles.

In almost every respect, SAS Institute seems like a throwback to an earlier era, to a time when there were long-term attachments between companies and their people, and large, progressive organizations such as Eastman Kodak, S. C. Johnson, and Sears offered generous, inclusive benefits in an effort to enhance the welfare of their workforce.[2]

Not all observers seem to approve of this form of employment relationship. Some people say that SAS Institute reeks of paternalism or a plantation mentality in a world otherwise dominated by marketlike labor market transactions. For instance, an article in *Forbes* stated, "More than one observer calls James Goodnight's SAS Institute, Inc., 'the Stepford software company'" after the movie *The Stepford Wives*.[3] In the movie, people were almost robotlike in their behavior, apparently under the control of some outside force. Another article noted, "The place can come across as being a bit too perfect, as if working there might mean surrendering some of your personality."[4] Of course, no one is forced to work at the company, and there are many nearby opportunities available.

SAS Institute is so inclusive and comprehensive in what it does for its people that it makes some observers, more accustomed to the arm's-length, occasionally adversarial relationship between employers and employees now so typical in organizations, uncomfortable.[5] Certainly, aspects of the company's generous benefits, spacious, campuslike grounds, and concern for the total welfare of all of its people seem out of place in contemporary management practice. What a puzzle! How can a company that operates like firms did fifty years ago succeed in today's economy—not only that, but succed in one of the most high-technology sectors of that economy, software?

SAS Institute poses a second mystery. The conventional wisdom is that turnover is endemic and inevitable in high technology in general and software in particular. In these industries there is a tremendous shortage of people, and job hopping is an accepted and even expected part of people's career strategy. But SAS Institute, with no signing bonuses, no stock options, no phantom stock—none of the gimmicks that have come to be taken for granted as ways of inducing people to join and remain in companies—has a turnover rate of less than 4 percent. Never in the more than twenty years of the company's history has turnover been above 5 percent.[6] SAS Institute is located in Cary, in the Research Triangle area of North Carolina. It is surrounded by numerous pharmaceutical companies, as well as by IBM, Northern Telecom, and many other high-technology and software companies, so SAS people would not have to move geographically if they wanted to change jobs. How in the world has SAS Institute kept its turnover so low and succeeded so well in wooing and retaining the talent that has permitted the company to flourish?

BACKGROUND

SAS Institute was founded in 1976 by Dr. James Goodnight, John Sall, Anthony Barr, and Jane Helwig. Goodnight, today the CEO, was an undergraduate in applied mathematics at North Carolina State University in the 1960s. The son of a hardware store owner, he helped pay his way through college by moonlighting as a programmer.[7] After graduating, Goodnight worked for General Electric on the ground control system for the Apollo space program before returning to North Carolina State to obtain his doctorate in statistics in 1971. He then joined the faculty on a so-called soft money appointment—a position in which you had to go out and get the grants to pay your own salary.

Goodnight and Barr, who had worked for IBM for two years developing an information system for the Pentagon and was now also working at State, thought it was wasteful to have to write a new program every time students wanted to do a new statistical analysis. "They decided to develop a uniform program that could be used over and over, and that could solve lots of different kinds of [statistical] problems."[8] Having developed such a system, they leased SAS (Statistical Analysis System) to other agricultural schools in the region and to some pharmaceutical companies. When the soft money began to dry up, they were told they could stay on at the university but would have to pay their own salaries. Instead, they left and formed their own company.

When that company, SAS Institute, Inc., began in 1976 as an independent entity, it already had 100 paying customers and was cash flow positive. Except for a mortgage on its first building, SAS Institute has never had any debt, nor has it ever had to raise outside venture or other equity capital. What about ownership of the intellectual property? "North Carolina State ceded them all copyrights on the program in exchange for free upgrades."[9] If this seems generous, consider that in the 1970s there really wasn't a software industry and no one knew what software was worth. As Jim Goodnight recounts, when his wife would tell people her husband worked in software, they thought it was some type of clothing or undergarments.

One of the cofounders, Anthony Barr, sold his 40 percent stake in the company for about $340,000 in 1979. Jane Helwig left to found another software company, Seasoned Systems, with her husband and then decided to attend medical school. She now practices obstetrics/ gynecology, and her stepsons, Mark and David Helwig, work for SAS Institute. Today, James Goodnight owns two-thirds of the company; the other cofounder, John Sall, owns the other third.[10] Goodnight's two-thirds stake of SAS Institute means that, according to *Forbes*, he is the forty-second richest person in the world. John Sall, also a billionaire, is not active at all in the management of SAS Institute and does not want to be. He sees himself "as a statistician and a software developer—not a businessperson or a manager."[11]

Over the years, the SAS program has expanded to become a twenty-module system for data warehousing, data mining, and decision support. "With 6.5 million lines of code, the massive program is used by the U.S. Census Bureau to count and categorize population, by the Agriculture Department to develop crop forecasts and by the long distance phone companies to figure out how much to charge for each call."[12] Banks use SAS Institute software to do credit scoring, hotels use the product to manage frequent visitor programs, and catalog companies use the system to help decide which people to mail particular catalogs. The original statistical analysis package that was the foundation of the company currently contributes less than 2 percent of total revenue.

SAS Institute operates on a worldwide basis. The company has forty sales offices in the United States and sixty-eight offices around the world, as well as licensed distributors in a number of other countries. Ninety-seven percent of the Fortune 100 companies use SAS software, as do more than 80 percent of the Fortune 500. In late 1997, SAS Institute had more than 8,000 customers and 31,000 customer sites throughout the world.

Because SAS Institute is privately owned, information on its finances is not publicly available. Table 5-1 presents information on sales revenues for the past eleven years. SAS Institute is currently the ninth largest independent software firm in the world and the largest privately owned independent software company. SAS Institute has enjoyed double-digit revenue growth since its founding.

The company has no single competitor that provides precisely the range of software products it does, but in segments of its business it competes with companies such as SPSS that offer statistical analysis

Table 5-1   Annual Sales Revenues for SAS Institute

Year	Revenue (millions)
1986	98
1987	130
1988	170
1989	206
1990	240
1991	295
1992	366
1993	420
1994	482
1995	562
1996	653
1997	750
1998	871

and graphics packages, with vendors of decision support and graphics software, and with database management companies such as Oracle. Although originally running only on mainframes, SAS applications today run on midrange computers, workstations, and personal computers as well as on a variety of mainframe platforms. The company is also beginning to use Internet- and intranet-based applications.

SAS Institute spends more than 30 percent of its revenues on research and development, an amount that has remained remarkably constant over the years and is about twice the average for the software industry. SAS Institute employs about 5,400 people, approximately half of whom work at corporate headquarters at Cary. Almost all of the company's software development occurs at Cary, with the other offices performing account management and service support.

If anyone thinks that SAS Institute's success was foreordained by its being at the right place at the right time, a comparison with SPSS is particularly revealing. SPSS was founded in the late 1960s by three Stanford University graduate students to offer packages for statistical applications. SPSS incorporated in 1975 and set up its headquarters in Chicago. In August 1993, SPSS offered stock to the public. SPSS applications originally ran only on mainframes, but in the 1980s they were migrated to a personal computer operating environment. In 1996, desktop revenues were almost 80 percent of total revenues. SPSS offers data analysis and graphics software, process documentation, and various management products. Although its origins in a university were similar to SAS Institute and it was founded at about the same time, the growth of the two companies has been quite different. In the fiscal year that ended December 31, 1998, SPSS had revenues of $121 million, less than one-sixth that of SAS Institute.

Strategy

SAS Institute's business strategy is built on relationships. As described in the company's 1996 annual report, "The Institute is founded on a philosophy of forming lasting relationships with our customers, our business partners, and our employees. These critical relationships, combined with our leading-edge software and services, together form the basic elements of our success."[13] Relationships are important because, unlike many software vendors, SAS Institute does not *sell* its products and subsequent upgrades but rather offers site licenses, provided on an annual basis after a thirty-day free trial. "The software is not cheap. A charge of $50,000 a year for 50 users is typical."[14] However, the licenses include free upgrades to new versions of the software and outstanding customer support. Initial first-year revenues are less than if the product were sold outright, but over time, revenues from a given customer will be higher as long as that customer remains with SAS Institute. The company's license renewal rate is over 98 percent.

Customer support is one key to maintaining satisfied customers. SAS Institute has one technical support person for every 100 customers.[15] Customer loyalty is intense. Like many software companies, SAS Institute sponsors user group meetings. One difference is the loyalty of the users who attend these meetings. "SAS veterans of previous user conventions wear up to 20 badges on their jackets as a demonstration of loyalty."[16] Howard Dresner, research director for the Gartner Group, sometimes speaks at SAS user group meetings and commented, "I was afraid that if I said anything negative they [the users] would lynch me."[17]

Product development at SAS Institute is also based on staying in very close touch with customers and giving them what they want and need. Jim Goodnight said:

> Listen to the customers. Give them the software they want. There is
> no reason to develop software they don't want. . . . Once a project is
> underway, we'll have a few of our customers come in that we know
> are interested in a particular area and have meetings with them and
> have them test the software we've developed. . . . [I]f we could make
> the product fit the needs of half a dozen companies through these
> strategic partnerships, it will pretty well fit the needs of other compa-
> nies as well.[18]

One way in which information is acquired is by meeting with users
in user group conferences. SAS Institute has six regional user groups
in the United States, one international group, and a dozen country-
specific user groups; it also sponsors a number of user group conferences throughout the world each year. At user conferences, the company holds a contest asking questions about the SAS software, for
which "customers have been known to study for days."[19] Each year
the company sends each of its customers a "ballot" asking what features they would like to see. From tabulating the results of that ballot,
the company decides on its development priorities for the coming
year.

The company does not have a focused product strategy, nor does it
engage in long-range planning. Goodnight believes that the industry
is evolving too rapidly for such planning and, as he puts it, "I'm not
as much of a visionary as Bill Gates, so I can't tell where the industry
is going."[20] The company will not turn down a product idea that
seems sound, even if the idea doesn't fit tightly into the existing product line. As David Russo, formerly the vice president of human resources, commented, the company operates on the philosophy of the
educator Maria Montessori, namely, that creativity should be followed, not led. Russo noted that "if you're hiring creative people, you
give them their head, you tell them that it's all right to take chances
and you mean it, they will do their best."[21] People at SAS Institute are
encouraged to try new things. David Russo commented:

> Have you ever heard us talk about the holes? He [Goodnight] says
> that he's dug a lot of holes. The only smart thing is knowing when to

quit digging. . . . We don't know if it's going to make a lot of money for the company or not. But the technology out there is exciting and it might turn into something. Go for it.[22]

As one consequence of this customer-focused, employee-initiated product development philosophy, SAS Institute is developing video games and is moving heavily into educational software. Neither of these areas is within the scope of its traditional focus on statistical and data mining products. These new products are being internally incubated, not obtained through acquisitions.

One other important element of SAS Institute's business strategy is its drive for market share and revenue growth. David Russo commented that the company, and Jim Goodnight, wants the software everywhere. "If it's a choice between making X dollars per sale and having more people have the software, he would rather have the software everywhere. He [Goodnight] thinks that there is no reason that any midsized or large enterprise shouldn't be using SAS. They should be using SAS for everything. So his perspective is, it should be out there. And as a result, he'll try anything."[23]

SAS INSTITUTE PHILOSOPHY AND VALUES

The fundamental way that SAS Institute operates has been the same since its inception and is premised on a small, consistent set of values and beliefs. One is the desire to "create a corporation where it was as much fun for the workers as for top management."[24] Two principles are inherent in that statement. The first is the principle that *all* people at SAS Institute are treated fairly and equally. In its practices and day-to-day operations, the company is a very egalitarian place. Neither Jim Goodnight nor anybody else has a reserved parking space. His health plan is no different from that of the day care workers. There is no executive dining room—everyone regardless of position can eat at one of the on-site company cafeterias, where high-quality, subsidized food is accompanied by a pianist playing during the lunch hour. Everyone at SAS Institute has a private office, not a cubicle. Dress is casual and decided by what the person feels comfortable wearing. As Goodnight explained, "Four of us started the business. When we started, there were no employees, we were all principals. What we tried to do was to treat people who joined the company as we ourselves wanted to be treated. . . . The company is characterized by an egalitarian approach."[25]

The second important principle is that the workplace should be fun and people should be treated with dignity and respect. This philosophy comes from Goodnight's early experiences. When he worked for General Electric on the Apollo space program, although the work was interesting, the job environment was not good: "We had guards at the door every day. . . . We had to sign in. You'd go down the hall and put your quarter in the machine and get a cup of coffee out. A lot of these things I found somewhat offensive."[26]

Essentially, SAS Institute believes in the power of reciprocity—that people feel obligated to return favors that are done for them. Or, more prosaically stated, if you treat your people well, they will treat the company well by being loyal and dedicated in return. Jim Goodnight has commented that he likes being around happy people. Who wouldn't? He and other SAS Institute leaders believe that if you take care of your people, they will take care of the company. As one manager put it, the basic philosophy "is one of trickle down—if you treat people well, things will take care of themselves."

A third, interconnected part of the philosophy that guides SAS Institute is a belief in and reliance on intrinsic, internal motivation. Part of trusting people is treating them like responsible adults and relying on them to do a good job. Barrett Joyner, vice president of North American sales and marketing, noted that "the emphasis is on coaching and mentoring rather than monitoring and controlling. Trust and respect—it's amazing how far you can go with that."[27]

The importance placed on people comes from the fact that SAS Institute operates in a business critically dependent on intellectual capital. David Russo, who was head of human resources for more than seventeen years, explained:

The best way to produce the best and get the best results is to behave as if the people who are creating those things for you are important to you individually. Every night at 6 o'clock, all of our assets walk out the door. . . . We just hope they come back at nine the next morning. . . . If you believe that, then it's just a waterfall of common sense.

It just means that you take care of the folks who are taking care of you. . . . *Why* we do the things we do is what's important. The things we do are secondary. . . . They are just a natural outgrowth of a philosophy that if you really mean that your people are important, you will treat them like they are important.[28]

The final part of the SAS Institute philosophy comes from an important insight about the business and economic benefits that come from creating an environment in which both the physical aspects of the workplace and the services offered to employees relieve the stress and the day-to-day concerns of people:

"We believe that an employee with some of the normal workday stresses relieved . . . is more productive, not only for that day, but comes back more refreshed and able to be more productive that second day . . . and so on," explains Russo.[29]

"The point of the strategy is to make it impossible for people not to do their work," by removing as many distractions and concerns as possible.[30]

The ideas that people are important, that if you take care of them they will take care of the company, and that taking care of them involves treating them as you yourself might want to be treated are not particularly novel or complicated. What makes SAS Institute fairly unusual is that it actually *lives* by these simple precepts. Implementing this philosophy requires taking a long-term approach. SAS Institute definitely thinks long term. Goodnight commented, "We only take a long-term view of all issues. Since any project will take at least one to three years to come to fruition, a long-term perspective is required."[31] This long-term perspective extends to the management of people at SAS Institute.

HOW SAS INSTITUTE MANAGES ITS PEOPLE

The management practices SAS Institute uses are all premised on the idea that in an intellectual capital business, attracting and retaining talent is paramount, and that the way to attract and retain good people is to give them interesting work to do, interesting people to do it with, and treat them like the responsible adults that they are. It is a management system based on trust and mutual respect. The fact that it is so unusual says something about most contemporary organizations and their leaders. The fact that the system works so well says a lot about human potential and what it takes to unlock that potential.

Benefits and the Work Environment

SAS Institute is probably most famous for its generous, family-friendly benefits and pleasant physical work environment. As already mentioned, everyone (including assistants) has a nice private office and is provided with the latest computer equipment. As in many organizations, the philosophy and practices reflect the founders' early experiences and their reactions to those experiences. Goodnight tells about interviewing for a job as a computer programmer—a job he did not take—when he was a young man: "The programmers sat in desk after desk, lined up row after row, in a building that was like an aircraft hangar. No walls, no privacy."[32]

Company headquarters at Cary consists of eighteen buildings scattered over a 200-acre campuslike setting with a lake and beautiful grounds and forests. The grounds feature outdoor sculpture and picnic areas, as well as hiking trails. People sometimes bring their friends and family to the grounds on the weekend for picnics or hiking. The buildings are architecturally interesting, with atriums and light wells. Goodnight himself oversees their design. They are beautifully decorated with art—something that a committee of four, including an artist-in-residence as well as Goodnight, attends to.

Company policy is for people to work about thirty-five hours a week, or a 9 to 5 work day with an hour for lunch and exercise. If you call after 5 P.M., the voice mail system tells you that the company is closed. As David Russo noted, if you shot off a ten gauge shotgun in the parking lot on a typical Wednesday at 7 P.M., you wouldn't hit anything. Goodnight and other senior leaders have the same schedule. Betty Fried, the director of corporate communications, has contrasted SAS Institute with other software companies, commenting, "You know that old joke about Microsoft having flex time, they don't care what 18 hours you work?" The company believes that people don't perform effectively when they are tired. Jim Goodnight commented:

> I've seen some of the code that people produce after these long nights and it's garbage. You throw it away the next day and start over. . . . You have got to be alert and sharp to be a good programmer. . . . I'd rather have sharp, focused people that write good code that doesn't need as much testing. I recently came back from a Microsoft conference and they said that now Microsoft has three testers for every programmer.[33]

The reduced work hours permit people to have both a job and a life. It means that women don't have to give up their careers if they want to see their children. As a consequence, at SAS Institute more than 50 percent of the managers are women, a relatively high percentage for the software industry. The company has been able to attract and retain both men and women with its work–family balance.

The company has a number of other amenities and benefits, such as an on-site 7,500-square-foot medical facility staffed by six nurse practitioners, two family practice physicians, a physical therapist, a massage therapist, and a mental health nurse. The average waiting time to be seen, if you have an appointment, is five minutes. When waiting times increase (for instance, because of the growth in the number of SAS people), the medical facility adds people, adjusts its hours, or does something else to reduce the waiting time. SAS Institute recognizes that time is money and that time spent obtaining medical care can't be used on work. The facility is free to employees and their families, although there is a small copayment required for the massage therapist.

The company's full indemnity health plan—not an HMO or a PPO, and with no managed care—has a $100 deductible per person, $350 per family, and covers first dollar costs for many things. Nonetheless, SAS Institute's health care costs are $1,000 per employee below the average health care costs for plans that aren't nearly as rich as theirs.[34] The SAS Institute health plan includes vision care, hearing, a good dental plan, free physicals, free mammography, and many other benefits. Gail Adcock, the manager of corporate health services, noted that the goal of her group was to keep people at work and to decrease turnover, not simply to save money.[35]

SAS Institute also provides on-site Montessori day care, with one staff person for every three children. Although the day care was originally provided completely free, SAS employees now pay about one-third of what the comparable fee would be in the market. Between the on-site and subsidized off-site care, SAS Institute provides child care for 528 children.[36]

SAS Institute has a fitness center that includes a large aerobics floor, "two full-length basketball courts, a private, skylit yoga room, and workout areas segregated by gender. . . . Outside, there are soccer and softball fields."[37] All of this is free to employees and their families. SAS Institute provides towels and even launders exercise clothes, also for free. The company estimates that 65 percent of its people use the exercise center two or more times per week.[38]

SAS is noted for its snack facilities—refrigerators and small eating areas—scattered throughout the buildings. Every Wednesday afternoon, plain and peanut M&Ms are distributed to these snack areas on every floor and every building. SAS Institute uses 22.5 tons of M&Ms a year.[39]

SAS Institute was one of the early companies to offer benefits for domestic partners. It provides on-site help in arranging elder care. The company provides financial assistance and paid leave for adoptions. The company's cafeterias provide excellent food at subsidized prices, with live piano music in the background. Families are encouraged to use this facility, and many parents will eat lunch with their children who are at the on-site day care facility. A program provides undergraduate scholarships to SAS Institute employees on a competitive basis. The company even helps with housing: It sells some of the land it owns to employees at discounted prices so they can build homes. The idea behind all of this is to remove distractions that keep people from focusing on their jobs and also to reduce the stresses that come from dealing with the common demands of life.

For SAS employees not working at Cary, every effort is made to provide similar levels of benefits and amenities, either on site or by purchasing them for employees at local vendors. The idea is to provide Cary-level care for everyone.

Performance Management

David Russo's theory of performance management is simple: Give people the tools to do their jobs and then let them do it, while holding them accountable. "Every SAS product manual includes the names of the developers and testers who created or updated the software."[40] Try finding the name of any person in the product manuals for most software companies, such as Microsoft. SAS Institute has eliminated the performance appraisal form. David Russo explained the decision: "We don't do performance appraisals. Why? Because they're stupid. Because everybody hates them. Because they take an inordinate amount of time with always a negative result."[41] Instead of formal appraisals, managers commit to spending time talking to their people and providing feedback on a regular basis, at least three times a year. In return for getting rid of the appraisals, managers also committed to walking around and talking to their people. Russo believes:

> [I]f there were a good performance appraisal process, everybody would be using it. . . . So what happens is companies institute a new performance appraisal process, it works for a while because it's new, and all of a sudden it starts to slide and then they start looking for something else. . . .
>
> I don't think you can really manage someone's performance. I think you can observe the results. . . . I think you can set short- and long-term goals. And you can sit back and see if it happens or it doesn't happen.[42]

The company's fundamental approach to performance management entails setting high expectations for both conduct and performance, which then become self-fulfilling, and giving people the freedom to do what they like to meet these expectations. John Boling, the director of the educational technologies division, said:

> When I've wanted to do research, I've had the opportunity. When I've wanted to travel, I've had the opportunity. When I've wanted to publish, I've had the opportunity. It's been pretty much my taking the initiative. . . . We assume that you have talent, creativity, and initiative. You have to be able to take that and run with it.[43]

SAS Institute operates on the basis of trust. Violations of that trust are not sanctioned. The company, therefore, has no sick days or sick leave policy. Nor does it have a sick child care program. Jim Goodnight believes if a child is sick, it should be home with its mother or father. Commenting on the company's sick day policy and the issue of trust, David Russo said:

> We don't have sick days. If you're sick for six months, you're going to get flowers, you're going to get candy, you're going to get a lot of concern and a lot of visits. If you're sick for six or seven Mondays in a row, you're going to get gone. It's a simple thing. . . . Now, do we have free riders? Absolutely, and guess who figures them out? Their peers. Management doesn't have to take care of that. They surface and they either get right or eventually . . . they get gone. It's just the way it is.[44]

Managers are evaluated principally on their ability to attract and retain talent. The company believes that in a business based on skill and know-how, if it can get and keep the best people, the rest will take care of itself.

Pay Practices

SAS Institute provides none of its employees with stock options, phantom stock, performance shares, or similar schemes. Goodnight has referred to stock options as Ponzi schemes. The company does contribute the maximum allowed by Internal Revenue Service regulations, 15 percent, to employees' profit sharing (401k) retirement plans. There is no matching—employees do not have to contribute anything. SAS Institute has done this for more than twenty years, a record unmatched by any other company. A small bonus based partly on the company's financial performance, typically on the order of 5.5 percent to 8 percent, is paid at the end of the year.

Base salaries are quite competitive with the industry and are adjusted annually, although people have taken pay cuts to work at SAS Institute because they value the work environment so highly. Salary increases are based on supervisors' assessments of an individual's performance, so in that sense, there is a merit pay system. However, SAS Institute tries to deemphasize the importance of financial rewards because most SAS managers don't believe money is a very effective motivator. As David Russo put it, "A raise is only a raise for thirty days. After that, it's just somebody's salary."[45]

It's one thing not to emphasize financial rewards in software development and administration. But SAS Institute eschews the typical piece rate system even for its sales organization. Account representatives do not receive commissions on sales. Goodnight noted, "[S]ales commissions do not encourage an orientation toward taking care of the customer and building long-term relationships."[46] Also, a commission culture tends to be more high pressure and high stress than what the leadership wants for their company. Barrett Joyner, head of North American sales and marketing, described their philosophy and approach to achieving performance:

> We have sales targets, but mostly as a way of keeping score. I want to make the numbers, but I want to make the numbers the right way. . . . I'm not smart enough to incent on a formula. People are constantly finding holes in incentive plans.[47]

He commented that many companies used incentive systems as a way of signaling what was important, that is, as a communications device. Joyner said that instead of using incentive schemes for this purpose, "Here, we just tell people what we want them to do and what we expect."[48]

To further downplay individual short-term performance, SAS Institute does not even post comparative sales data by name. Some observers believe that this kind of pay system does not encourage the best people to join and remain in the organization. Instead, the thinking goes, these high-potential people will go to places where they can do better financially. There is, of course, no way of definitively answering this concern. However, Barrett Joyner had the following comments on this issue:

> As you know, we move people around a lot at the Institute, so even though we have low turnover, account representatives may change assignments. I frequently get calls from customers that say, "I don't want to lose my account executive." How many software firms do you know where that happens?[49]

Training, Career Development, and Mobility

SAS Institute believes in training, but it is almost all internally done. New employees receive an orientation program from senior managers that includes a history of the company, its vision, and its values. New employees learn about the products, the organizational structure, the business model, and the customers. Long-time employees really enjoy and value helping with this socialization. A lot of technical training takes place. For instance, in a nine and a half month period in 1997, about 400 technical training seminars were held that had a total of about 3,000 people in attendance. In the sales organization, new people received two weeks of training in Cary, but the company is moving to a five- to six-week program delivered over a six-month period to beef up the sales training effort. SAS Institute does not offer tuition reimbursement for outside classes. Although it has sent people to outside management or leadership training programs on rare occasion, the emphasis is very much on doing things internally.

SAS Institute tries to make it easy for people to move laterally—there are no functional silos. As David Russo noted:

> There are no silos of research and development, there are no silos of marketing and sales, there are no silos of technical support. Everything's based on a tool kit. If your tool kit fits this division's model for business and you want to do that, chances are pretty good you'll get to do that. And if two years later you see something else you want to do and it's across three organizational boundaries, you get to do that. . . . In an intellectual capital organization like ours, the most important thing you can do is engage the individual's energy so that they can apply it to the thing that excites them most, their work.[50]

SAS believes that people will have three or four careers during their working lives—it would like for all of those careers to be within SAS Institute.

The company has a very flat organizational structure. Depending on the particular division, there are only three or four levels in the company. Jim Goodnight has twenty-seven direct reports. He noted that "my general management style is to let people manage their own departments and divisions with as little interference from me as possible."[51] The company structure is fairly informal, and the firm does not have a formal organization chart.

One of the most important aspects of careers at SAS Institute is that every manager is a working manager—they do their own jobs as well as managing others. This model even extends to Goodnight, who spends about 40 percent of his time programming and leading product development teams. He noted, "running a big company like this is pretty boring."[52] Another dimension is the ability to move from an individual contributor role to a managerial role, and back, without penalty. A number of people have preferred less managerial responsibility and more programming activity, and this is possible. This practice is consistent with Russo's previously cited philosophy of letting people do what they're good at and what they want to do—and permitting them to discover what they like and are good at by doing it.

As one might imagine in a company with a strong culture, fit is important in hiring, promotion, and retention decisions. SAS Institute wants people who are team players, not those who seek to stand out, to be particularly important, or to be treated like stars. Barret Joyner encourages people to think about what they really want out of their jobs and to be clear and direct about this. In considering this question, one former employee said, "I want to be able to have performance that permits me to do whatever I want. When I walk down the hall, I want to feel like 'I'm the man.'" Joyner told this individual that this sounded like a wonderful goal and that he (Barrett) would help him achieve it—at another organization. As David Russo has noted, SAS is not a good place for someone who wants to feel like a star or feel particularly important. At SAS Institute, *everyone* is important, and the contributions of all are valued and recognized.

Outsourcing and the Use of Temporary Help

SAS has a simple policy with respect to the practice of using contract programmers supplied by so-called body shops (for instance, in India or Pakistan), a practice common in high technology, particularly in the Silicon Valley. It doesn't use them. It also has a simple policy with respect to contracting things out—it doesn't. SAS Institute used to have an outside public relations firm, but has now taken this work back inside. SAS Institute does its own training; develops and prints its own materials, including marketing materials and product manuals; and even runs its own publishing organization that publishes books about the SAS program, including those written by outsiders.

Why does it do this? Barrett Joyner said, "If you want something done right, own it and control it."[53] He noted that most companies contracted out activities in an effort to save on costs. They frequently got products or services that may have cost less, but were also of lesser quality. The question soon becomes, How little can one get away with? SAS Institute is not that focused on short-term costs in the first place, so cost savings are less critical. It is focused on doing things in a quality fashion, and it believes the best way to ensure quality is to manage the process internally.

But why not contract out "nonessential" or "noncore" activities such as health care, day care, the food service, and so forth? The answer is actually quite simple: Those activities are viewed as being "core" at SAS Institute. If the company is organized around the attraction and retention of talent not through throwing money at people but by providing a good work environment, then activities involved in building that work environment are actually quite central to the company's operations. Many people at SAS comment on how other firms make poor decisions about what are and are not core activities and get themselves into trouble in the process of ostensibly saving money.

LESSONS FROM SAS INSTITUTE

One central question concerning SAS Institute is whether it is a relic of the past or the wave of the future. As Peter Cappelli, an astute observer of labor market trends, noted, "Most observers of the corporate world believe that the traditional relationship between employer and employee is gone."[54] And there is no question that this statement is empirically true for most companies in the United States. But it is not true for SAS Institute. In fact, the idea of limited attachments, in both duration and scope, between people and their companies is not true for all the companies we write about in this book. Why?

One possible answer is that these companies are simply interesting anomalies, the products of unique circumstances. Thus, for instance, some people look at SAS and note that the company is privately owned by two people who are both billionaires, so they can do what they want.[55] A second possible answer is that processes of market selection and competition don't reach everywhere simultaneously, so these management approaches will be doomed eventually. We think both of these answers are wrong.

SAS has a business model that has permitted it to successfully affect the competitive dynamics in its industry segment and that provides numerous economic benefits. For instance, consider two consequences of SAS Institute's low turnover. First, the company saves money. If the average turnover in software is 20 percent, a conservative estimate, and SAS Institute's is 3 percent, the difference (17 percent) multiplied by the size of the SAS workforce means that about 925 fewer people per year leave SAS than other companies. What does it cost to replace someone? Most estimates range from one to two times the annual salary. Even with a conservative salary estimate of $60,000 per year and an estimate of 1.5 times salary as the replacement cost, SAS Institute is saving more than $100 million per year from its lower turnover—from a revenue base of about $800 million. This is a lot of money in both absolute and percentage terms.

Second, the lower turnover helps build and maintain customer relationships both directly, by providing continuity in the providers of customer care, and indirectly, by helping to provide better products with fewer bugs. In a software firm with about 30 percent turnover, not unheard of in the industry, about one-third of a product development team's members are learning the product, the team, and how to work together; one-third of the members are on their way out, looking for their next job and consequently not too focused on their current tasks; and about one-third are actually focused on the product and have enough experience to be effective. In a company with high turnover, customers are always making new friends because their inquiries are met by different people each time. Customers soon come to believe they are providing on-the-job training, a comment we often hear about accounting and law firms. It is not a model designed to build customer loyalty. And customer loyalty is an important ingredient for profitability, particularly given SAS Institute's business model of software licensing rather than sales and its product strategy that relies heavily on customer input.

Why does the SAS management system work? First, because of its uniqueness. When many companies provided cradle-to-grave benefits and the promise of a long-term career, any given company providing such an environment was just one of the pack. Ironically, as fewer and fewer companies engage in behavior that demonstrates care or concern for their people, the benefits to those that do, such as SAS Institute, increase. SAS Institute gains by being an anachronism in the software industry.

Second, the management practices work because they produce a system that generates real value for both customers and employees. From the customers' point of view, SAS, not driven to meet quarterly profit goals dictated by Wall Street, does not fill its distributors' pipelines full of product as a way of pumping up sales. Because it does not feel compelled to meet arbitrary quarterly sales figures, SAS Institute does not have the same incentive as many of its competitors to ship products before they are debugged, so it can then *sell* upgrades later, something common in the software industry. Instead, the company focuses on building long-term customer relationships and providing outstanding service.

From the employees' view, SAS Institute, although obviously not for everybody, offers interesting work in an environment designed to build, rather than destroy, families and mental health. Why do many employees in Silicon Valley want to get stock options and make a lot of money? So they can quit and do what they really want to do! So they can have a life. At SAS Institute, people can do interesting work with colleagues who are both nice and smart in a comfortable environment that permits them to have both a job and a life. SAS Institute has one of the important characteristics we use to judge organizations: a work environment where people stay even when they can afford to leave.

The company's business model, premised on long-term relationships, and even its products and product strategy, benefits mightily from the kinds of people and low turnover its management practices have produced. And, as we have seen so many times, these management practices are themselves internally consistent. The absence of short-term financial incentives is consistent with the concern for customer service rather than cramming the product down the customer's throat. The emphasis on trust in all of the management practices, ranging from eschewing managed care—a system premised on distrust and adversarial relationships—to getting rid of formal performance appraisals and emphasizing interpersonal communication, helps build a consistent culture and send a consistent message. SAS Institute has not succeeded in spite of what it has done but because of what it has done. Nor is it some quaint relic of a bygone era. Talk to its customers. Talk to its people. It has a business model that works, one that permits it to obtain the full benefits of the talents and dedication of its people.

Chapter 6

PSS World Medical: Opening the Books

PSS WORLD MEDICAL headquarters is located on the top two floors of an ordinary-looking building in an office park just off a busy freeway on the outskirts of Jacksonville, Florida. The lobby, although pleasant, decorated in dark wood paneling with comfortable furniture, is not showy. A small shelf contains a few of the medical supplies the company distributes to physicians, and an interior staircase leads to the fourth floor. Even the people, at first glance, seem like pleasant and friendly, albeit regular, people. Few have graduated from elite educational institutions—there are a lot more people from Florida State than Harvard—and the firm hasn't hired MBAs. Pat Kelly, the CEO, has commented, "We've tried to hire MBAs, but they've all failed. They're too structured, too hard core in their beliefs that they've got the answers."[1] Certainly no one would mistake this for a Wall Street investment firm, a prestigious consulting practice, or the bustling center of a high-tech start-up company. What is extraordinary about PSS, however, is its history of growth and financial performance, all built with ordinary people working in a highly competitive, low-margin industry—the distribution of medical supplies—who have performed in a most extraordinary way.

PSS World Medical offers several mysteries as we seek to understand how companies are able to accomplish extraordinary things with their people. First, the company operates in one of the most fiercely competitive industries in the economy—distribution. It is an industry undergoing constant change as both evolution and revolution in supply chain management continue. The company has been very successful, nonetheless. As of late 1999, its five-year growth rate in revenues was 52 percent and its five-year growth rate in earnings per share was 31 percent.[2] PSS World Medical's return on equity, return on assets, and profit margin were all more than twice the industry average.[3] But if you look at the company, nothing about it seems exceptional. How has it achieved such great results?

There is a second mystery. The evidence is overwhelming that most mergers and acquisitions are economic disasters, albeit not for the shareholders in the firms that are acquired, who receive a large financial premium. Mark Sirower found that about two-thirds of all acquisitions produce negative returns,[4] and a study by the Hay Group reported even worse results, with 80 percent of the acquisitions providing negative economic benefits.[5] However, PSS World Medical's growth has been achieved largely by acquisition. The company's founder and CEO, Pat Kelly, has stated:

> If I had my way, we'd expand entirely by acquisition. An acquisition is just a whole lot easier than a startup. The facilities are in place. The reps have well-established relationships with physicians. . . . An acquired company, even one that's losing money, can be turned around and made profitable much more quickly than a startup.[6]

So, what does PSS World Medical do to manage its growth and acquisitions?

A third mystery also exists. It is well known that rapid growth strains companies, particularly companies that have strong cultures. Assimilating lots of new people and imparting the company's values and practices are difficult. Simply managing the logistics of growth, in terms of the demands on facilities, systems, and finances, is taxing. That is why managing hypergrowth is considered to be a substantial managerial challenge. PSS World Medical has grown extremely fast virtually since its inception—a rate of almost 60 percent per year compounded. For instance, it went from $170 million in sales in 1993 to more than $1.5 billion in 1999. How has PSS World Medical been able to successfully manage this rapid growth?

If we can understand what PSS does to grow rapidly and integrate acquisitions, and how it has been successful in such a competitive industry, we can learn a lot about building management practices that produce sustained success. So, let's solve the mystery of PSS.

BACKGROUND

On February 8, 1983, Pat Kelly, then thirty-five years old, was vice president of sales and marketing at Intermedco, a $41 million company headquartered in Houston and owned by British Tire and Rubber. He had worked in medical supply sales and distribution almost his entire career. Kelly, who was raised in an orphanage and at the time was married with two small daughters, learned that day that the parent company had decided to freeze all officers' salaries for a year. When he told his boss he might have to look for another job, his boss took that statement as a resignation. When he told his boss he really didn't want to resign, his boss told Pat he was fired. Pat Kelly became a reluctant entrepreneur. He and some partners founded Physicians Sales and Service (PSS) on May 2, 1983.[7] PSS has enjoyed remarkable growth since its founding. Table 6-1 shows its recent financial performance.

Business

"PSS World Medical is a specialty marketer and distributor of medical products to physicians, alternate-site imaging centers, long-term care providers and hospitals through more than 100 service centers to customers in all 50 states and five European countries. . . . Medical products distributed to physicians [through the PSS subsidiary] include various types and sizes of paper goods, needles and syringes, latex gloves, specimen containers . . . blood chemistry analyzers . . . exam tables and furniture . . . vaccines and numerous other items. The company serves more than 100,000 physicians' offices (about 50% of such offices). . . . Image offerings [through the company's Diagnostic Imaging subsidiary] include wet and dry laser cameras, automated film handling equipment, mammography systems . . . and magnetic imaging equipment. In addition, the company provides on-site maintenance, emergency service, and parts for a large number of its imaging

Table 6-1 Selected Financial Information for PSS World Medical

	1994	1995	1996	1997	1998	1999
Sales (in millions)	170	236	483	691	1,289	1,565
Operating income	4.7	8.5	21.2	20.7	82.7	102
Net income	1.6	3.7	0.2	4.4	16.0	43.7
Cash	0.1	0.1	86.3	28.7	82.5	41.1
Total assets	59.7	86.4	271	298	677	743
Long-term debt	21.2	11.1	0.5	0.6	128	152
Earnings per share	0.12	0.19	0.01	0.12	0.23	0.61

Note: Years ended on March 31.

products. The Gulf South Medical supply unit . . . distributes personal care items, wound care supplies, exam gloves, nutritional supplements, oxygen supplies, and related items [to nursing homes]."[8]

In late 1998, the company employed about 4,500 people and operated a fleet of about 1,000 vans and delivery vehicles. Approximately 50 percent of its sales were in the physician supply business, with about 25 percent in both the long-term care and imaging markets, and only 2 percent internationally. The markets in which PSS World Medical operates are extremely competitive. There are about 200 locally owned companies serving the physician supply market, 300 locally owned companies serving the imaging market, and 100 locally owned companies serving the long-term care market; a number of large national firms also compete in these markets. The industry has experienced rapid consolidation in recent years, reflecting government regulation and the cost containment pressures in health care. The CEO of a $14 billion electronics distribution company described this business of consolidation and delivery as "a dirty little business" with low margins and fierce competition.[9]

Strategy

The PSS strategy has two core elements: rapid growth, and differentiation based on outstanding customer service and a very broad product line with exclusive distribution agreements with a number of suppliers. Kelly sees growth as critical for future success and has, from the beginning of the business, established audacious goals for the company. In 1988, when PSS did $20 million in business with 150 employees in seven branches, he set a goal of becoming the first national physician supply company.[10] In 1993, with sales of $170 million, Kelly set a goal of doing $1 billion in business by 2000. Now, PSS World Medical seeks to be a *world* distributor of medical products.

By setting audacious goals, Kelly doesn't mean just financial targets. In his view, real goals have to do with accomplishing something meaningful, something that gets people's juices flowing. He notes that coaches of sports teams don't motivate players by setting goals for percentage of shots completed or time spent on offense. They convey the idea of winning. He acknowledges that although there may be differences of opinion about strategies and tactics to attain the goal, there must be absolute clarity and agreement about what the goal is. This focus is critical in a fast-changing marketplace. Without this, it's easy to veer off track. This focus also helps in decision making.

But PSS World Medical isn't pursuing growth just for its own sake. Kelly ticks off some rewards from being number 1. First, you shift the balance of power in the marketplace, with suppliers soliciting you. Second, competitors use you as reference point in setting prices. Third, customers take pride in doing business with you. It is also the case that in an industry experiencing consolidation, you either grow or get acquired. Moreover, growth provides greater opportunities for people in the company to assume more responsibility: Company growth helps foster personal growth. And, growth is exciting. For Kelly, growth is most easily achieved through acquisitions, and the company has made more than sixty of them since 1989. To make a successful acquisition, however, you have to add value. PSS does this by replacing the old business model with its own. Sometimes this may mean increasing the number of sales reps in a territory by four to five times the old number. The company also teaches the sales force how to sell at higher margins. This means bringing in a PSS leader to run the operation.[11]

PSS's differentiation strategy is founded in part on a broad product line that permits its customers to deal with only one distributor for virtually all of their supplies. The company stocks about 35,000 products in its physician supply business, more than 4,000 products in its imaging line, and more than 18,000 medical products in its long-term care division. Because of PSS's broad relationship with its customers, it can sometimes negotiate exclusive distribution agreements with its suppliers, for instance, Abbott Laboratories, Hologic, Critikon (a division of Johnson and Johnson), and SonoSite. When PSS is the only distributor for a product, it can earn higher margins on that portion of its business. Customers can't shop other distributors for price, and distributors need PSS to sell their product, so they will offer better margins. PSS also uses broad market coverage and its size to negotiate discounts from manufacturers. What the vendors get in these agreements is the attention of the best field sales force in the medical distribution business (and one of the best sales forces in any industry) and broad geographic coverage even while dealing with a single organization.[12]

PSS also differentiates itself on the basis of superior delivery and responsiveness to customers. Whereas most of its competitors distribute products through common carriers such as UPS, PSS provides same-day service to all of the customers it can reach through its branch network. One of the drivers in Jacksonville commented, "My job is mostly making sure the customers are happy. You call. We haul."[13] PSS also offers a no-hassles return policy under which delivery drivers can take back any merchandise a customer doesn't want for any reason. The company does not charge customers a restocking fee for returned merchandise. Also, unlike virtually all of its competitors, no minimum order sizes are imposed on customers. A physician can order one box of tongue depressors.

To deliver outstanding customer service, decisions are decentralized. Delivery drivers have business cards with their name and "CEO" on them, because Pat Kelly believes "when you're standing in front of the customer, you *are* the CEO."[14] PSS's customer service relies on a proprietary information system, the Instant Customer Order Network (ICON). This system permits salespeople to write up and transmit their orders immediately after visiting the customer, not just at the end of the day, thus improving delivery service. The system also provides salespeople the ability to manage their business by giving them the information to check a customer's buying history, see what the gross margins are, and so forth, all from their personal portable computers. Warehouse employees also understand the importance of inventory management and of meeting customer requirements (no out of stock items). Drivers are taught not simply to rush into the customer's office and dump the package, but to know where the supplies go and to help unpack and shelve the items. A driver commented, "When I walk in, I like to spend a few minutes with them, asking if everything is okay, because if there's something special, then we want to do that."[15]

In describing his approach to strategy, Kelly distinguishes between understanding the *business* you are in and understanding your *business model*. The former refers to your industry; the latter is *how* you do business. For Kelly, this means the kind of company you create and what kind of value you bring to the customer. He maintains that Diagnostic Imaging's business model is identical to the PSS model: setting a service standard higher than anyone else's, putting in place systems to guarantee those service commitments can be met, and managing in ways such that people have fun, learn and grow, and share in the wealth.[16] For Kelly, the secret to diversification without losing focus is to enter a new business without losing your business model. This means understanding how each business is different and not blindly copying every procedure. As an example, he points out that each of PSS's three divisions has the same top twenty rules and the same values, but each has different practices. He believes that the closer you stay to your business model as you diversify, the more successful you are likely to be.

PHILOSOPHY AND VALUES

In talking about how PSS implements its strategy, Kelly begins by talking about the importance of the PSS people and the company's values. "Business people don't like to talk about values. But without these, all business is about is making money," and this isn't enough. Kelly sees business as "people working together to deliver value to a customer."[17] He argues that it matters a great deal how people work together. For him, no achievement of business goals is worth sacrificing your values.

PSS World Medical is built on a culture of trust and mutual respect. The company has a set of core values and a philosophy for managing that provide the foundation for everything the company does. Some of those values are as simple as teamwork, respect for people, and having fun. The company's management practices, such as calling people at all levels by their first names, all derive from four central ideas. The first is to run an open company. The company not only practices open book management by sharing lots of financial information, but also has an open door policy and encourages people to ask questions. When Pat Kelly or the other officers attend meetings in the branches (called "stores"), they carry $2 bills with them and give them out to anyone who asks a question. Any question is legitimate and must be answered. For instance, Eric Miller, the controller in the PSS division, said that if someone asked him his salary, he would, under the norms, have to answer. "The right to communicate with anyone, anywhere, without fear of retribution is one of the core values."[18]

The second idea is to give people authority and accountability. Kelly believes it is easier to ask forgiveness than permission, and he encourages people at all levels of the firm to take initiative, to make decisions, and to be responsible for their own performance and behavior and that of their unit. Michael Weise, the operations leader in Jacksonville, said, "At PSS, you get an opportunity to shine."[19] The company gives out "Don't Grow on Trees" awards to people who take initiative to provide outstanding customer service. People aren't fired for making honest mistakes, because mistakes are to be expected if people are taking responsibility and making decisions. And the only way to learn is to try new things.

The third idea is to share the wealth. PSS World Medical has an employee stock option plan and numerous bonus and incentive programs. The idea behind these programs is that the people who help create the financial performance should share, generously, in what they have created.

Finally, the fourth idea is to have lots of leaders, not managers. You won't hear the word "manager" at PSS World Medical. There are no sales managers or operations managers—there are sales leaders and operations leaders. Kelly believes in the concept of servant leadership, something we find also at The Men's Wearhouse and at ServiceMaster, a $6 billion industrial cleaning company that has also learned how to unleash the potential in its largely unskilled workforce. Described by Mahatma Gandhi, the idea is that a leader is the servant of the people he or she leads. The leader works for those who are led, in the sense of having the responsibility to provide coaching, teaching and development, and feedback and guidance so that those people can reach their true potential.

PSS World Medical also has a set of twenty core values, shown in figure 6-1, which it posts in every office. Many of these values have to do with the importance of people and the need to treat each other with trust, respect, and dignity. Many companies have similar values; what is different about PSS, though, is how it lives these values.

The integration of Taylor Medical, in Dallas, Texas, illustrates the PSS philosophy about people in action. Pat Kelly described the initial situation and the company's response:

> When I went to Dallas about three years ago, the warehouse was chaotic. We had bought Taylor Medical. The culture was bad. They had cameras throughout the warehouse, and the manager sat in his office watching all the employees. And we knew we were going to make a change there. The day after we closed the deal, I called Gary Corliss in

---

Figure 6-1   PSS's Top 20: The Company's Values

To: SERVICE all our customers like they are the only one we have.

RECOGNIZE our people as our most valuable asset.

ALWAYS communicate without fear of retribution.

ENCOURAGE ideas and creativity at all levels.

ENCOURAGE self-development and individual entrepreneurship.

ALWAYS strive to share the wealth.

ALWAYS promote from within first.

EARN profits and value for our entrusted shareholders.

PROVIDE an environment of trust and honesty.

MINIMIZE excuses and maximize getting the job done.

INVOLVE family in all social aspects of the company.

ENCOURAGE and develop pride and esprit de corps.

ENCOURAGE all PSS people to be shareholders.

TREAT all company assets like they are your own.

SUGGEST and encourage better ways of doing things.

MINIMIZE paperwork and memos.

BE professional at all times.

ANTICIPATE and capitalize on market needs.

DO what's best for all PSS.

RECOGNIZE PSS as a family that cares.

Minneapolis and said, "I want you to go to Dallas and I'll introduce you to the employees there."

So I went and put Gary in charge. And Gary said to the people, "Folks, can you plan on sticking around tomorrow night? I'm going to have dinner brought in and let's just talk about PSS, what it's going to do, what's going to happen."

I was out of town that evening. I get a voice mail from Gary about midnight the next night. He said, "Pat, I know we just spent all this money for Taylor Medical. But you need to know first hand from me that I just managed to destroy $10,000 worth of cameras and video in the building tonight. So, if you would, just please write that down, and if you have to, take a payroll deduction against me." Gary had walked into the meeting with a baseball bat, and he asked the employees, "Tell me everything you hate." And he knew what was going to be the first thing they mentioned. They pointed at the cameras. And Gary took a swing with the baseball bat. Knocked the camera off the wall. . . . Then he says, "Does anyone else want a bat?" And they threw blankets over the cameras and destroyed all of them. And that started the whole conversation about cultural change. Now, they haven't had any turnover in a truck driver in six months.[20]

ORGANIZATION AND MANAGEMENT PRACTICES AT PSS

Organizational Structure

PSS World Medical has a flat organization consisting of three divisions (PSS Medical, Diagnostic Imaging, and Gulf South) with a small corporate headquarters. There is no written organizational chart. The company's structure is similar to many geographically structured U.S. distribution firms. Each division consists of a small number of regional units (typically three or four) that oversee the separate branches or service centers.

Each branch is equivalent to a small business, with its own P&L, responsibility for gross margin, and complete discretion to set prices and determine its operations. For instance, each branch is responsible for its own janitorial and maintenance activities. At virtually all the branches, cleaning and routine maintenance are performed by the employees themselves. The typical branch is headed by a sales leader (never referred to as a manager) responsible for sales and an operations leader responsible for the warehouse, distribution, and back office (accounting, billing, and collection functions). Smaller branches may have only a single head, but most use a dual leadership approach. The typical sales leader is charged with supporting an average of ten sales representatives who call on thirty customers daily, versus an average of twenty visits to customers for other medical supply firms. The typical operations leader has a warehouse staff, administrative staff, and an average of ten truck drivers, who are responsible for the same-day delivery of products to the customer.

All this is pretty standard stuff. But it is what is not on paper that makes the organization of PSS different. In describing how PSS is organized, Kelly begins by saying, "I've always been bothered by structure. I'm bothered by how structure will become an excuse for why people can't perform. I became a devout believer that we are not going to have a lot of things in writing."[21] He sees his job as eliminating the "corporate arthritis" that sets in when bureaucracy takes over.

This translates into several unique features within PSS. First, there are no policy manuals. The company emphasizes personal communication rather than putting things in writing. The company's policy guidelines are written on a large, colorful foldout brochure called "Rules of the Game." The sheet describes guidelines in seven areas: equal opportunity; sexual harassment; rules of conduct; alcohol, drugs, and firearms; absence of unions; guidelines for leave and holidays; and complaint resolution procedures. Second, there are no memos. Kelly's rule is that everybody is required to read the first memo they get each month, and none thereafter. This means that if you need to send a memo and want to ensure that it's read, you stay up until midnight on the last day of the month and send your memo.

PSS has a relatively lean corporate staff: seven people in the corporate human resources department, a three-person business development group looking for acquisitions, corporatewide financial reporting (although each division has a controller and financial staff), and a corporate development department that includes PSS University. Kelly believes that staff should have line experience and should serve, not direct, the frontline people. "Staff to me means a mentor. Staff is an advisor . . . to help people solve problems. . . . I think the best staff leaders are people who have been in a line role, and vice versa. If you look at the three chief financial officers in our divisions, they all came in as accountants, and they all went out and operated companies."[22]

Recruiting and Selection

Finding the right people with the right attitude and values is important at PSS. PSS does recruit some experienced salespeople and experienced operations people, including truck drivers, from other companies. But its preferred recruiting pool is right from school. Because PSS is headquartered in northern Florida, many of its sales representatives come from Florida schools, such as Florida State. The company for the most part has not recruited from elite institutions or sought out people with graduate degrees. In fact, credentials aren't very important in the company. Gene Dell, the president of the PSS division, does not have a college degree. The downplaying of formal credentials is partly because the nature of the business—sales—probably won't appeal to people with elite or advanced degrees. Nor would the company's practice of starting almost everyone in operations. Moreover, PSS leaders believe that much of what the company needs to do to be successful is best learned on the job or at PSS. Because the company tries to get people early in their careers and has grown rapidly, it is a relatively young organization. The average age of PSS people is thirty-five.

Recruiting is based in large measure on personal referrals. Michael Weise, operations leader at Jacksonville, commented:

> I don't use newspapers. Our recruiting is word-of-mouth. What I try to do is promote my company so much that people actually enjoy being here . . . make it fun so they tell other people. And so when I'm looking for somebody, I normally go right to the drivers and say, "I'm looking for a position. Does anybody know anybody? If you do, just let them call me." And boom, we fill the position.[23]

Jane, a driver in Jacksonville, was recruited by someone who worked at PSS, and she took a pay cut to join the company. Many of the sales representatives come to the company through personal networks. Salespeople calling on hospitals or physicians' offices naturally meet others working for the competition. They learn who is good and who would fit the PSS culture; this informal network is an important recruiting method. The company also recruits on college campuses, occasionally uses agencies, and obtains people when it acquires companies. Nepotism is not discouraged, and people will get not only their friends but also their relatives to apply for jobs.

Charlie Alvarez, vice president of corporate development, says that "We hire people like ourselves. I like to be associated with people who are ambitious, driven, competitive, athletic. . . . I don't care how good a sales rep is, how much money he drives into the branch, if he's negative and brings the branch down, that person is going to get a talking to."[24] Recruiting for attitude or fit is important. As Pat Kelly put it, "If you want to build a company of CEOs, you have to hire people who are capable of becoming CEOs. . . . You can teach people *how* to accomplish great things. It's much harder to teach them to *want* to accomplish great things."[25]

No one is hired at the company until that person is interviewed by an officer. The hiring process takes six to eight weeks. One of PSS's methods is not to call people back for interviews. After the first recruiting contact, candidates are given a phone number to call for a follow-up interview. If they don't initiate the contact, the process ends. Next, the applicant will go to a local branch for interviews. Even if this interaction is positive, people from PSS will not call back. Rather, at the end of the interview, the candidate is invited to contact the manager of another branch. This requires more initiative and provides the opportunity to further evaluate the candidate. And so the process continues through several more rounds. The company wants to see if people are interested enough, entrepreneurial enough, and aggressive enough to pursue the job opportunity on their own initiative. Often interviews will be done on Saturday, to see if the people will come in, and if they do, if they are hung over from Friday night.

Early in its history, PSS hired with less care and relied on washing out the new hires who didn't fit or weren't working out. But people realized that this wasn't cost effective, and so the company developed a behavioral interview guide. The guide consists of a series of about thirty questions each interviewer can use for screening applicants, along with suggestions to the interviewer about what to listen for in the answer. The interview begins with some questions to break the ice and then moves to more revealing questions, such as what type of relationship the person wants with coworkers (PSS is looking for people who want more than just a business relationship). Interviewers also ask what a candidate finds attractive about sales (they look for independence and a desire for unlimited earning potential and are wary of answers that emphasize "talking to people").

Training and Career Development

Pat Kelly believes that if a firm's whole competitive edge is built on doing things differently, it follows that training in how to do things is a critical first step. In 1991, the company brought all its training activities together under the rubric of PSS University. Prior to that, training had been done in the branches. Putting its money where its values are, PSS spends about 5 percent of its payroll budget each year on training, an amount that is now about $5.4 million. Kelly says that in a sales company, training is the firm's research and development. In 1999, about 1,000 people went through PSS University.

The company has an orientation program for new hires. People are also expected to attend various other training classes as a way of becoming acculturated and of meeting others in the company, building enduring social relationships in the process.

Training at PSS World Medical has several unique aspects. First, its sales training is different from what most medical supply companies do. New sales recruits attend PSS University upon joining the company (previously, trainees spent time in the field before attending the university). After an orientation week, "there's 12 weeks of field training during which they shadow veteran reps and, Kelly says, 'do all the manual work we can push on them'—from cleaning bathrooms to driving trucks to stocking warehouse shelves—to learn how the company works from the bottom up. Then it's back to PSSU for two weeks of sales development training."[26]

Most companies train their people in product information. PSS expects training at the branch to provide the necessary product information. Instead, sales training at PSS University uses role playing to emphasize selling skills. Greg Griffing, director of PSS University, described it this way:

> Usually about the end of the week we say, "Okay, let's just talk about some of the objections you get and how we would overcome them." My philosophy is we're not here so much to teach as they are here to learn. And when you have 20 people with a lot of knowledge, you're going to learn more from the people around you than you do from Charlie and I and Susan getting up and talking.[27]

In addition to sales training, there is Creativity Week—about 150 people went through that program in 1999—and leadership training. The training experience not only imparts knowledge (people are exposed to various books, such as Covey's *Seven Habits of Highly Effective People*) and skills, but also creates bonding among the participants. People stay at one of four corporate apartments instead of at hotels, or they will stay at the homes of people who staff PSS University and even at the homes of officers. Even if they don't stay there overnight, they will have dinner with each other and with corporate officers. Charlie Alvarez commented on the importance of this for building rapport: "One of the guys said, 'I was at J & J [Johnson and Johnson] for 15 years. I didn't even know my division president's wife's name. And here I am rummaging through Pat's cigar humidor, picking out my favorite cigar.'"[28]

Another unique aspect of the training is the emphasis on peer learning, discussion, and teaching as a way of learning. The instructors don't do a lot of talking, but instead, ask a lot of questions. PSS distinguishes "teaching" from "learning," and emphasizes acquiring skills and knowledge by confronting hypothetical situations and by sharing knowledge with others. For instance, in Creativity Week, the company will run more than one section during the week. A student from the day before becomes the teacher for the material the next day.

At PSS World Medical, there is an emphasis on promotion from within and moving people around to different divisions and different roles. For example, Michael Weise, an operations leader who has been with the company nine years, began by training in Dallas and driving a van and working in the warehouse. Then he moved into sales in Dallas and subsequently sold in Phoenix. He then moved to operations. People move from headquarters to the field and back. There is increasing movement across the divisions. This provides people more opportunity for learning and advancement. The idea is to learn the various aspects of the company and its operations by doing them all. Almost everyone who starts at the company, particularly those hired right out of school, begins by driving trucks, selling, and becoming intimately familiar with the work of PSS.

Moving into leadership is very much a voluntary decision and one that requires sacrifice, particularly in the sales track. As one leader commented when asked why people wouldn't want to move up to leadership roles: "It means giving up freedom. The sales rep has a lot of independence. The sales rep has ultimate control of his or her financial gains versus a sales leader who has to depend on other people." Moreover, leadership in PSS World Medical means something different than in many other companies. "In other companies, moving up to a leadership role, you become more powerful, your income

---

Figure 6-2   Leadership Training Vignettes

Mark could not get Steve Block motivated. Sure, Steve was on commission and not hurting the company, but he was missing his forecast. Mark had his hands full. Corporate had just pulled a couple of his top sales pros as leaders and given him a bunch of rookies. To add insult to injury, one of the rookies Corporate gave him a year ago was not making it, and Mark had positioned a trainee to replace the failing rep.

One afternoon at 2:00 P.M. Mark was returning from a customer and decided to stop by Steve's house. His wife had a gift for Steve's wife and had asked Mark to drop it off. What a surprise to find Steve in blue jeans, watching soap operas. Steve made excuses, but Mark blew him away and stormed back to his car.

With all the transition that's going on, does he fire Steve now? What would you do?

Dr. Harold Barnsley [all these names are fictitious] is one of PSS's best customers, but has a tendency to get behind on his bills. Tom Arnold is the leader of the branch and has to put Dr. Barnsley on credit hold nearly every other month. John Dandy is the sales rep, and John is pulling his hair out trying to keep Dr. Barnsley off credit hold.

Right now it's March and Dr. Barnsley is on credit hold. John asks Tom for relief because he is confident Dr. B. can work out of it. Then Dr. Barnsley's office calls up: They need syringes urgently, because of a rash of inoculations. Customer service informs Tom. Tom says sorry, no way they can ship the product out. Dr. Barnsley is furious. He has been slow, he knows, but he always pays his bills, including the service charge for late payment. He tells the nurses never to buy from PSS again.

If you were Tom, what would you have done?

---

increases. In our company, going into leadership means you're giving up income. You're actually losing some job security because you tend to get moved around a lot more. And what we get is people going to leadership for the right reasons, and not going into it for a pay increase. They do it for the challenge, and they do it for the internal drive, and their interest in helping other people be successful."[29]

The leadership selection and development process begins when a successful branch employee who wants to become a leader volunteers for a one-week course conducted at PSSU. After an intense week during which they discuss fifty real-life leadership problems (see figure 6-2 for an example) and receive plenty of feedback on their strengths and weaknesses, the individual must decide whether he or she really wants a leadership position. At this point, about 40 percent of candidates recognize that being a leader isn't for them and return to sales positions. The others make the decision to become a leader for the "right" reason; that is, they choose to become leaders for the responsibility and challenge it provides, not because they were selected or see it as a way to make more money. After this decision, all future PSS leaders then attend a second one-week training session, called Creativity Week, which entails spending three days with PSS senior leaders in intense discussions about fifty real-life problems faced by PSS leaders.

Rewards

PSS has a clear compensation philosophy: The wealth should be shared, but shared in such a way that people earn what they make and then get to keep what they earn. There is never a cap placed on sales representative commissions. When a salesperson joins the company, at first he or she gets paid mostly on a base salary. Each month, as the person learns more about the business and selling, the base salary goes down and the commission goes up. After about a year, salespeople are paid strictly on commission. There are also some more collective incentives. For instance, branches are eligible for bonuses if they meet certain financial targets. However, if salespeople don't make their forecasts, they are not eligible for a share of that bonus.

In many companies, people don't really know what they have to do to get a raise or bonus, or how the amount of the bonus is determined. If they know, they may have limited ability to affect it. At PSS, everyone knows the numbers and how they fit in. The bonus plan is expressed in terms of a game that everyone can play and everyone can win. Known as the "Field of Dreams" (based on an analogy with baseball), the rules are as follows:

- The bonus is paid semiannually.

- You have to have been an employee for six months to be eligible.

- Sales reps are not eligible for a share of the branch bonus unless they achieve their gross profit forecast. Operations people must attend ten of the twelve Challenge meetings (monthly meetings) during the year to be eligible.

- The bonus pool is shared among employees, not the leaders in the branch.

- The bonus pool for each branch is the amount by which the branch's net income exceeds 6 percent of sales. The branch can receive up to 20 percent of this bonus pool.

- The branch gets 5 percent for hitting the forecast, in terms of percentage returns.

- The branch gets another 5 percent (of the total pool) for hitting or exceeding its dollar objectives.

- The branch gets another 5 percent if it keeps its asset days (inventory and receivables) below a target level.

- The branch gets the final 5 percent and hits a home run if it exceeds its forecast by an additional 2 percent of net income as a percentage of sales. So, if the branch was forecasted to do 7 percent (net income as a percent of sales) and it achieves 9 percent, it has hit a home run.

Eric Miller, the PSS controller, checked his records and indicated that in the first six months of 1998, six branches of the fifty-six in PSS Medical had hit "home runs" and more than thirty-five branches were awarded some bonus. The largest individual bonus for the six-month period was $4,145, not bad if you were a truck driver making about $16,000 a year.

In addition to sales commissions for the representatives and the branch bonuses, PSS World Medical encourages all of its employees to own stock in the company. In the Jacksonville branch, for instance, about 70 percent of the truck drivers own stock. After three years with the company, all employees receive stock options.

Open Book Management

Open book management originated at PSS World Medical partly from Pat Kelly's philosophy and values and partly because, early in the company's history, it was financially strapped and sold stock to the employees. As Kelly explains, "When my neighbor pulled his financial support and the bank kicked us out, we had to raise money. The employees bought stock in the company. All of a sudden, we became an employee-owned company and I had to share information. From that point on, we became an open book company."[30]

Kelly recognizes that if you want a really effective organization, everyone has to be involved, not just the managers or salespeople. To get people to act like CEOs and rise to the occasion, he believes that you have to run an open company. This means people have to see and understand all the information so that they can see where they fit and how their efforts contribute. He sees typical companies as dens of secrecy with departments not knowing (or caring) what other groups are doing. Only the people at the top see the overall numbers or can truly understand how they contribute to the larger effort.

Eric Miller, controller for the Physician Sales and Service division, described the open book management process at PSS and its advantages. By the tenth of each month, he and his staff send to the operations leader in each branch a preliminary profit and loss statement that is a detailed presentation of the revenues and expenses for the branch. All of the financial information is posted at the branch, including sales by individual representatives, compared with last year and to the budget. "It's posted in such a format that they look at each expense item that exists in that branch and how they're matching up to their forecast. . . . [T]hey know if they're going to get a bonus, they've got to be able to hit their bottom line and so they look at each expense item."[31] People in the branch have the ability to bring up the details behind these numbers on the firm's intranet, download them into an Excel spreadsheet, and look at the specific transactions that make up a particular expense category. They can question specific items that they think are inaccurate. Miller commented:

This is a good control for us because it gives them the ability to go through and make sure we haven't double paid an invoice. . . . So in my mind, aside from them understanding their own business, it also gives us an extra pair of eyes that knows their particular branch better than we do to make sure that if an employee has been terminated and perhaps our HR department didn't get the paperwork in on time, that the person doesn't get overpaid. . . . And so they submit their questions. We go through them. We respond to them. We make any corrections . . . and then we go back and issue the final P&Ls, and those are the ones that would get posted at their branch.[32]

At least once a year, at one of the monthly Challenge meetings, where the entire branch gets together to talk about business issues and have some fun together, there will be a review of elements of the profit and loss statements. People will explain what makes up the various expense categories. They will explain what depreciation is, what interest expense is, and so forth. Because earning a bonus depends on hitting the numbers, people are interested in learning about operations and the branch's financials. Obviously, people vary in both their interest and sophistication, but the level of understanding generally is quite good. Eric Miller commented, "they'll understand it if it means money in their pocket."

One problem with financial objectives and measures, as Kelly sees it, is that in most companies the goals seem to be plucked out of thin air—at least it often seems this way to the majority of people who are charged with meeting these numbers. At PSS, open book management works because from the very beginning of the forecasting process for the next year's budget, people are heavily involved in setting the goals. The process is one of bottom-up forecasting. It begins in January, three months before the end of the fiscal year. At that time, corporate headquarters creates a financial model for each branch based on the previous year's sales history, expenses, and growth. This is sent to each of the branches. The branch fills out the forecast based on its own assessment of its capabilities, what is going on in the market, and what the people in the branch will commit to achieve. This includes a line-by-line forecast of expenses and a specific forecast for each sales representative in the branch. For example, this forecast will include all estimates of employee raises, whether there needs to be another delivery truck, and so forth. The key number that everyone looks at is the percentage of sales flowing to the bottom line. During the next three months the CEO and senior managers visit every branch for a four- to six-hour review meeting to go over the forecast on a line-by-line basis. Once the forecasted budget is agreed upon, it is signed by the branch leaders, the regional vice president, the division president, and Pat Kelly.

Integrating Acquisitions

When PSS buys a company, regardless of its size, it is not operated autonomously but rather is expected to become part of the PSS culture. PSS leaders talk about the difficulty of getting the new people to adopt the PSS way, but nonetheless are determined to do it. Jean Collins, the vice president of human resources, described the process:

> We just keep talking. We bring them to the University. We have their leaders come in, and we just try to keep pumping it into their heads. Then Pat, one of the division presidents, or one of the regional guys goes to those locations, and we just keep trying to tell them, this is the culture of PSS. . . . Sometimes it takes about a year, in some people. Some of them are very excited right away, especially in the sales and the leadership. They feel there's such an opportunity, especially if they were in a small company.[33]

Susan Parker, a corporate trainer in PSS University, described what happened when the company acquired Gulf South:

> The acquisition closed I think March 26th. And the first weekend in April, we invited every single one of their sales reps here to be part of the work we call the field support. They came down. They met with these new people and learned who they were. We had a large barbecue for them. In just four days, they learned some really unique things about this company. We're all on a first name basis. We all socialize together. All their leaders were part of it. With the Gulf South acquisition being so big and all at once, we said we're not going to be able to piecemeal it. So, they were all brought here, 125 people for four days.
>
> During the four days, they also met with their regions individually about how this was going to affect them. They met with who was now the new leadership. I think they were absolutely amazed at how open everything was. Every question they asked we would answer. If we didn't have the answer already, someone would get out their laptop and get the information and share it. . . . We were more honest with them than we had ever been with an acquisition. We said we've seen the cycle. The first three months, we're going to drive you crazy. The next three months, you're going to drive your customers crazy, be-

cause it's going to take them about that long to figure out that it's not going to be the same. And the last three months, it's going to be an accounts receivable nightmare. But just having come here and being introduced to the feeling of welcome and excitement, made them go back into the field accepting it more easily.[34]

THE PSS CULTURE AND HOW IT IS MAINTAINED

PSS is a values-driven company with a strong culture. Jean Collins described the culture as energetic, outgoing, and workaholic. Charlie Alvarez is the vice president of corporate development, but informally his title is "CEO of Culture." He talks with passion about the importance of culture for PSS and its success. The culture is built and maintained through PSS University, through the selection process for new employees, through the meetings and social events, including the monthly Challenge meetings, and through practices that build accountability into the organization. The culture and values have been unchanged over the years—despite growth, expansions of the focus of the business, and the various challenges the company has faced.

Every organization has its unique cultural rituals, stories, and practices that make its values and beliefs real. At PSS World Medical, these unique cultural practices help to exemplify the basic belief in people and their importance. They include the ability to "fire the boss," efforts to drive fear and distrust out of the workplace, an emphasis on having fun, and practices that ensure accountability and consistency in how this rapidly growing, geographically dispersed company operates.

Firing the Boss

At PSS World Medical, the idea of empowerment is taken so seriously that people can actually fire their boss. Although this idea may seem radical at first, Kelly believes that it isn't radical at all. If the job of a leader is to make a branch or other unit work, and that person is failing at his or her task, then "if leaders can't deliver, the *customers* will fire them."[35] PSS would rather solve the problem sooner with fewer consequences for performance. Also, as Kelly commented, "ultimately, your people will fire you anyway. They fire you two ways. One, they don't perform. Two, they quit. So, what we try to do is to provide an environment for our employees and for our leaders to understand that, if your employees can fire you, maybe you need to be listening to your employees and taking care of your people."[36]

The process begins by someone calling Pat or another officer saying that the group is upset with their leader. Then Pat or another very senior executive will go to the facility and meet with the entire team, without the leader present. Very often the complaint is from just one person or a very small group of people, and other people think the leader is doing a great job. After some open discussion, the leader will be brought in. As Pat Kelly puts it, "we just create an environment where they can start talking." Regardless of the outcome, there are no sanctions against the people who raise the issue. In fact, senior leaders publicly praise them for getting problems and concerns out in the open. Kelly summarized PSS's experience with "firing the boss" as follows:

> 80% of the time, the people don't get fired by their people. It's just more opening up communications. Sometimes, they do get fired. We offer soft landings to those, to go back to the level of what they can do. And many of them come back. I had been saying for a long time that about 30%–40% of our officers have had a soft landing in their career. I got reminded more recently at an officer retreat that it's more like 60% of our officers have screwed up somewhere along the line, had to be repositioned back, and they subsequently got moved ahead and were very successful as officers.[37]

Driving Out Fear

One of the company's core values is never punishing people for making an honest mistake. Everyone at PSS is promised a "soft landing." Clearly, the practice of rapid promotion means taking risks regarding people. It also means an increased chance that people will fail. In most companies, failure in a job means failure in a career. This creates tension that often makes people cautious and organizations risk averse. At PSS, this isn't the case because of the "soft landing" policy. If a person does well in a $5 million branch but not in a $20 million one, the company needs to end the experiment quickly. For this reason, PSS keeps a careful eye on the numbers and listens to the opinions of people in the branch as well as to customer feedback. If a leader is in trouble, it is the job of the regional vice president to help as much as possible. However, if the poor performance continues, the company moves quickly to find a replacement. But if the company wants to keep people and truly develop them, the answer is not to shunt the poorly performing person into a dead-end job or to encourage him or her to leave—the policy followed by many organizations. At PSS, the soft landing policy means that the company will help the person find another job at which they can succeed. The company is filled with examples of successful people who failed multiple times before succeeding.

The company also practices open communication, something that extends beyond an open door policy. The idea is that there are no secrets and that chains of command, in terms of information sharing, aren't very important. People should feel free to talk to others about their ideas for making the company better. When there is a board of directors meeting, Kelly will invite employees to attend receptions and dinners and talk to the directors. He and other corporate officers spend time in the field visiting branches and, while there, talk to as many different people as possible. There is no standing on ceremony.

Accountability

PSS World Medical has a culture that emphasizes accountability and accepting responsibility. It also wants to be a company that operates with consistent values and beliefs across its divisions and across its many dispersed locations. One of the ways that this cultural consistency is built and maintained is through "Blue Ribbon" inspections.

The Blue Ribbon Tour is a cornerstone of the culture. Twice each year one of PSS's senior leaders shows up unannounced at every single branch for an inspection. Everyone in the company has a booklet entitled "The Blue Ribbon Scorebook—A Foundation for PSS Culture." This lists 100 items detailing the way every branch should look and operate. The senior manager evaluates the branch on all 100 items. These assessments operationally define the culture and include things such as the following: Are the trucks clean? Are there refreshments available for guests? Is there a map showing all PSS locations? Are truck maintenance logs maintained? Is there a Wall of Fame celebrating employee accomplishments? Is the phone answered on three rings or less? Are all visitors asked if they would like coffee? Every question has a yes or no answer, resulting in a possible total of 100 points.

The inspection usually takes between three and four hours and involves meetings with employees, who are asked questions about customer service, product knowledge, inventory, and goals. Rather than being a solemn event, the inspection often becomes a raucous social occasion with employees shouting out answers and prodding their colleagues with hints. Two-dollar bills are handed out for all questions asked, and $20 bills are given to those who pass on-the-spot quizzes. This is not seen as a visit from Big Brother but rather as something done in a spirit of fun and celebration. Branches compete vigorously to be among the top ten highest scoring branches—both for bragging rights and for the $2,000 per employee awarded to the top branch ($1,500 for second place, $1,000 for third, $750 for fourth, $500 for fifth place, and $250 per employee in the branches that finish sixth to tenth).

Commenting on the culture of accountability, Michael Weise, an operations leader, stated:

> When it all comes down to it, you've got a group of people that are responsible for everything. And we all want to hit blue ribbon numbers. We all want to get bonuses. We all want to save money. We are all bound to each other. So when you see something out of the ordinary, out of whack, you're going to say, "Hey, don't do that, because that's wasting us money." So, we're all a little company ourselves.[38]

Fun

Kelly believes that you need to take business responsibilities seriously, but you also need to have fun. People spend too much time at work not to. This means you have to have fun all the time, not just on special occasions. Leaders throughout the company thus set regular times for people to get together and enjoy themselves. The annual sales meetings, held in resorts, are filled with celebration, humor, and fun. Once a month, everyone in the branch gets together after work for a Challenge meeting. If a person attends ten out of twelve meetings, the individual receives 100 shares of PSS stock. Challenge meetings are usually held at a theme park or amusement center and always begin with a twenty- to twenty-five minute session playing the Challenge Game, modeled on the TV show *Family Feud*. Participants are formed into two teams and compete to answer questions about the company ("What is amortization?"). Points are awarded for correct answers and are redeemable for PSS merchandise contained in a catalog. After the game, everyone eats and enjoys himself or herself. These activities emphasize the importance of practical learning and having fun. Eileen Delaney, the operations leader of the Diagnostic Imaging branch in Jacksonville, believes that these meetings are a good way to educate people and ensure that leaders communicate with their people.

People are also encouraged to get together on their own time. For instance, at corporate headquarters, people get together once every three months and go somewhere. This is a surprise and is announced the night before; for example, everyone goes surfing or attends a party at which prizes such as a free trip to Hawaii are given out. The annual picnic is held over a weekend near a theme park. Families are invited and a competitive volleyball tournament is held. The idea is that your colleagues will become your friends and you will enjoy going to work to be with them. They're part of the family.

LESSONS FROM PSS WORLD MEDICAL

As we consider what PSS World Medical does that leverages their employees' talents, several things become clear. First, the answers to the three mysteries posed at the start of the chapter are quite interrelated. What the company does to successfully integrate acquisitions also permits it to manage rapid growth and enables it to achieve outstanding financial results in a competitive environment. That's because solving each of these issues entails the same thing: building a system, a set of management tools and practices, that helps people do their best and permits the rapid integration of new people (whether from internal growth or acquisition) into the organization.

Second, most of what PSS does is not rocket science. Recruiting people who will fit the culture, sharing information so that people know what is expected and how they are doing, providing people incentives to do well both individually and collectively, making it safe to try new things and take on new responsibilities, being consistent in behaviors and connecting behaviors to the company's core values, and measuring what matters—the key elements of culture and behavior—seem like obvious things to do. In some sense, they are. However, a number of considerations make these things difficult to implement. And it is in actually implementing management practices that PSS World Medical excels.

What makes this all harder to do than it appears? One element is the need for consistency and alignment among the various management practices if they are going to achieve all they can. What management does, beginning at the top and cascading down through the organization, sends a set of messages about what is important and how to think about the business. If these messages are inconsistent, people get confused. Achieving consistency and alignment is hard work. It requires attention to all the myriad details of day-to-day management. PSS is similar to the other companies we have seen in this book in that it has achieved a tremendous congruence and consistency across its various management practices. If you are going to give people responsibility and accountability, then they need training, and PSS provides both the opportunities and the training necessary to capitalize on them. If you are going to hold people accountable, then they expect to be rewarded for their accomplishments, and PSS does this also. If you are going to build a company of motivated, ambitious people, then you need to recruit the right people in the first place, people who are interested in the challenge. PSS's hiring for fit, its rigorous selection process, and PSS University all help to build consistency in core values and beliefs. If you are going to be flexible and cope with rapid growth and change, you can't be bureaucratic. PSS's flexible, decentralized structure and absence of rules help build adaptability.

Doing what PSS has done also requires enormous attention to detail, not only to achieve consistency across activities but to structure each management practice with enough forethought that it produces the attitudes, values, and behaviors crucial to the firm's success. Think of the Blue Ribbon inspections and the need to consider all of the things that are important to success—answering the phone promptly, being polite to visitors, knowing certain facts about the business, meeting certain delivery targets, having branches look a certain way to provide visual cues that guide behavior, and so forth. This level of detail is easily ignored by those who attend only to the "big picture" or the grand strategy and ignore the myriad details of day-to-day implementation.

Managing this way requires immense patience and persistence, qualities that are often in short supply. It takes time to train people in the financial concepts that enable them to understand the business, and it takes time to recruit selectively. And achieving consistency and performance once is not enough: The need to engage in management practices that build the core capabilities of the company and are consistent with its values is ongoing and ever present. As Pat Kelly remarked, "[T]he key to our success is the people you've got to motivate and fire up every day to want to get out there and do something a little bit better."[39] Note that Kelly talks about "every day," not "occasionally." Every day PSS sales representatives and drivers are in the field building and maintaining customer relationships that are crucial to the company's success. And so, every day, the company must be sure that it has motivated and trained people to perform the thousands of interactions with its customers and suppliers that determine its financial performance.

We see that PSS has built a set of capabilities that have permitted the company to change the competitive dynamics in its marketplace. PSS competes on service: no-hassle return policies, no restocking charges, same-day delivery, no minimum order sizes, helping the customers shelve the products. But these activities all take time, time is money, and the medical supply distribution business is fiercely competitive and subject to stringent cost pressures from purchasers of medical services.

PSS World Medical's success is very similar to that of Southwest Airlines, The Men's Wearhouse, and AES (described in the next chapter). Each of these organizations is managed in a way that leads to immense productivity from their employees. Southwest does this through their fifteen-minute turnarounds, which gives them higher levels of productivity than their competitors can achieve. The Men's Wearhouse invests in people, who then sell more merchandise than their competitors. AES, a company that runs power plants, reaps a similar reward by running their plants with greater efficiency than the competition. PSS has sales reps who call on 33 percent more accounts on average and are better at meeting the customer's needs. Each of these firms does this not by pressuring or "pushing" people but by giving them information, opportunity, training, coaching, and a fun place to work. The secret of these companies is no secret at all—it simply requires more attention to detail than many managers are willing to devote. Success is in the small operational details, not the grand strategic decisions that entrance many senior managers.

But PSS is not perfect. Although they have successfully met one of the great leadership challenges—unleashing the potential in their workforce—their success is not guaranteed. Recently, after a large acquisition, accounting irregularities were uncovered that caused Wall Street to punish their stock. They have also learned that their business model may not work as well in the long-term health-care sector as it does in the medical supply business. So, for the moment, PSS is in a period of retrenchment. But their same-store sales continue to grow and their people remain committed. What remains true, in spite of their current difficulties, is that PSS has built a set of management practices that has helped them tap the energy and enthusiasm of all their people.

This is a challenge that many of the companies we have seen in this book have met. To do this requires a different mind-set about where business success comes from and how to produce it, and a different set of values about people and how to manage them than can be found in most companies. Regardless of their current difficulties, PSS has done this.

Chapter 7

AES: Is This Global Company Out of Control?

THUS FAR, we have seen numerous examples of companies that have been able to achieve extraordinary results with their people—results achieved by taking myriad interrelated, aligned actions that unleash the energy, ideas, and talent of everyone in the firm. But, to this point, all of our examples have been companies based solely or primarily in the United States. That raises a question: Can these same ideas apply to a global corporation, and if so, how? Can you practice open book management and share information with people all over the world? What about building and managing a company based on a set of core values? Certainly values must vary with national cultures, so that having one set of strongly held values that operates all over the world would be infeasible. It is one thing to operate a global company in a consistent fashion all over the world when the management practices used to do so are based on standardized accounting and financial reporting and a model of incentives presuming that people work mostly for money. The management approach of companies such as Citicorp and Asea Brown Boveri (ABB) comes to mind. It is quite another thing to try to implement humanistic values—such as those we saw in The Men's Wearhouse—and a management system based on trust in countries all over the world with people who speak different languages and who don't share a common history or tradition.

Examining the AES Corporation, an independent electric power producer operating more than 110 power plants and distribution systems in sixteen countries all over the world, gives us a chance to explore an important mystery: Can the same ideas and approaches really work in a global firm, from Pennsylvania to Pakistan, from Connecticut to China, from New York to The Netherlands?

AES poses another mystery as well. As we will see, the company believes strongly in decentralizing decision making and delegating authority. It also abhors specialization and has virtually no centralized staff functions. There is no strategic planning department; no specialized staff in human resources, quality assurance, or environmental compliance; no legal department to speak of; and the chief financial officer sees his job primarily as helping and training other people to raise capital and perform the treasury functions. Business development is the responsibility of almost everyone in the firm, including relatively junior people, not just something done by senior executives or a business development group.

When executives from other companies see how AES operates, many are worried, in spite of the company's outstanding economic success. And successful the company certainly is. In late 1999, AES's return on equity was 178 percent of the industry average and its profit margin was 203 percent of the industry average.[1] Even with some charges associated with the Brazilian currency problems, the company had achieved a five-year growth rate of 41 percent in revenues and 18 percent in earnings per share. The total return to shareholders over the previous five years was a whopping 531 percent,[2] far exceeding the return for other benchmarks, and particularly remarkable given that this company was not some Internet, e-commerce, or computer company but operated in the more prosaic business of generating and distributing electric power.

But in spite of its historically outstanding performance, executives worry about AES's operating style and practices. After all, AES builds capital-intensive electric generating plants with long economic lifetimes and has to raise a great deal of money to do so. In 1998, AES raised about $6 billion and was the fifth largest raiser of private capital in the United States that year. Furthermore, much of the company's new growth is in emerging markets in Asia and Latin America, markets that present numerous financial and political risks. To some observers, the company seems like it is out of control given its decentralization and absence of specialized staff. And so the other mystery to explore as we consider AES is, Can a radically decentralized company that operates in the manner AES does be in control? Is the company, in fact, out of control?

BACKGROUND

AES, originally called Applied Energy Services, was founded in 1981 by Roger Sant and Dennis Bakke. Sant, a Harvard MBA graduate, left a position teaching finance at Stanford Business School in the mid-1970s to lead energy conservation programs at the Federal Energy Administration (FEA) under John Sawhill.[3] Bakke, a 1970 graduate of Harvard Business School, had worked in the Department of Health, Education, and Welfare and in the Office of Management and Budget before working with Sant in the FEA. The two of them moved to the Mellon Institute's Energy Productivity Center in Washington, D.C. There Sant and Bakke wrote a book entitled *Creating Abundance: America's Least-Cost Energy Strategy.* The book reflected their emerging view that the answer to the energy crisis wasn't rationing or hoarding energy but "to produce those services—heat, light and power—at the lowest possible cost."[4] The two decided to start AES as a provider of consulting services in the energy industry. Raising money for the new company was not easy. They spent about a year talking to venture capitalists trying to raise $3 million, but could only raise $1.3 million. Those people who did make an initial investment did very well— $10,000 invested in 1982 was worth about $20 million in 1999.

Both Sant and Bakke wanted to start a company that would be the opposite of what they had experienced in the government: flexible rather than hierarchical, and completely unbureaucratic rather than burdened with rules and procedures. In addition, Bakke, raised in a Norwegian family of faith (his father and two brothers are ministers) in a small town in western Washington, wanted to build a company in which he could live his religious values. At around the time they were founding the company, *In Search of Excellence* by Tom Peters and Robert Waterman appeared. The founders were intrigued by the ideas in the book. AES recruited Waterman to serve on its board of directors, an invitation that he accepted so that he could see how and if his ideas could actually be implemented. Bakke has described Waterman as his soul mate, and Waterman's influence on how the company operates is evident.

AES eventually decided to move beyond just providing consulting services and actually operate an independent power plant. The company began operating its first power plant in Houston, Texas, in 1986. AES went public in 1991 to raise equity capital to continue its expansion in the market for producing electric power. Since that time, AES has achieved phenomenal growth. In 1996, *Inc.* magazine named AES the twelfth fastest growing U.S. company (see table 7-1 for recent financial statistics). The company has grown both by acquiring exist-

Table 7–1   Selected Financial Statistics for the AES Corporation

	1999	1998	1997	1996
Revenues (in millions)	3,253	2,398	1,411	835
Net income (in millions)	228	311	185	125
Earnings per share	1.28	1.69	1.09	0.80
Total assets (in millions)	20,880	10,781	8,909	3,622
Shareholders' equity (in millions)	2,637	1,794	1,481	721

ing plants in the United States and elsewhere and by developing new, greenfield plants.

The company's business, in terms of source of revenues and fuels used, was described as follows in its 1998 annual report:

Electricity sales accounted for 97% of total revenues in 1998. . . . AES's generation business represented 58% of total revenues for 1998 compared to 74% in 1997. . . . AES now operates and owns (entirely or in part) a diverse portfolio of electric power plants . . . with a total capacity of 24,076 megawatts (MW). Of that total, 29% are fueled by coal or petroleum coke, 24% . . . by natural gas, 33% are hydroelectric facilities, 6% are fueled by oil, and the remaining 8% are capable of using multiple fossil fuels. . . . AES is also in the process of adding approximately 5,254 MW to its operating portfolio. . . . AES also sells electricity directly to end users. . . . AES's distribution business represented 39% of total revenues for 1998 compared to 20% for 1997.[5]

The company operates power plants in the United States (about 20 percent of its total generating capacity), England, Northern Ireland, Wales, the Netherlands, Argentina, China, Hungary, Kazakhstan, Republic of Georgia, Canada, Brazil (about 25 percent of the total capacity), the Dominican Republic, Panama, Australia, India, and Pakistan. It has plants under development in Mexico, Sri Lanka, and Bangladesh. Recently it has also gotten into the power distribution business, for instance, in Brazil, El Salvador, and Argentina.

The electric power generation business is both competitive and complex. Many subsidiaries of large U.S. electric utilities and gas companies with substantial financial resources have entered the independent power business in a search for growth opportunities. The growth potential exists because much of the world does not have access to reliable electric power—in 1997, 40 percent of the world's households had no electricity.[6] In addition, there is a growing movement to privatize government-owned power generation and distribution facilities. The complexity comes not so much from the technology of electric power production but from the various ownership and financing arrangements frequently required. Either purchasing or building a new power plant invariably requires governmental approvals and often requires between two and five years to complete. AES's financing and ownership arrangements vary widely. It owns some plants itself, whereas others are owned under various joint venture arrangements. "For instance, the Medway plant in England was a joint venture between AES and two privatized British utilities. . . . The plant in San Nicolas, Argentina[,] was owned by a partnership in which AES held 70% interest and Community Energy Alternatives, Inc., and the people at the plant held the rest."[7]

Although AES has pursued opportunities to buy power plants from utilities in the United States, much of the company's growth opportunities have been overseas as countries privatized facilities and systems that had been owned by governments. Many of these opportunities were in emerging economies in Central and South America, Eastern Europe, and Asia. In early 1999, AES publicly reaffirmed its commitment to continue to invest in Central and South America in spite of the various currency crises and other financial problems then plaguing the region. "The essence of AES's mission to the world makes it inevitable that we will endeavor to serve in areas that some consider unstable."[8]

Strategy

AES, without a centralized corporate strategic planning function, likes to claim it doesn't really have a strategy. Dennis Bakke maintains that the company follows Robert Waterman's idea of "ready, fire, aim," or retrospectively figuring out what your strategy is after you have done something. Since Wall Street wants to know the company's strategy, Bakke claims he tells them, "[W]e try a bunch of stuff, we see what works, and we call that our strategy."[9]

Certainly AES does not believe in central planning or central control, even of new business development opportunities. "It is not senior executives . . . who do the deals. It is the 300 team leaders all over the globe."[10] Bakke and Sant have described the company's strategy as "disciplined opportunism." It is opportunistic in that virtually anyone in the company can propose and work on a new business development project. AES is also opportunistic in the sense that the company does not believe that financial capital for good investments is scarce, so the company sets no limits on how many deals it works on or completes. The company is disciplined in that it sets a reasonably high hurdle rate (of about 20 percent return) as the threshold for projects and will not buy its way into a business or sacrifice economic returns just to close a deal.

AES doesn't have a "strategy," but it does have a goal: to be the leading global power company. Roger Sant, chairman and cofounder, commented on the importance of this stretch goal:

> The biggest target we have is to be the leader. I can't tell you how important that is. . . . It was magical how it transformed the way we did

business. . . . It's a big statement to make. It's very different from saying we want to grow 20 percent per year. . . . I think it indicates that we were operating under some constraints before, when we asked ourselves, "How do we get rid of those constraints? If we're really trying to be the leading global power company, would we have done this or that?" . . . The company just exploded thereafter.[11]

Strategy is about developing competitive advantage. Another way of asking about AES's strategy, therefore, is to ask what differentiates the company from its competitors and helps it succeed. In response to a question about what makes AES so successful, Roger Sant answered, "I suppose our underlying assumptions about people—especially AES people—is the most important. It's the first time in my experience where an organization has assumed that their people are good, that they really want to make a difference; that you don't need to control them; that you can depend on them."[12] Dennis Bakke, addressing the same issue, noted:

There are some things about the way we do things in terms of freeing up people that are amazingly adaptable to a world that's going topsy turvy and changing all the time. . . . We're faster than anybody in the world. We may be one of the fastest companies in being able to act and respond to the world that's ever been created. . . . We have more people, in more places, spending less money than any other company in our business. We're just everywhere.[13]

Robert Waterman commented that the AES management system "was designed to make people happier in the way they work. It probably is more efficient. . . . [T]here's a lot of peer pressure and lot of advice from all over the world in how these deals get analyzed."[14] By giving a lot of responsibility, fun, and learning opportunities to essentially everyone in the company, AES inspires "smart young people to produce prodigious amounts of work."[15] In addition to the advantages gained from having people who like what they do and help each other, Waterman noted that the company was able to leverage capital by using nonrecourse project financing, where the debt is secured only by the specific generating asset, not by the company as a whole.

PHILOSOPHY AND VALUES

From its inception to the present, AES has emphasized a set of core values and beliefs. The company's 1998 annual report discussed the results of its thirteenth annual survey on principles and shared values. The company's four core values are fun, fairness, integrity, and social responsibility, which it defines as follows:

> Integrity . . . Integrity comes from the Latin word "integra," which means "wholeness." By carefully weighing all factors . . . AES strives to act with integrity in all of its activities.
>
> Fairness . . . [T]he term "fairness" means "justice." Often "fairness" is confused with "sameness". . . . We don't mean that. AES aspires to give everyone special treatment.
>
> Social responsibility. The most socially responsible thing a corporation can do is to do a superb job of meeting a need in society. Therefore, companies must carefully manage capital, employees, and intellect to meet a societal need. For AES, the first step . . . is to ensure that every generating plant is operated in a clean, reliable, safe, and cost-effective manner. But we have chosen to go beyond the essentials. . . . That is why we plant millions of trees to offset carbon dioxide and build new schools and take . . . other steps to improve our environment and build communities.
>
> Fun . . . For us, "fun" means establishing an environment in which people can use their gifts and skills to make a difference in society without fear of being squelched.[16]

AES is committed to the value of fun. The company provides fun by giving its people interesting things to do, decisions to make, challenges to meet, and lots of opportunities to learn and try different things. AES will readily trade the gains from having people do the same thing over and over again—specialization—for the interest and enthusiasm generated when people get to take on new, challenging assignments.

AES adheres to its values so strongly that when it offers stock to the public (for instance, in its initial public offering) the company is required by the Securities and Exchange Commission to list its adherence to its values as a possible risk factor:

Adherence to AES's Values—Possible Impact on Results of Operations. An important element of AES is its commitment to four major "shared" values. . . . [I]f the Company perceives a conflict between these values and profits, the Company will try to adhere to its values—even though doing so might result in diminished profits or forgone opportunities. Moreover, the Company seeks to adhere to these values not as means to achieve economic success, but because adherence is a worthwhile goal in and of itself.[17]

Most of the AES people we talked to found it amusing, if not incredible, that adherence to values would be listed as a "risk factor" for a company.

In addition to having and living a set of core values, AES has a relatively unusual philosophy regarding profits and the role of the corporation. Dennis Bakke believes that businesses exist "to manage resources and nurture relationships to meet a need in society."[18] Maximizing profits is not the primary goal at AES. Bakke has stated, "Profits are to a corporation much like breathing is to life. Breathing is not the goal of life, but without breath, life ends. Similarly, without turning a profit, a corporation, too, will cease to exist."[19] He and other AES people reject the idea that shareholders are preeminent and that the primary task of the company is to maximize shareholder value. He has written, "Where is the justice in placing the wealth of shareholders above that of quality products and low prices to customers? . . . Isn't capital just the stored product of *past* work? Why should the corporate purpose give higher priority to the product of past work than to the product of *current* intellectual capital?"[20] AES people believe that no group—for instance, employees—is primary. It is, therefore, the job of all AES people to balance the conflicting interests of all of the various AES stakeholders.

Another important component of the AES philosophy is that leaders are the servants of those who are led and should voluntarily give up their power. Dennis Bakke has a statue of Christ washing the feet of St. Peter in his corporate office, and the idea of servant leadership certainly has a moral and religious foundation. But it is also based on some beliefs about how people should be treated in their work environment in order to make that environment as much fun as possible. Bakke commented:

We come out and we work hard to be king, and then at AES we say that you're supposed to be a servant. I can't overestimate how difficult that is, but . . . it's the most central thing to what we do. I was in Argentina a few months ago and I got the best answer I've ever had to this question. I asked an AES person what happens when your supervisor exercises power and makes a decision in your particular area of responsibility. He said, "I don't have a job." The essence of human beings, who we are as people, is our ability to analyze and make decisions. . . . [I]f you don't have that, you can't even experience full humanness.[21]

Bakke maintains that this willingness to give up power is rare and difficult and is one of the reasons that few other companies would adopt the AES model:

I think it is natural to give away power, as natural as it is to keep power. It's just that in our society, when you're educated, you expect and deserve to have power. . . . Everyone who's come to watch and study AES, especially other competitors, say, "this is exciting." Then some of them get it. They turn and walk away slowly because the price is too high. . . . [A]re you willing to pay that price, which is, in effect, to become a servant instead of a king? Are you willing to give up power so that others can flourish?[22]

AES has a unique perspective on its people: "The people of AES are not principally economic resources. We are not tools of the corporation. Rather, we hope the corporation is structured to help individuals make a difference in the world that they could not otherwise make."[23] The company hates the term "human resources," which it finds demeaning to people. The company also doesn't like to say "people are its most important asset." Dennis Bakke has commented, "I thought about the word 'assets.' What do we do with assets? We depreciate them. We sell them. When they're used up, we throw them away. It's not exactly the image of a person that I really want to put across."[24]

Because of the value it places on fun and because of its view of people, AES also doesn't like to talk about efficiency. Efficiency is a concept from engineering, a ratio of output to input. It is a concept that sees people as analogous to machines, and is consistent with a

Tayloristic, scientific approach to management. This is anathema at AES.

MANAGEMENT PRACTICES

Dennis Bakke, Roger Sant, and other leaders in AES maintain that the management practices must come from the company's core principles and values. Otherwise, "it's just technique."[25] What is important is not just what AES does, but why it does it. Most of what the company does is not that different from other companies we have seen in this book. These practices make the values and principles come alive and reinforce each other, maintaining consistency and alignment in how the company operates.

Recruiting and Selecting for Aptitude and Cultural Fit

AES believes in hiring people not for specific skills but for their general competence and talent and their ability to fit into the AES culture. This approach makes sense given the company's tendency to move people around to different jobs and different locations and its emphasis on learning new things. In the plants, hiring is done by the plant personnel. People from all levels and positions, particularly from the area in which there is a vacancy, volunteer to look at resumes. Based on the evaluation of the resumes, telephone interviews are conducted. Two of the questions in the telephone interview guide are "Why are you looking for a new job? and "What are you looking for in your next job?" For those candidates who pass the phone interview screen, there are a number of personal interviews, followed by a group interview. The personal interviews ask questions that help determine the person's fit with the AES culture. For instance, some interview guide questions are "What does fun on the job mean to you? Should everyone be treated equally? Why? What have you done to become more effective in your job? What do you do when something needs to be done and no procedure exists? Tell me about [your] two most important achievements."[26]

  If there is interest in the candidate after the group interview, the individual receives a so-called sales pitch interview from the plant manager. At this point, the process is as much to sell the organization and the specific employment opportunity as it is to screen the individual. During the hiring process, if any AES person believes the candidate does not fit, the person does not get the job.

The hiring process takes a long time for all positions—anywhere from one week to a month or more. That is because getting the right person is viewed by AES people at all levels as one of the most important things the company can and must do to ensure its success. Candidates are often surprised that they are not asked about specific technical skills, but AES people believe that technical skills can be learned. As one AES person said, "[W]e hire people who want to keep learning new things."[27] AES people are quite clear and consistent about what would make a bad hire, or someone who wouldn't fit in the company:

> Someone who is a chronic complainer, who is not happy, who blames others, who doesn't take responsibility, who's not honest, who doesn't trust other people. A bad hire would be someone who needs specific direction and waits to be told what to do. A poor hire would be someone who wasn't flexible and who says, "It's not my job."[28]

AES has relatively low turnover, which provides some evidence for the effectiveness of the hiring process. The plants that AES buys are frequently tremendously overstaffed, particularly if they were previously government owned; governments often used these plants as ways of creating jobs. AES believes that overstaffing is bad for people because jobs aren't as much fun if people don't have sufficient challenge and enough to do. Consequently, AES will often reduce the workforce substantially. In that process, the company will have some opportunity to signal its culture and values and have those who don't feel like they are a good fit leave voluntarily.

Delegation of Decision-Making Authority

Selecting the right people is critical because AES gives those people a lot of challenge and variety in their work. Probably the most unusual feature about AES is its radical decentralization of authority and responsibility, even to people who may not have had extensive experience doing the job. Some examples are given in this section.

Oscar Prieto, a chemical engineer who had worked for AES for just two years in his first job in the power industry, had turned around a power plant in Argentina. In May 1996, he was visiting corporate headquarters in Arlington, Virginia, when Tom Tribone, a senior executive, asked him to come to a meeting about buying a business in Rio de Janeiro. He was then asked to take the lead in AES's involvement in Light, a Brazilian distribution company. Eighteen months later, Oscar Prieto was a major leader of AES's rapid expansion into South America. His division serves a combined customer base of more than 8 million people, and he oversees hundreds of millions of dollars in construction projects.[29]

In another case, "[w]hen AES raised . . . about $350 million . . . to finance a joint venture in Northern Ireland, two control room operators led the team that raised the funds."[30] That is typical. Most financial decisions at AES are made by members of project teams who may not have had any formal training in finance. Paul Burdick, a mechanical engineer without an MBA, led the complex financing on the $404 million Warrior Run project in Cumberland, Maryland.[31] "Hard as it is to imagine, CFO [Barry] Sharp has raised less than $300 million of the approximately $3.5 billion of funding for AES's 10 power plants. The multidisciplinary project team working on each new plant is charged with that task, even if the team has little finance experience."[32]

At the Thames, Connecticut, plant, the maintenance group of about fifteen people volunteered to take responsibility for investing about $12 million in cash reserves held at the plant. As Bakke explained,

> They didn't have a clue about how to invest short-term money in the market, but they thought it would be fun to learn. So they hired a teacher who told them what a spread was, who to call on Wall Street . . . and so forth. After a few weeks of studying, they started calling up brokers and looking for the best vehicle for investing. . . . By the third month, they actually beat the returns of the people who were investing the money for the company's treasury at home office. They were so proud . . . [T]hose people will be changed forever. They have become better businesspeople.[33]

At Thames and most of the other plants, a budget task force composed of frontline people formulates the budget. Budgets are not determined unilaterally by the plant manager or the superintendents. Technicians in an area may get an idea for capital improvements. They will obtain bids, do a financial analysis to see if their ideas are economically sensible, and, if they are, will implement the proposals. Budgets are seen as guidelines, not as hard and fast constraints, and are set by talking to people in the plant about what they think they will spend next year based on what they spent last year and what they think they need to do the job.

AES distinguishes between its practices and typical participative decision making. In most systems of participation, people are asked for their advice, but the decision remains with the boss. At AES, people throughout the organization get real responsibility and accountability for making substantive decisions. Others will offer advice, and of course, there will be reviews of the decisions to see how things went. But the decisions remain with individuals throughout the company. Bakke provided an example:

> We have a team member in India; he's been with us for three years. He and his team wanted to buy two coal plants. Most board members . . . were very interested in getting those plants, and we urged him to bid $170 million. He said no. . . . [T]he returns weren't good enough, he believed. . . . He bid $143 million—and he won. The important point is this: even with advice from the most senior people in the company, the decision belonged to him . . . and he made it.[34]

One way AES encourages delegation of authority is to keep the formal structure quite flat. Even today the company has only five levels, and adding hierarchical levels is done with great reluctance. Roger Sant commented, "the more authority figures you have above you, the more likely it is that you won't make decisions yourself."[35] The flat structure and absence of hierarchy extends to the plants themselves. Plants operate typically with just three levels: the plant manager, some superintendents, and the frontline people. Moreover, most of the plants operate without shift supervisors.

Training and Developing People

Giving people responsibility, letting them move to new jobs, and holding them accountable for their decisions is the best way AES has found to develop future leaders and encourage people to learn. Bakke has said that because people know they have to make decisions, they know they have to get educated. AES does not have an "AES University" or company-sponsored or mandated training programs. Rather, people are responsible for their own education and development. Experienced employees train newcomers, and operators in a plant train other operators. If people think they need a course, they organize and book it. There is extensive cross-training, accomplished by encouraging people to move to different jobs. So, for instance, someone in accounting in a power plant might work for a while in materials handling, unloading coal. AES has a tuition reimbursement program for taking classes at local educational institutions. The company will advance 80 percent of the funds for tuition and fees. People receive 10 percent more if they earn a B in the course, and 10 percent more than that, or 100 percent of their tuition and fees, if they earn an A.[36]

AES practices promotion from within—with a vengeance. It can do this because people learn quickly in an environment in which they have real responsibility. For instance, Peter Norgeot began as a boiler room technician at AES's Thames plant in 1988 after working at Northeast Utilities following his graduation from the Massachusetts Maritime Academy. Within five years, he was designing the company's 688-megawatt plant at Medway, in the United Kingdom; at the age of 32, he managed the Barry plant in Wales.[37] Of the twenty-three people who stayed longer than a few months working with the then-plant manager, Dave McMillen, during the start-up of AES Thames in 1988, "two are AES Vice Presidents-Group Managers, seven are Presidents of individual AES businesses and eight are plant leaders."[38]

If you put people in new jobs and give them lots of responsibility, they will make mistakes. Errors are part of any learning process—think of learning to ride a bicycle. AES encourages people to take on new responsibilities and try new things by not punishing honest mistakes. For instance, at the plant in Barry, Wales, "[w]hen a technician forgot to submit a bid to the government pool on a day when demand was high and prices at a peak, he cost the company $150,000 in a single hour. Norgeot [the plant manager] didn't fire him, and the technician later proved his worth by designing a daily, fail-safe alarm so the mistake would never happen again."[39]

If you put people in jobs they have never done before, they may not be immediately successful. AES gives them time to learn. Ian Miller, a design engineer with technical experience, was assigned by

AES to peddle surplus power to local utilities in Ireland. He did a terrible job. His reward: eight months of training in the AES values at headquarters. Then Miller went to Japan, where he spent fifteen months working with Mitsubishi, the builder of an AES plant in Pakistan. In this assignment, Miller claims he made mistakes that cost the company $600,000. However, the Pakistan projects were ultimately completed on time, and more recently Miller helped design the new Ironwood plant in Pennsylvania. This is what he says about AES's tolerance for mistakes and for taking the time to learn: "Most utilities waste small fortunes making sure no one makes mistakes. And no one does because no one does anything."[40] Miller has articulated an important lesson: Preventing "mistakes" costs money, and fear of making an error causes decision paralysis, which is deadly in a company that competes on the basis of speed and innovation.

Organizing in Teams

The basic organizational unit at AES, particularly in the plants, is the team, with task forces formed to handle special tasks or assignments:

> The plants and business development activities are grouped into 11 regions. . . . Every plant has a manager as well. He or she oversees 5 to 20 teams within the plant, each containing about 5 to 20 people, including a team leader. . . . [T]here's a team that oversees the control room and one that oversees everything having to do with fuel for the plant. There's almost always a water treatment team. . . . We're moving toward a system in which each team has total responsibility for its area both in terms of operations *and* maintenance. . . . [W]e want people to take ownership of the whole. . . . When something goes wrong, you own the problem, from start to finish.[41]

Decisions that would normally be handled by a specialist group, such as human resources, are handled by task forces and committees at AES. So, for instance, at the Thames plant there is an audit task force, an environmental task force, and a safety task force. An ad hoc group makes decisions on things such as health insurance, and a group reviews holiday and vacation day issues. Task forces and committees in AES are staffed largely by people who have volunteered to participate because they are interested in the particular issues.

Teams at AES help in the information sharing and transfer process and help provide advice and support in this very decentralized structure. They also provide a context in which people can more easily learn from each other, because a lot of training and development takes place within the teams, task forces, and committees.

Sharing Information

If people are going to make decisions, they need information so they can make those decisions as effectively as possible. In keeping with its philosophy of decentralization and continuous learning, AES shares lots of information with all of its people. In fact, it shares so much information that all of its employees are considered to be insiders by Securities and Exchange Commission guidelines.

For instance, at the Thames plant information on financial and operating performance is shared once a month at a communications meeting. During the meeting, each operations area of the plant talks about its projects, reports on personal news, and discusses anything that concerns people or is on their minds. Some people voluntarily come to these meetings even on their day off.

The company focuses on plantwide or companywide measures of performance, and there are comparatively few "micro" measures. This measurement system recognizes the interdependence among people and keeps people focused on global indicators of success. For instance, at the plant level, the monthly report focuses on the percentage of time the plant is operating and the percentage of rated capacity power produced, both for the month and year to date; the overtime used; the safety record; and environmental compliance with emissions and water standards. AES operates its facilities at an average of just 60 percent of permitted sulfur dioxide emissions and 44 percent of permitted nitrous oxide emissions.[42]

Although at present the company does not share information about everyone's salary, it is considering doing so. Because salaries are set mostly by task forces and by people talking to each other about these decisions, it is unlikely that there is much real salary secrecy in any event. For instance, Paul Stinson, vice president in charge of the Silk Road Group, which oversees AES plants in Central Asia, "furnished each of the dozen members . . . with a list of the salary, bonus, and stock options paid to each person in the group, as well as comparative compensation data for all AES employees with similar responsibilities" so that the members could, after a group discussion, determine their own salaries.[43] This practice is likely to spread to more parts of AES because it is consistent with the company's core assumptions that AES people can be trusted and are capable of making decisions.

Reducing Status Distinctions

AES's philosophy, structure, and competitive strategy are premised on the idea that *all* AES people are "creative, thinking individuals . . . [who] are responsible[,] . . . desire to make positive contributions to society, associate with a winner and a cause, like a challenge[,] . . . are unique persons, deserving respect, not numbers or machines."[44] Therefore, AES seeks to treat all people as similarly as possible and largely eschews demarcations that separate people by rank or status.

One of the things that the company particularly dislikes is the distinction between hourly and salaried positions, categories that, at least in the United States, are embodied in labor law. Hourly people get paid overtime; salaried people do not. AES has offered people the opportunity to voluntarily move from hourly to salaried status. From 1995 to 1997, the company reduced the proportion of people being paid on an hourly basis from about 90 percent to 50 percent. In the company's 1998 annual report, it noted: "In two years, the percentage of the 10,000 or so people listed by name in this report who are paid on an all salary basis has gone from 29% to 52%. . . . Allowing people to convert to salary, bonus and stock option pay packages . . . is not an elixir that makes every person a business person. But for many, it is a giant step in that direction."[45]

To keep AES senior management in touch with what happens in the field, *every* senior manager in the company (except for Roger Sant, who recently cut back his involvement to 60 percent time) spends one week in one of the plants the company operates. During that week, the managers do actual jobs in the plants. As Sant explained, "I think it gives us more insight into what operations are all about. . . . [Y]ou learn enough to make you appreciate what kind of contribution is being made by our plant people. I think that it changed the relationship of people to the point that there was considerably more mutual respect."[46]

Two other concrete actions also reduce status distinctions at AES. First, there is a great deal of salary compression. In 1998, Dennis Bakke, the president and CEO, earned $500,000 (salary and bonus). In 1997, he was ranked number 560 of the 800 top CEOs in the country in terms of total compensation.[47] Beginning in 1999, Bakke's cash compensation was reduced to $0. "Mr. Bakke will be compensated solely by the grant of stock options (in lieu of a cash salary and cash bonus)."[48] No executive officer received more than $750,000 cash compensation in 1998, the amount paid to the CFO, Barry Sharp. As noted previously, a lot of discussion about wages and a lot of information sharing about all personnel matters and, indeed, all decisions takes place. This sharing of information throughout the company helps everyone feel truly involved and important.

Second, the language used at AES is watched carefully because the leaders strongly believe that "Words are important."[49] The company dislikes the phrase "human resources" because steel is a resource, not people. AES people are called just that: AES people. You will not hear or see words like "employee" or "worker" in AES materials or in conversations at the company. In fact, the company does not even like or use the term "management." "We don't allow that word to be used in our company."[50] It's not that AES people prefer "leader," but that they don't like to distinguish between people on the basis of job titles or hierarchical positions.

Compensation

Pay is determined, as discussed previously, by looking at what others are being paid for comparable positions, both inside individual plants and across the company. There is no set salary schedule for each job. AES tends not to pay the highest rate in the industry for its jobs. As one person at the Thames, Connecticut, plant noted, "If you pay the highest, people will fake it in terms of liking the culture and the values."[51] AES wants people in the company who really like the place, believe in the AES system and philosophy, and enjoy what they do. About two-thirds of the people in the Connecticut plant took a salary cut from their previous job to work at AES. As part of this philosophy of having people work because they like the environment, not just for the money, AES has only a five-year period for the vesting of retirement benefits rather than the more typical ten-year period. This avoids the problem of having people stay around just to get their retirement package.

Raises are given once a year. Individuals engage in a self-evaluation process, and those who determine salaries will look at this as well as talk to the person's peers and others who may have come in contact with the individual. In addition to the salary, there are three other forms of compensation: individual bonuses; a plant performance bonus, based on safety, the environmental record, costs, and electricity production; and a companywide bonus based on the overall results. The plant performance bonus is distributed equally to everyone in the plant. The company bonus has typically been about 10 percent of an individual's salary. Almost everyone owns stock in the company, either directly or through his or her retirement plan.

One of the questions about stock ownership is how people feel when the stock price goes down. At AES, most people want to buy more when the stock price is low (a policy that, over the years, was quite profitable). One person at the Thames plant commented, "We feel we're part of the entrepreneurs. The fluctuation in the stock price reinforces the fact that we're responsible. If there were only upside, we're taking a free ride. The fact that the stock price fluctuates and that they gain and lose accordingly makes people feel like they are more of an owner of the company."[52]

Integrating Acquisitions and Going Global

AES believes that its core values, philosophy, and operating principles will work all over the world. So, in 1998 at the Tisza II power plants in Hungary, AES people voluntarily converted from hourly to salaried wage packages after three months of discussion.[53] The AES way of operating is quite radical, but it is just as radical in the United States as in any other place. Dennis Bakke explained the company's philosophy and views about operating outside the United States:

> It's easier for us to implement this [system] in some places outside the U.S. than in the U.S. I challenge you to be less American-centric in

your ideas. On risk and everything else. On Wall Street everybody's worried about everything outside the U.S. . . . . Everything is bad two miles from your home, or fifty miles from New York City. We say the whole world of business is risky. We don't differentiate between the risk in Pakistan and the risk in the U.S. I illustrate that by saying we've had one political expropriation of a business in our 17 years of history, a painful one. It was in Florida.[54]

AES operates by its core values even in plants it acquires. Of course, there is a transition period, and of course, making the transition from a traditional, command-and-control hierarchical system to the AES way is not always easy or smooth. But the company does not permit compromise of its basic values and philosophy in how it operates. Bakke described the process:

> We start by telling them [the people in the acquired plant] what we believe. Sometimes that's a plant manager or someone coming from afar, usually bringing in some new leadership. . . . We bring in somebody who really believes the stuff, who's an outsider. If you're going to do something radical . . . you are probably better off having somebody from outside, someone who can communicate the values and principles. There will be other people that will infiltrate the plant, too, not just at the top leadership. Enough people so that folks can ask them and they can model what we're talking about. I come sometimes . . . and I teach. We do a values survey immediately, and we do it every year, asking people the questions. It doesn't really matter how they answer it. What it does is force people to think about what all of this is about. Then we bring people to orientation and have them experience the AES way. We let them go to other plants to look at what really happens.[55]

In Pakistan, initially the plant manager didn't think the company had the right people. He thought that only 20 percent of the people were going to make it. Bakke said to him, "Well, 20% is better than zero. We can keep working on it." Six months later when Bakke returned to the plant, the manager reported that everything had changed. Now he thought that 80 percent of the people were understanding and believing AES philosophies, values, and management practices. AES is both patient and persistent in instilling its principles and culture. The company understands that it does things differently and that it will therefore take time for people who are used to more traditional ways to adjust. It gives people that time, but is unrelenting in measuring its values and remaining committed to them.

LESSONS FROM AES

As Dennis Bakke has noted, AES's management practices are both interrelated and focused: "They're like an ecosystem. Everything about how we organize gives people the power and the responsibility to make important decisions, to engage with their work as businesspeople, not as cogs in a machine."[56] AES's underlying core principle of a belief in and trust in people has led to an organization composed of truly self-managing teams in which people feel responsibility for not only their own work but also the welfare of the whole. Bakke has described the company as a real "learning organization" in which people are encouraged to learn new things all the time. The company has fostered a whatever-it-takes mentality, whereby people work with others and do what is necessary to get the job done and to overcome problems and obstacles as they arise, which, of course, they invariably do.

The development of skill and teamwork and a whatever-it-takes attitude has led to AES being able to operate its power plants at much higher utilization rates than average for the industry. In 1997, AES plants had an average availability, including scheduled and unscheduled maintenance, of 93 percent, compared with an industry average of about 83 percent. Plants acquired by AES improved from an availability of 81 percent to 85 percent in one year. In 1997, the AES plant at Thames, Connecticut, was available an amazing 98 percent of the time.[57]

Because of the company's trust in its people, information is widely shared and decision-making responsibility is widely dispersed. Because of the company's belief in the importance of all of its people to its success, senior leadership makes relatively few decisions and enjoys few status distinctions or perquisites. Rather, the role of the senior leadership is that of coach, cheerleader, reminder of accountability, and perhaps most important, keeper of the organization's unique culture.

To return to our mysteries, is AES in control? In the first place, control, to the extent it interferes with fun and letting people be businesspeople, is not much valued at AES. More important, the answer to the question depends very much on how you view management and the management process. As Dennis Bakke has noted, in most organizations there is "a fundamental belief that people can't be trusted and won't work unless they're told what to do. . . . There is a belief that some people are thinkers, some are leaders and visionaries, and the others are the doers."[58]

If that is your belief about people, then AES is clearly not "in control."

But in large organizations, one of the great challenges is to have everyone feel as if his or her work and ideas are important. It is all too easy for people to come to believe that what they do doesn't matter, and that the work and thoughts of others will compensate for their own deficiencies or lack of effort. At AES, this absence of involvement and commitment is largely avoided because everyone has decisions to make and has accountability for his or her actions and decisions. Moreover, by building a team structure and hiring people who work well with others, and by creating the expectation that people will ask for advice from their peers and that such advice will be forthcoming, the company has built a strong system of mutual control. People ask for advice and help via the company's e-mail system, and AES organizes conferences (for instance, for plant managers) so that people can build social ties and share information and knowledge. It is our observation that both knowledge and learning flow and develop as effectively at AES as they do in any company we have either seen or read about. In that sense, the company is very much in control.

As for the mystery of how AES operates as it does all over the world, on reflection, that isn't much of a mystery at all. AES has tapped into some human values that are virtually universal. Who doesn't want to have fun? Who doesn't want to be taken seriously and be treated with respect? Who doesn't want to be treated fairly and to treat others fairly? The record at AES suggests that its values, philosophy, and cultural practices work well everywhere it has gone so far. In fact, its cultural values and management practices have helped transform some of the places it has opened for business.

The ability of AES to improve the operations of plants it acquires, both in the United States and overseas, provides some evidence that the company has developed a system that unlocks the value hidden in its people. The ability of AES to develop talent, to create a learning system, and to fill so many positions from within even as the company has expanded dramatically in both size and scope provides further evidence for this assertion. There is no doubt that AES has talented people. But there's also little doubt that these people are, in some ways, not much different from those to be found in many companies. The difference is a system that truly unleashes their ideas and their energy.

Chapter 8

New United Motor Manufacturing, Inc.: Transforming People and Systems

WHEN WE TELL people the stories in the preceding chapters, we typically get the following response. These companies—Southwest, AES, SAS Institute, PSS World Medical, Cisco, and The Men's Wearhouse—have a long history of being managed in the way we describe. In several cases they were founded by their current CEOs, and in any event, they "got it right from the start." What about companies that haven't had a track record of success? What about companies that haven't been led on the basis of some philosophy or overarching values? Can they be changed? Can you teach an old dog new tricks, and reinvent and reinvigorate culture? The answer, of course, is yes. Continental Airlines went from being worst to first in on-time performance in a year and substantially improved its customer service. British Airways changed its culture to provide better service, and then unwittingly has changed it back because it got too caught up in short-term financials and lost sight of what produced those financial results in the first place. This chapter provides yet another and perhaps the most compelling example. New United Motor Manufacturing, Inc. (NUMMI) was born from a closed General Motors (GM) plant in California—in the same building, with largely the same workforce and the same union, the United Auto Workers (UAW). The lessons from NUMMI are important in understanding how to change a culture in a unionized workforce in a very competitive and demanding industry in order to achieve exceptional returns with the *same* people.

NUMMI is an exception in the U.S. automobile industry and particularly in the General Motors system. During 1998, poor union-management relations between GM and its unions resulted in a fifty-four-day strike at two parts plants in Flint, Michigan. Parts shortages resulting from the strike idled nearly 200,000 UAW members, with an average loss of $1,240 a week in wages. The state lost $37 million in tax revenue. The shortage of critical parts also resulted in a shut-down of most of GM's automobile assembly plants, with an estimated loss to GM of $2.5 billion—enough for GM to build two brand-new assembly plants.[1] For consumers who bought a new GM car, the strike meant an average cost of at least $200 more than if there had not been a strike. Labor troubles were not the only problem confronting General Motors. In 1997, estimates were that GM lost an average of $104 per vehicle whereas crosstown rival Ford made $1,520 per car sold.[2] Even worse, GM has been losing market share in the United States for over a decade.

Now suppose we gave you the following data about an automobile plant and asked you to identify this plant's location:

The plant employs over 4,000 unionized workers and produces an average of eighty-seven vehicles per worker, an average far above the fifty cars per worker at both Saturn and Buick City, the most efficient GM facilities.[3] In 1998, this plant won the National Association of Manufacturers' award for excellence.[4] The award noted that this plant managed a changeover to a new model in the remarkable time of only five days and took only thirty days to reach full production. The quality of the new vehicles, already one of the highest rated, was nearly 50 percent better than the old version, while the cost-reduction targets through the launch were exceeded by 86 percent. In addition, the workforce made over 3.2 suggestions per person in 1998, of which 81 percent were adopted. Over 86 percent of the plant's team members made suggestions that year.[5]

Where is this plant? Not in Japan, but in Fremont, California. More amazing is the fact that this plant, NUMMI, is a joint venture begun in 1983 between Toyota and General Motors. The plant was founded after GM closed its Fremont assembly facility and laid off the same workers that later formed the core of the NUMMI operation. Even

more remarkable is that since 1983, GM has spent an amount estimated to be over $80 billion on technology designed to improve the
quality of its automobiles and enhance productivity.[6] Yet, in spite of
the immense investments in technology, in 1998 the most efficient
plants in the GM system were 40 percent less productive than
NUMMI. What's more, as GM and its unions continue their bitter and
costly labor disputes, NUMMI turns out the highest-quality automobiles in the GM system in an environment characterized by comparative labor peace.

Why is NUMMI able to outproduce GM? It's not because it
has some special workforce. The plant employs ex-GM workers.
It's not the technology. From its inception, NUMMI has relied
on older technology and is not as automated as many competitive
plants. It's not that NUMMI is a nonunion workplace, because
the company has the same union (and originally even the same
union leaders) as at the old GM-Fremont plant. How has NUMMI
been able to continually produce with such high levels of quality
and efficiency when they began by reopening a plant that was
probably one of the worst in the GM system at the time it was
closed in 1982? Why has General Motors been largely unable to
replicate the lessons of NUMMI in its other facilities? These are important mysteries to solve, for they lie at the heart of a broader phenomenon: How can one management achieve extraordinary results
when the previous management failed miserably with the same people?

To solve this puzzle, we need to examine it through the eyes of a
real expert—a manager with long experience in automobile manufacturing. Jamie Hresko, a fifteen-year veteran of GM, undertook a remarkable personal experiment to learn how NUMMI really operated.
Seeking to understand the secret of NUMMI, Jamie took a job there
building cars on the line. To enable you to solve this mystery in turn,
we begin with Jamie's account of his experience on the assembly line
and then describe the history and operating principles of NUMMI. As
you read this description, ask yourself what the fundamental differences are between NUMMI and the old GM-Fremont operation. But
be careful, because the differences are as subtle as they are important,
and the more obvious differences may be less important than they
first appear.

JAMIE HRESKO AT NUMMI

Jamie Hresko joined GM in 1982 as a production supervisor at the Buick City plant and has been with the company in manufacturing ever since. In 1997, Jamie was selected by GM to attend the Sloan Program at the Graduate School of Business at Stanford University—a one-year accelerated master's program for high-potential managers making the transition into general management positions. Prior to attending the Sloan Program, Jamie was an operations manager for one of GM's North American assembly plants. This facility is one of GM's most complex assembly plants and employs over 4,000 people. The plant produces five different midsize and luxury automobiles on one assembly line.

Jamie was a manufacturing person and was familiar with some of NUMMI's accomplishments. For years at GM he had seen the comparative productivity and quality numbers from NUMMI. He had been at quarterly manufacturing meetings with his peers from Fremont and other North American plants for discussions of the Toyota manufacturing system.[7] He had even sent people from his own plant to NUMMI to learn from them. But, like many GM managers, he also harbored a certain cynicism about NUMMI's success. Although NUMMI had been building cars since 1984, there was a lingering question of whether the company could sustain its performance. Jamie was committed to GM and cared deeply about helping GM improve its manufacturing operations. He knew that GM was running well behind Ford in productivity. A recent *Business Week* article reported that GM was the least efficient of the U.S. auto producers—20 percent less efficient than Ford, even though GM had shed some 60,000 workers since 1992.[8]

This background led him to undertake a remarkable experiment. Since he was heading to California for the Sloan Program, he decided to test the NUMMI production process for himself. Early in 1997, Jamie arranged to be hired as a production worker at NUMMI. Only a few members of the NUMMI management team knew of his previous connection to GM or suspected that he was anything more than a slightly older guy looking for a decent job. The fact that Jamie is young looking and comes from a blue-collar background helped him fit in. For two weeks, Jamie worked on the line and, using his deep knowledge of manufacturing operations, tested the NUMMI system to see whether it was as good as the numbers suggested. He tried every trick he knew to subvert the process and test its limits. It was an amazing experience that left him convinced that NUMMI was every bit as good as he had heard.

On the Line at NUMMI

Jamie began his experiment by calling a manager at NUMMI and describing his request. He didn't want the usual tour. What he wanted was simply to be put into the hiring process with other applicants for jobs at the plant. No one was to know who he was or what his purpose was. He was to go through the usual steps.

> I had the opportunity to go through the hiring process, including written tests, interviews with other hourly people, and the training program. I was amazed at all the levels of testing and educational training that they provide new recruits. The majority of NUMMI applicants were referrals from people already working in the plant, family members and the like. In this sense, most applicants already had a pretty good idea of what working on an assembly line was like.
>
> The initial training and orientation program takes three months, so I only got the short version. The formal training is 30 days and includes aerobics, instruction about the Toyota production system, how the suggestion system operates, the importance of standardized work processes, scrolling, welding, the team process, and lots of discussion of the importance of having the right attitude. It gave a very realistic picture of what it's like to work on the line. NUMMI doesn't want people unless they have the right attitude and are capable of performing the aggressive work requirements. They have to fit with the company.
>
> After this initial training, new employees are sent out to the line for a couple of days a week. Their work time on the assembly line then increases over the 90-day probation period. About 80 percent of the applicants drop out by the end of the program.[9]

Jamie was placed in the body shop building radiator supports, a physically demanding job that required him to run three machines. He was assigned to a team of four. The team leader, another hourly employee, was responsible for training him. It was clear that all team members were expected to take an active part in improving productivity and quality, with the team leader asking for suggestions or ideas for improvement.

The informal norm within the team was to rotate jobs every couple of hours to give people ergonomic relief and to share the burden. Jamie noted that it was hard for people to complain about their jobs if other people did the same work. There also was an expectation that if the job was too difficult or unsafe, the team would redesign the work. Jamie described some of the feelings within the team:

> Everyone seemed to agree that all team members must be on board if you're going to survive and compete in today's competitive market. There was a sense that the system wasn't designed to squeeze people or destroy them but to help them be competitive. The peer pressure is intense. Most people were willing to stay after their shift to finish their job if necessary. I wasn't accustomed to this type of attitude. People at NUMMI just go do it. They believe that their job is to protect the customer by never shipping a bad product. But this isn't because of a fear of being fired. It actually appears to be harder to fire people at NUMMI than it was in my old plant.
>
> For example, the team leader made it clear to me that I wasn't to worry about slowing down production. I was to make a quality part. During my first few days when I would get behind, other team members would come over and help me catch up. In fact, the team really handled not just the work but also the discipline. When one team member came to work late a couple of times, he was strong-armed by the entire group. The peer pressure is really big-time. Teams can really impact the decision to keep a person or let them go.[10]

After learning the job, Jamie set out to test the system by violating some of the production and safety regulations regarding error proofing, cycle time, and material handling. For example, he attempted to build up a buffer of extra parts, a common ploy used by workers to get ahead so they can use the buffer to rest. He also attempted to stack parts on the floor, a safety violation, to make his job easier. He tried extending his lunch break by two minutes and not doing some of the quality checks he was supposed to do. All of these attempts drew reprimands immediately, mostly from other team members rather than the team leader.

Most days I never saw a supervisor [group leader], but I was always called on any violation. When I came back two minutes late from lunch I was told that others would cover for me if it was important, but that I hurt the whole team when I did this and I had better not do it again unless there was a good reason. When I missed a couple of quality checks, an operator down the line picked them up and stopped by to make sure I didn't do it again. But there was also a willingness of operators to help me fix errors and do a better job.[11]

After working for two weeks, Jamie marveled at how the entire system was oriented toward helping the worker on the line do a better job.

There was a continual effort to make the jobs safer and more efficient. The suggestion system is set up to quickly implement suggestions. Team leaders and coordinators do a lot of the scheduling, budgeting, and other administrative tasks that in another GM plant would be done mostly by managers and engineers. From the very beginning, there is complete clarity and honesty about what's important. These are reinforced with plenty of visuals around the plant with indicators of quality, productivity, safety, and attendance. There are team meetings twice a month for 30 minutes when the line is stopped so people can review their performance. It's impressive how familiar people are with these performance indicators. Even the union preaches the importance of productivity and apparently won't support workers who are out to destroy the company. The culture is one of a willingness to help each other, friendliness, discipline, honesty, hard work, and one that stresses the importance of productivity and quality. It's a remarkable place.

As a manufacturing manager, I have always believed that supporting the hourly technicians is the most important factor in winning in the automobile industry. I was overwhelmed by how much the NUMMI process is geared toward helping line workers. Here, production really is king. As a team member, you can always get engineering help. The goal is to support the operator. I feel that establishing processes and systems to engage hourly technicians and team support is the key to success. I simply haven't been able to accomplish it to this level in my career.

Part of NUMMI's success is that HR is accountable for hiring, approving budgets, contract changes, training, discharge procedures, and running the plant. If you want to make a process change, you have to go through HR. Because they actually administer the plant, they don't make stupid mistakes. You have HR people who really know how to run the plant. At GM, HR has a more limited role and is much more removed from the whole manufacturing process.[12]

NUMMI'S HISTORY

To understand how NUMMI operates, it is important to appreciate its history. In 1963, General Motors opened an automobile assembly plant in Fremont, California. With a large population, California is an important automobile market. Given its distance from Detroit and other Midwest manufacturing plants and the high transportation costs for automobiles, it made sense to locate production in this large and growing market. By 1978, the Fremont plant employed over 7,200 workers. By 1982, it was closed. The reasons for closing the plant were sound: GM-Fremont ranked at the bottom of GM's plants in productivity and was producing one of the worst-quality automobiles in the entire GM system. A militant union averaged 5,000 to 7,000 grievances per three-year labor contract. The plant was characterized by high use of sick leave, slowdowns, wildcat strikes, and even sabotage. First-line managers were known to carry weapons for personal protection. Daily absenteeism was almost 20 percent, and drug abuse and alcoholism plagued the workforce. There was a climate of fear and mistrust between management and the union. George Nano, union representative at the old GM plant, described labor relations succinctly: "It was war. At GM we had to fight for everything." Under the old system, Nano said, "Management just didn't seem to care. And when management doesn't care, workers won't care either."[13]

In 1983 Toyota and General Motors signed a letter of intent to reopen the plant, now named New United Motor Manufacturing, Inc., or NUMMI. Toyota's goal in entering the joint venture was to gain a foothold in the U.S. market, learn about working with U.S. suppliers, and see if their manufacturing and management approaches could work with U.S. employees. GM needed a small car (the Nova) to add to its product line and hoped to learn about Toyota's production system. Doug Fraser, then UAW president, saw the opportunity that working with the Japanese presented and committed the union to work with the new venture. Don Ephlin, UAW head for GM and an individual interested in developing new models of work, also committed himself to the new venture.[14]

Under the joint agreement, Toyota and GM agreed to invest roughly $100 million each, with another $200 million in debt for the new entity. Toyota was to operate the facility. Although Toyota originally wanted to operate a nonunion plant, GM felt it had to push to keep the UAW to avoid trouble with the union in its other facilities. In the end, NUMMI agreed to recognize the union and to offer recall rights to the workforce laid off when GM closed the plant. The company also agreed to pay union-scale wages. The UAW agreed to accept the Toyota production system, to greatly increase the flexibility of work rules, and to simplify the myriad job classifications. The first page of the new agreement reflected this new relationship:

> Both parties are undertaking this new proposed relationship with the full intention of fostering an innovative labor relations structure, minimizing traditional adversarial roles and emphasizing mutual trust and good faith.[15]

Reflecting this new relationship, Toyota agreed to reappoint the same twenty-five-person union bargaining committee that existed under the old GM system. George Nano and Tony De Jesus, union leaders under the old system, assumed the same roles at NUMMI. This committee was the beginning of the establishment of a new culture based on trust and respect. The committee was also important in crafting a vision for the new plant that reflected the mutual interests of workers and management. As one experienced GM labor relations manager observed, there was a significant risk in this approach at the beginning:

> These guys were tough as nails. They'd strike GM as fast as you could snap your fingers. They hated General Motors and they didn't want to change. . . . But, I knew that if we didn't bring in the leadership of the

old GM local, they'd be settin' across the street pitchin' firebombs at the place. There was no way Toyota could have opened the plant without them.[16]

The New Company

Under the terms of the joint venture agreement, Toyota assumed responsibility for all plant operations, including product design and engineering as well as marketing, sales, and service for vehicles with the Toyota marque (i.e., the Corolla and subsequently the Tacoma pickup). GM assumed responsibility for the marketing, sales, and service of GM-branded vehicles (initially the Chevy Nova and more recently the Prizm). In addition, GM was to assign to NUMMI, on a rotating basis, a limited number of managers and coordinators to learn the Toyota manufacturing system.

NUMMI's management was initially headed by Tatsuro Toyoda, son of Toyota's founder. Other NUMMI management came from Toyota (Kan Higashi), Ford (the head of manufacturing), and General Dynamics (the head of human resources). Eighty-five percent of the initial workforce of 2,200 came from the pool of laid-off GM employees. In the first year, NUMMI built almost 65,000 Novas—a car that was rated by *Consumer Reports* as one of the highest-quality small cars in the world. Absenteeism was less than 3 percent, and only a handful of grievances were filed.

Kan Higashi, the second president of NUMMI, recalled that at first Toyota was concerned that American workers and the UAW would not understand the Toyota production concepts. But, he said, "We found people here to be capable and flexible" and he didn't see much difference between American and Japanese employees. He noted that management treats people not as part of a machine but as human beings deserving trust and respect. The result? "Basically the NUMMI plant is the same as the plant in Japan—only smaller."[17]

As the joint venture started up, both union and management stuffed envelopes, sending job applications to 5,000 former employees. Three thousand replied and 85 percent were rehired. The only group of former employees not offered employment at NUMMI were former first-line supervisors. Of those who applied, many voluntarily dropped out during the screening process when they learned what would be expected of them in the new operation. Only 300 applicants were actually rejected, mostly for unusually poor work histories or drug or alcohol problems. The demographic composition of the initial workforce at NUMMI closely resembled that of the original GM-Fremont plant, suggesting that few people from the old plant who wanted to work at NUMMI were actually not rehired.

At the outset, Toyota sent 400 trainers from Japan to teach the Toyota production system. NUMMI spent more than $3 million to send 600 of its new employees to Japan for training. This included three weeks of classroom and on-the-job training working side by side with Toyota workers.

The NUMMI Production System

The primary goal of the Toyota manufacturing system is to reduce costs and maximize profits through the systematic identification of waste. At NUMMI, this goal was broadened from reducing the cost per vehicle to include continually improving quality and securing safety. The vision for NUMMI was to produce the highest-quality, lowest-cost vehicles in the world. Using a strategy of *kaizen* (continuous improvement), Toyota has consistently been ranked as among the most efficient producers of automobiles, both in its Japanese facilities and at NUMMI. For instance, the company employed 2.62 workers per vehicle produced in 1996 compared with GM's 3.62—a 20 percent productivity advantage. The Toyota system also produced automobiles of the highest quality—approximately 80 defects per 100 cars in 1996 compared with around 110 for GM.

Kaizen places an unrelenting emphasis on the identification and elimination of waste in all of its various forms: inventory, buffer stocks, equipment, material flow, manpower, and work design. These forms of waste stem from poorly designed plans and processes, local suboptimization, improper automation, poor standardization, a lack of communication, and poor cost accounting practices. Importantly, waste is seen as having deleterious effects on people, leading to physical and emotional fatigue, frustration, stress, and a tendency to blame others. The shared belief is that everything can be improved and that all improvements, no matter how small, are valuable. This approach further recognizes that people are the foundation of this system and that their ideas are the true source of improvement. This means that *kaizen* must be built on the cornerstone values of safety, trust, fair-

Table 8-1 Productivity and Quality Comparisons among Four Automobile Plants

Productivity	FRAMINGHAM 1986	GM-FREMONT 1978	NUMMI 1986	TAKAOKA 1986
Overall productivity				
Hourly (hours/unit)	36.1	38.2	17.5	15.5
Salaried	4.6	4.9	3.3	2.5
Total	40.7	43.1	20.8	18.0
Corrected (adjusted) productivity				
Hourly	26.2	24.2	16.3	15.5
Salaried	4.6	4.9	3.3	2.5
Total	30.8	29.1	19.6	18.0
NUMMI's advantage (%)	57.1	48.5	—	−8.2
Quality indicators				
GM audit	125–130	120–125	135–140	135–140
Owner survey	85–88	NA	91–94	92–94

Source: John Krafcik, "Learning from NUMMI," working paper, International Motor Vehicle Program (Sloan School of Management, MIT, Cambridge, Mass., 1986). Reprinted with permission.

ness, teamwork, security, and involvement—for both workers and suppliers. Designed using this philosophy, the NUMMI system ensures continuous increases in efficiency and quality at lower costs.

In 1986, John Krafcik, a former NUMMI engineer working on a study of automobile manufacturing plant efficiency, reported comparative data showing that NUMMI was almost 60 percent more efficient than a comparable GM plant at Framingham (see table 8-1). With a current payroll of more than 4,000, NUMMI now produces the same number of automobiles as the old GM-Fremont plant but with much higher quality and half the workforce. All this for a total investment of roughly $1.5 billion.

Employee Reactions

The most frequent explanation for this turnaround offered by cynics who had never worked at the plant is that laid-off workers would do almost anything to get their jobs back. But knowledgeable insiders and outside observers discount this explanation. After all, the threat of plant closings has done little to enhance performance at other GM plants. In fact, one study contrasting NUMMI with the GM assembly plant in Van Nuys, California, (since closed) explicitly noted that fear, quite present at Van Nuys, did not guarantee the replication of NUMMI's success.[18] The success of NUMMI comes from an integrated set of human resource and manufacturing processes that align the interests of employees, managers, and the company and involve the workforce in a way that simultaneously empowers them while managing the interdependence inherent in a complex manufacturing process.

One NUMMI team member described his previous experience at GM as follows:

> But you know, they made us build cars that way. One day I found a bolt missing. I called the supe over and he said, "What's the matter with you boy, you goin' to buy it? Move it!" Then when the plant failed they blamed us.[19]

Contrast this incident with the fact that well over 90 percent of current NUMMI workers report that they are proud of the cars they build now. A seventeen-year veteran said that the biggest difference was management's attitude toward line workers: "It's the way they treat people. You've got a say now in how your job is done. It makes a person feel important."[20]

One team member commented that "I look forward to coming to work here. There's more responsibility and challenge [at NUMMI] but with no one pressuring me. People get along well. People listen if you have ideas. But it's fast-paced, not like the old plant." Another said "We're the future of American industry. We want the same thing as management. We want success. I like the way we're all involved. We have to be flexible to survive." Another team member described how their group leader was on medical leave for eight months and the teams worked without management supervision until he returned. One former union radical summed it up:

> I have 31 years experience at GM. I'm 56 years old. For the first time in my life I got a pin for not missing any work. I find it exciting. I

think it's fun. Our team dictates what we do and how we do it. Our group leader comes by about a half-hour per week. I feel that the team members are what's most important. We can function without management.[21]

Over 50 percent of NUMMI's workforce comes from minority groups—a fact of which employees are proud. Management identified three principles that they believe are key for their success:

- Both management and the union realized that their futures were interdependent and required a commitment to a common vision.

- Employees needed to feel that they would be treated fairly before they would become contributors.

- The production system requires great interdependence, which mandates teamwork, trust, and mutual respect to operate.

THE NUMMI MANAGEMENT SYSTEM

People are seen as the foundation of the NUMMI production system, with the company being only as good as its people, individually and collectively. For this reason, the primary function of management and staff is to support the production people. Based on these guiding principles, the *NUMMI Team Handbook* states:

Our HR philosophy guides us in the development of our full human potential to enable us to build the highest quality automobiles at the lowest possible cost by:

- Recognizing our worth and dignity
- Developing our individual performance
- Developing our team performance
- Improving our work environment

The practices that foster mutual trust and respect, equity, involvement, and teamwork include the following: job security (a no-layoff policy), concern for safety in the plant, individual responsibility for quality, active involvement in the decision-making process, no time clocks, common eating and parking areas, and no distinctions in dress. The core values that are constantly reinforced include customer satisfaction (quality and cost), dignity, trust, teamwork, consistency, frugality, continual improvement, simplicity, and harmony.

No-Layoff Policy

The no-layoff policy was initiated by Toyota as a first step in establishing a culture of fairness, trust, and mutual respect. It stipulates that no one will be laid off unless the long-term viability of the company is threatened. Before anyone is laid off, the contract specifies that all outside contract work will be dropped and that the top sixty-five executives will take pay cuts. This policy has now been tested four times. For instance, in 1988 NUMMI was forced to reduce production 40 percent because of a slump in sales. During this period the line speed was slowed, workers were offered voluntary vacations, and team members were retrained in the basics of production, teamwork, and problem solving and worked in special *kaizen* project teams. A survey showed that over 80 percent of NUMMI employees felt that job security was the most important aspect of working at NUMMI.

Selection and Orientation

Before being hired, each hourly applicant goes through a three-day assessment that includes production simulations, individual and group discussions, and written tests and interviews. Evaluations concentrate on the applicant's ability to function within the NUMMI philosophy, his or her ability to follow instructions quickly and safely, and teamwork. The assessors are team leaders, themselves union members.

Once hired, team members attend a four-day orientation conducted by team members and managers. There are classes on the team concept, the Toyota production system, quality principles, attendance requirements, safety policies, labor management philosophies, cultural diversity, and the competitive situation in the automobile industry.

The Team Concept and Organizational Structure

NUMMI is a team-based organization with a flat, three-level management hierarchy. This contrasts with the five to six levels common in many GM plants. All employees are part of multifunctional teams composed of three to six people. Teams are run by a team leader, who is not a part of management but is a union member selected jointly by management and the union. Team leaders receive a 50 cent hourly premium to coordinate teamwork and training, replace team members on the line when necessary, and to build a sense of team interdependence and unity. To help ensure that teams are a tightly knit social group, each team receives a small social budget that the team can use for group social activities. Team members are allowed to request a transfer to another team only after one year on the job.

The goal is for each team member, through education and training, to become and act like a businessperson and to understand how his or her team contributes to the larger goals of the organization. Team members are responsible for the design of their own work and rotate jobs within the team. Each team member is thus obligated to understand team concepts, accept responsibility for quality and continual improvement, perform all job functions (including housekeeping and maintenance), and work within the NUMMI philosophy.

The role of first-level management (group leaders) includes planning for the group, training team leaders, and supporting the continuous improvement effort. The responsibilities may encompass assisting in the resolution of engineering problems and breakdowns, implementing the suggestion system, solving problems, and supervising any corrective discipline or counseling issues that team leaders raise. Group leaders are also expected to be available to work on the line if needed.

Second-level managers have similar responsibilities and are expected to be more process oriented than results oriented. In addition to responsibility for budgeting, planning, and training, managers are expected to encourage openness concerning problems and to see that problems are resolved at the lowest possible level.

This approach is very different from that used in the typical U.S. manufacturing operation and requires different management skills. One NUMMI manager noted that for the line to work efficiently, managers must respect their employees:

One of the key concepts is respect for the worker, the team member. The Japanese know that to make things more waste-free and stream-lined, they have to work with the people on the line. They have to work with their people, to listen to them for ideas, and to work with them to support theirs. . . . They trust their team members are doing their best. When something breaks down, managers feel it's their re-sponsibility and they're apologetic out of respect for their team mem-bers.[22]

When Gary Convis, long-term executive vice president at NUMMI, was first promoted to vice president of manufacturing, Kan Higashi, then NUMMI's president, cautioned him, "I would like you to man-age NUMMI's manufacturing operations as if you had 'no power.' Ev-eryone knows you are the vice president; however, in your day-to-day job, your listening, coaching, mentoring, and gaining consensus around key initiatives will be most appreciated and effective."[23]

Higashi emphasized that Toyota understood the importance of us-ing all means available to establish a climate of fairness—including fewer levels of management, no executive perks, and a blurring of dis-tinctions between managers and team members. This also meant overcoming a tendency on the part of Japanese employees to associ-ate only with others who spoke Japanese. Higashi noted that this ap-proach was designed at NUMMI to signal the company's vision and intent. Kosuke Ikebuchi, NUMMI's first head of manufacturing, used to emphasize to his managers, "Never forget, management is the beneficiary of our team members' hard work. Our job is to support their efforts. This way the company will be successful."[24]

Job Design

Another system explicitly designed to foster fairness and efficiency is the design of jobs. Under the old GM system there were eighty-one separate job classifications. Under the NUMMI system there are three, each with the same wage rate. The new system makes all employees responsible for quality and safety and provides a method (the *andon* cord) for any person to stop the line to get help with a quality or safety problem—even though the estimated cost of line downtime is $15,000 per minute. The cord is routinely pulled over 100 times per day. Commenting on this, one person stated, "Any worker on the line can stop production if they see a problem. . . . They're actually required to do so. Why? Well, because quality depends on it, and the survival of our company depends on our quality. Only because of this level of involvement on the part of every employee were we able to take #1 on the J.D. Power survey."[25]

Unlike the old GM mass production system (or "push" system), which could tolerate conflict and adversarial relations, the new lean production system (or "pull" system) minimizes the buffers of inventory and demands interdependence and cooperation throughout the assembly line. Under this approach, the emphasis is on *kaizen,* or continuous incremental improvements in efficiency.

The responsibility for quality does not reside in management supervision and inspections but is pushed down to the worker under the principle of *jidoka,* or identifying problems the moment they occur and responding to them immediately. Problems are resolved at the lowest level possible. The assembly line is kept constantly alert, with the emphasis being on doing the operation correctly every time. Responsibility lies with the individual to call attention to a problem whenever a defect is observed. This places a premium on people being able to identify problems and to quickly adjust and correct errors. This is almost the opposite of the old GM line, where few people beyond the superintendent had authority to stop the production line. At NUMMI, management recognizes that downtime is a signal that workers are taking their jobs seriously. As one manager said, "When there's no down-time, I know that my people are sending junk through or they're trying to be superstars."[26]

Team members are responsible for designing and improving their jobs, including the industrial engineering. This includes generating detailed definitions and sequencing of jobs, completing standardized work sheets, and adhering to these instructions. As one employee said, "We're responsible for timing our own jobs. We're always involved in making changes—not to add tasks but to improve safety and efficiency."[27] Team members often take the initiative and contact suppliers to improve the quality of parts.

The Reward System

The NUMMI system relies on a flat wage structure that serves to equalize rewards and foster a perception of fairness. There are no incremental rewards for learning new skills or tasks. This flat structure helps reinforce the belief that the company's fortunes depend on everyone's efforts. This is a difficult concept for some U.S. managers to grasp because of a deeply ingrained sense that employees will work hard only if given incremental monetary rewards. As one NUMMI senior manager noted:

> Our team members are ready and willing to change as long as they feel they are being treated fairly and equitably. We've tried to avoid favoritism and to level out the harder jobs. A single pay level is fundamental to the success of this company as is security of employment. We have learned . . . the importance of tying the company's success, and the success of the individual, to things they can control.[28]

The reward system at NUMMI goes beyond wages. For example, employees can qualify for drawings for a NUMMI-built vehicle based on attendance records. Conversely, too many absences and the employee either loses the company's contribution to his or her 401(k) plan or risks a "no fault" dismissal. Suggestions are sought from every team member and are rewarded with the equivalent of frequent flyer points good for merchandise, not cash, from a catalog sent to the person's home. Group leaders are responsible for initiating the evaluation process for all suggestions. In 1995, over 86 percent of the employees participated in the suggestion system, leading to savings estimated at over $27 million.

Training

Under the Toyota system there is continual training. As one plant manager said, "People should be given the opportunity to develop— given adequate training so they can get promoted."[29] The approach is characterized as a "lifetime training system." For example, a manager noted that a group leader "should be a kind of an instructor—not a commander. You can't do this without training."[30] Newly promoted supervisors are given thirteen weeks of training in how to treat people.

Aside from the ongoing training programs in problem solving, creativity, quality improvement, industrial engineering, and leadership, there are also periodic special training sessions designed to support annual goals. A program to help employees get their high school diploma also exists. Martha Quesada, a team member, reflects the prevailing attitude that "the company feels that the more employees know, the more well-rounded they are, . . . the more valuable they are to the company."[31]

Information Sharing

To increase employees' sense of interdependence and teamwork, NUMMI makes plant performance highly visible. This is done in part by hanging standardized work and *kaizen* charts in public team areas. Attendance boards with individual ratings (green, red, and yellow markings) and defect records are displayed prominently throughout the plant. Maintaining these records is a team responsibility. There are also daily meetings of forty to fifty team leaders, group leaders (first-line managers), and assistant managers to discuss defects found in a random sample of cars. Managers are put on the spot to explain the reasons for these defects and the corrective measures they plan to take. This discussion is done in a blame-free spirit in which the focus is on solving the problem rather than holding an individual responsible. Team leaders pass this information on to all team members so that all employees understand on a daily basis how the plant is performing.

Labor Relations

From the beginning, the NUMMI system has relied on a unique relationship between the union and management. UAW Local 2244 has supported the NUMMI production system, including the team concept, three job classifications (production, tool and die, and general maintenance), a no-fault attendance policy, nonconfrontational problem solving (asking "why," not "who"), and unique work rules (e.g., a thirty-minute paid lunch break). Under the old GM system the labor contract was contained in eight booklets totaling over 1,400 pages. The NUMMI contract is contained in a single booklet of less than 100 pages. Under the old system the contract language stipulated that the UAW and GM "recognize their respective responsibilities under federal, state, and local laws relating to fair employment practices." The language now states that the UAW and NUMMI "will exhibit mutual trust, understanding, and sincerity, and, to the fullest extent possible, will avoid confrontational tactics." Under the old system, the wording was that "Employees will be laid off and rehired in accordance with local seniority agreements," with management giving twenty-four hours' notice. Under the new system, the agreement states that "The company will take affirmative measures before laying off any employees, including such measures as the reduction of salaries of its officers and management."[32]

With the new system, union leadership preaches and practices union-management cooperation. For example, the union is actively involved in the selection process for new employees and for team leaders. One union leader commented, "It's hard to say what's the role of the union, what's the role of the company. It doesn't work that way. It's a partnership. It's a total rethinking of your role."[33] In exchange for this cooperation, management has agreed to be completely open with the union and to work with them to ensure a harmonious and mutually productive work environment. There are approximately twenty full-time union personnel plus almost 100 UAW coordinators, all paid by the company. This relationship relies on the informal resolution of disputes and tries not to waste time and money on formal grievance procedures.

Summary

Obviously, the NUMMI production system is characterized by a constant tension and quest for improvement. There is always a danger, on one side, of becoming complacent or, on the other side, of reverting to old top-down methods of driving production. Balancing this tension requires consistency in adhering to the principles of the system and requires maintaining a level of cooperation and trust between management and employees. Trust of this sort is indispensable in the NUMMI system. And building this trust requires a genuinely open, data-driven decision-making management style, but not necessarily one that is democratic or permissive. It is one of disciplined analysis and constant questioning and listening, not one of speed and individualism.

Managing this process also requires continual change. To do this effectively over long periods of time requires that managers continually "renew the spirit," as one manager put it—that is, find new ways to reenergize employees to push for improvement and to avoid the complacency that success brings. These efforts involve the usual buttons and banners but also involve defining new challenges with which to engage the employees' interests and energies.

The results aren't perfect. Employees always acknowledge that it is an ongoing effort. Says team member Martha Quesada, "It's not always a honeymoon. We still have a lot of problems and there are still some conflicts, but we're working constantly to keep improving. We have a foundation for communication and teamwork, and that's what's important."[34]

NUMMI managers and employees recognize that the quest for continuous improvement is never over. The answer isn't in some high-tech solution but in the people. Bill Childs, vice president of human resources, believes that "It all centers around the treatment of people and the dignity you give the hourly person on the line."[35]

LESSONS FROM NUMMI

So, what explains NUMMI's success? It would be easy to suggest, as many observers did, that the original layoff of workers by GM provided the key motivation. Of course, this had an effect, but it cannot explain NUMMI's continued success since 1983. Most of the current team members at NUMMI did not work under the old GM system and were never laid off. It would also be easy to blame the union, as many journalists have when they describe GM's current woes. But the UAW also represents workers at NUMMI, albeit under a contract with different provisions. As we have described, the differences in performance are not caused by technology or by workers from a different gene pool.

The explanation for the mystery of NUMMI's success rests on something far more subtle—the values of trust, respect, and continuous improvement that characterize relations within the plant, and the consistency with which these are applied in *all* the operating systems and management practices. This consistency in alignment is manifest in how people are selected, trained, rewarded, and supervised. But this explanation probably seems simplistic and unsatisfying. If it were this easy, why can't smart managers at GM and elsewhere adopt this same approach? It also may seem unlikely that something so straightforward would offer any competitive advantage.

This system is so difficult to imitate because of something fundamental and not very amenable to change, namely, the basic assumptions that management begins with in developing relationships with employees. At NUMMI, like the other companies we have described, the fundamental belief on the part of management is that people are responsible and want to contribute. Unleashing their potential requires that they be treated accordingly. At GM, the assumption appears to be that people do not want to work hard and will take advantage of any opportunity to shirk. In the language of economics, people are assumed to be effort averse.

The tragedy is that, as we have seen, these implicit assumptions lead managers to design systems that produce the very behavior they were designed to prevent. Under the old GM system, these assumptions about people produced narrow job designs that required little training or thought from the workers. The thinking and job designing were reserved for industrial engineers and managers. Because the employees needed little skill, no real effort was made to select those with positive attitudes. Instead, the assumption was that all people were lazy and needed close supervision; hence, supervisors and strong punishment systems played large roles. Faced with this environment, bored employees reasonably looked for ways to beat the system. With strong management control, people also felt the need for strong union representation as a countervailing force. In this crucible, employees and management had little common interest. Management's role was to coerce unwilling workers to produce more for less. Workers and their union wanted less work and more money. The result: GM-Fremont was the worst plant in the GM system, hated by employees and managers alike.

The NUMMI approach begins with a different set of basic values and assumptions. The underlying belief is that all the people in the plant have a common interest. In a highly competitive global automobile market, success for everyone requires that NUMMI produce the highest-quality car at the lowest possible cost. Doing this will ensure profits for the company and job security for the employees. Further, management believes that the line employee is the key to accomplishing this goal. It is this person who knows the job best and is best able to offer suggestions for improvement. Critically, the assumption is that employees understand this, can contribute, and genuinely want to build a quality product. These assumptions led to the design of a system calculated to unleash the power of the workforce, from how people are selected to how jobs are designed and improved and to how employees are supervised and rewarded. It is a system predicated on the belief in a common fate and one that rests on mutual trust and respect for the contribution of all members of the organization.

But let's be realistic. This sounds like some academic fairy tale. The cynic would note that there are people in all organizations who will take advantage of opportunities to abuse the system. Like any other organization, NUMMI has these people too. But the company has not designed its systems in a way to catch the few who are likely to abuse the system. Instead, it has carefully built a system that provides autonomy for teams and opportunity for people to contribute. Realistically, it has also built some safeguards into this system to weed out those who do not fit: for example, the careful screening process, the no-fault attendance policy, and a heavy reliance on teams. The philosophy of the system, however, is predicated not on catching the few who will abuse it but on capturing the potential of the majority who do want to contribute. The results are manifest.

To understand why this system is so difficult to replicate, consider the following thought experiment. Suppose that a competitor, after studying NUMMI, concluded that NUMMI's success was explained by the careful alignment and consistency of its management practices and the NUMMI production system. Believing this, suppose this smart observer was able to carefully replicate all the NUMMI policies and practices, but without embracing the underlying values. That is, the competitor set up another plant identical to NUMMI in all respects except that the management of this new plant did not share the same values and philosophy about people as NUMMI. What would the outcome of this experiment be?

If all the policies and practices were faithfully copied, the plant would, at first, likely be successful. However, over time, cracks would appear in this new world as people came to understand that management did not truly believe in the stated values. This evidence would leak out in the expressed attitudes and behavior of management—in how they talked and how they responded to problems. For example, confronted with the need to modify or adapt the system, the tendency of conventional managers who believe that people are effort averse would be to rely on the use of external controls, subtly signaling that the rhetoric about trust and common goals was more words than real beliefs. Efforts by managers to correct any abuses would likely tighten the control systems even further. The reaction from employees and the union would be to test the system and sincerity of management. Soon, it is likely that a cycle of self-fulfilling predictions would result in a confirmation of people's worst fears: Management would see that employees really could not be trusted, and employees would learn that management wasn't walking the talk. The system would quickly devolve into blame, finger-pointing, and escalation of retaliatory actions.

For these reasons, the success of NUMMI, and of the other companies we have discussed, is difficult for any manager or organization to imitate—unless the underlying values and philosophies are deeply held and there is a genuine commitment to live these values. Although the specific systems are important in enabling the NUMMI system to operate, a focus on the *how* of its operation will miss the underlying *why* of its real success. Like many mysteries, the solution to NUMMI's continued success may be obvious with hindsight. Finding it in the first place is what is difficult, because it requires that we examine some of our deeply held and unexamined assumptions. In our view, this is why NUMMI succeeds whereas GM continues to struggle.

Chapter 9

Cypress Semiconductor: What's Missing?

YOU HAVE NOW learned about seven remarkable companies. But learning only from success can be dangerous. Simply imitating successful companies has several risks. First, unless you are sure that the characteristics being copied are a source of competitive advantage, there is a danger of imitating irrelevant practices that have nothing to do with performance. It may also be that failed or less successful firms had the same characteristics. But since these companies are less interesting to authors or are no longer around to be studied, no one noticed that they were doing many of the same things. To really understand long-term success, we must understand what successful firms do that is *different* from those that are less successful.

For this reason, we now offer you the real test of your understanding of the success of people-centered companies—a profile of a company that does many of the same things as the successes you have read about but has not realized its full potential. Your challenge is to figure out what is missing. The mystery is why Cypress Semiconductor has not fully unleashed the power of its workforce in spite of the many things it does that are similar to the previous companies and in spite of its avowed attention to achieving success through its people. Although Cypress does many things well, it has not had the breakthrough success of the other firms in this book. If you can solve the puzzle of what's missing at Cypress, you will really understand what it takes to unlock the hidden potential of an organization's people. You will also better understand why would-be imitators so often fail in their attempts to emulate what successful companies do.

In its own way, Cypress is an amazing company. Called by the *Wall Street Journal* "a quintessential entrepreneurial company," Cypress ranks in the top fifteen U.S. semiconductor companies.[1] It has survived in the brutally competitive market for integrated circuits against much larger competitors, and attributes its accomplishments to the ability to tap into the skills and motivation of its employees. Since its founding in 1982, Cypress has grown to a $500 million revenue company with 3,000 employees and a market capitalization in June 1999 of $1.7 billion—by any standard a successful record. Yet Cypress has not succeeded in reaching its oft-stated goal of being a billion-dollar company by the year 2000. During the past five years, Cypress's revenue growth and return on assets have lagged behind its industry peers, and it has lower revenue per employee and lower gross margins than its average competitor. As a consequence, its stock price has experienced "a protracted period of under performance."[2] These unfavorable economic results occurred because Cypress has struggled to execute its current strategy of competing in the high-volume, low-margin business of static RAM (SRAM) chips while simultaneously generating innovative, high-margin products in low-volume niche markets. So, the mystery is, Why has Cypress not lived up to its promise or its initial potential? What's missing?

BACKGROUND

Cypress, headquartered in San Jose, California, was founded by Thurman John (T. J.) Rodgers, then thiry-five years old, and six others in 1982. Table 9-1 presents recent financial data for the company. Cypress went public in 1986 as one of the largest IPOs of its time. Its business strategy has evolved over time:

> Initially, the company targeted select niche markets which it believed would be ignored by major, established . . . semiconductor manufacturers. In 1992, the company modified its strategy to focus on selected high-volume products, particularly memory products. Since 1996

**Table 9-1   Selected Financial Statistics
for Cypress Semiconductor**

	1996	1997	1998	1999
Revenues, in millions	570	598	555	705
Operating income (loss), in millions	54	8.5	(120)	53
Net income (loss), in millions	25	7.5	(105)	91
Net income (loss), per share	0.28	0.08	(1.03)	0.87
Total assets, in millions	834	978	824	1,117
Shareholder's equity, in millions	512	645	499	698
Long-term debt, in millions	135	224	211	226

prices for memory chips have declined sharply. . . . More recently, the company has attempted to diversify its product base into more proprietary, non-memory chips.[3]

Today, Cypress's competitive advantage comes from continuous improvement in the cost efficiency and productivity of operations, the implementation of programs for reducing cycle times and inventory, and the constant introduction of innovative products.

The Philosophy and Values of Cypress

Cypress is very much a reflection of the vision and values of its founder and CEO, T. J. Rodgers.[4] With a Ph.D. from Stanford and a patent for a special chip technology, Rodgers began work in 1973 at AMI (American Microprocessors, Inc.). In Rodgers's memory, AMI was a relaxed, supportive, nurturing environment where people seldom raised their voices and managers seldom held people accountable. Rodgers notes, "Today, AMI is a Silicon Valley memory. The building where I worked has been dismantled, the land returned to orchards. It's like evolution in reverse. And that, to me, is the ultimate hypocrisy of warm-and-fuzzy cultures that don't deliver. Life is cordial right up to the day the company dies. Winning is what matters. And if winning means being tough, demanding, impatient, then that's what you have to be."[5] In Rodgers's view, Cypress is characterized by five principles that underlie all of the organization's practices:

- No secrets

- No politics

- No distractions

- No confusion

- No waste

Whether abhorred or revered, the sometimes-controversial CEO of Cypress has always garnered his share of media attention. He has made *Fortune*'s list as one of the country's toughest bosses, describing himself as tough but not mean. When dealing with subordinates, Rodgers says he questions their rationalizations, "and there are some people who can't handle that and say I'm too tough and blunt. I don't care. In that case . . . they can go work somewhere else."[6] Rodgers's management style is very much hands-on. For example, because of his strong technical background, Rodgers actively participates in meetings and has been known to take over presentations, even going so far as to write changes on a presenter's overhead transparencies and redirect the discussion. For some individuals, this can be disconcerting, particularly if Rodgers detects either flaws in the logic or what may be an attempt to cover up problems—resulting in a phenomenon referred to as "rock turning," which, to some, can be seen as a cross-examination. The combination of a take-no-prisoners approach and the associated fear of failure creates stress and burnout, resulting in an employee turnover rate of 19 percent.

Rodgers's vision—and competitive personality—are succinctly reflected in the company's statement of core values (see figure 9-1). He also recognizes that "You don't create core values from the top— from the big guy going to consultants and coming back and telling everybody what the company stands for, because they'll be laughing at you from the back of the room."[7] He and his senior team spent a year developing the set of five values, beginning with a statement of purpose: "Cypress is smart, tough people who work hard, thrive on competition, demand victory, and will not tolerate defeat. We exist to invent, make, and sell the world's best semiconductor products." This

**Figure 9-1   Cypress Core Values
(What We Stand For)**

1. *Cypress is about winning.*
   - We will not tolerate losing.
   - We thrive on competing against the world's best.
   - Individuals can choose to compete and win in business at Cypress.

2. *Cypress people are "only the best."*
   - We are smart, tough, and work hard.
   - We tell the truth.
   - We value knowledge, logic, and reason.
   - We deplore politicians.
   - We are aggressive problem solvers who take ownership and get results quickly.

3. *We do what's right for Cypress.*
   - We are company owners.
   - We choose "Cypress wins" over "looking good."
   - We reward personal initiative.
   - We are loyal and fair to our people.
   - We follow the spec or change it.
   - We keep our commitments to customers.

4. *We make our numbers.*
   - We gain market share while we make excellent profit.
   - We each set aggressive, quantitative goals—and we achieve them.
   - We constantly improve.
   - We do not tolerate waste.

5. *We invent and make state-of-the-art products.*
   - Our technology challenges the world's best head on, and we spend a fraction of what they do.
   - Our first silicon always works on schedule.
   - We manufacture at the world's lowest cost.
   - We manufacture with excellent quality.

process included brainstorming sessions that involved hundreds of employees and managers.

For Rodgers, management philosophy and personal ideology are inextricably intertwined. His scorched-earth approach to winning can be seen in an episode involving not another high-tech CEO or Washington bureaucrat, but a Catholic nun from Philadelphia. As the beneficial owner of Cypress shares, Sister Doris Gormley of the Sisters of St. Francis wrote Rodgers and Cypress shareholders a form letter expressing the view that a company "is best represented by a Board of qualified Directors reflecting the equality of the sexes, races, and ethnic groups." The letter went on to say that it was the congregation's policy to withhold authority to vote for directors of boards that didn't include women and minorities and concluded by exhorting him "to enrich the Board by seeking qualified women and members of racial minorities as nominees."

Rodgers responded with a public six-page letter railing against the political correctness of the sister's position, calling the operating principles expressed in her letter "not only unsound, but even immoral." Rodgers claimed that the Cypress board of directors was not a ceremonial watchdog but a critical management function whose members required experience as CEOs of technology companies and knowledge of the semiconductor business. He went on to say, "I am unaware of any Christian requirements for corporate boards; your views seem more accurately described as 'politically correct,' than 'Christian'. . . . Bluntly stated, a 'woman's view' on how to run our semiconductor company does not help us, unless that woman has an advanced technical degree and experience as a CEO."[8] "I would rather be labeled a person who is unkind to religious groups than as a coward who harms his employees and investors by mindlessly following high-sounding, but false, standards of right and wrong," he wrote.[9] He subsequently pointed out to Sister Doris that there seemed to be an absence of women in the college of cardinals and suggested she might be better advised to begin her quest there.

The Original Cypress Management Model

To implement his philosophy and world view, Rodgers initially conceived of Cypress as a federation of companies with a self-contained economy. The original organizational design had all factories and product lines as profit centers that had their own balance sheets and income statements. Product lines negotiated prices with manufacturing. Factories competed with each other on price, service, and delivery. Cash changed hands in these deals, even if it was an internal sale. If a product line could get a cheaper price from an outside producer, they could contract with them. Rodgers believed that anything that's free will be used inefficiently. "Therefore," he said, "nothing at Cypress is free." In this spirit, he was quoted on the cover of one Cypress annual report saying, "If it doesn't make for faster circuits, happier customers, or motivated employees, we don't spend a nickel on it."[10]

Rodgers's goal was always for Cypress to be a big company, but he worried that it might not be possible to run a billion-dollar company with the speed, discipline, and energy that Cypress had in its early history. "We want the muscle and staying power of a big company with the drive and agility of a startup." To do this, he proposed the idea of building a federation of small companies. "Why not build a collection of companies—each small enough to maintain its intensity, together big enough to matter?"[11] This, he believed, could be a system of "perpetual entrepreneurship" and could help Cypress avoid becoming one of the slow-moving, self-satisfied large firms that he often referred to as "bloated rhinos." To make this happen, he created subsidiaries, each with its own shares whose value was contingent on meeting long-term performance targets.

One result of this structure was that members of subsidiaries became productivity zealots. Cypress was therefore able to bring wafer fabrication facilities on line in much shorter times and with less capital than its competitors. The philosophy behind this approach was designed to create an energy level, sense of mission, and spirit of determination that Rodgers doubted could be achieved in a large company. As such, Cypress was a self-contained market economy rather than a self-centered bureaucracy. People benefited directly from success—through stock options and bonuses tied directly to their autonomous operations.

Problems and Change

A sobering loss of $21 million in 1992 caused a reappraisal of whether this organizational structure was appropriate for a billion-dollar company. Rather than "niche-ing" its competitors to death, Cypress was "niche-ing" itself. Rodgers explained, "The high-performance niche-market approach was a good way to get from zero to $100 million, but it ran out of gas in 1992. The problem with niche products: Each one realizes only $1 million a year. This drives too much inventory, and you need Einsteins in the field who know all things."[12]

This experience changed Rodgers, who publicly acknowledged his responsibility and embarrassment. As a result, Cypress changed its strategy to emphasize production efficiencies for high-volume markets and new products to drive revenue growth. From its peak of carrying 3,500 different integrated circuits, it has cut its product portfolio almost in half. Gone too are the incubator ventures and subsidiaries. Rodgers also moved assembly and testing offshore, sold some assets, and was forced to lay off employees. He admits that he made some bad business decisions: "There was too much autonomy and not enough control. There were also discipline and leadership problems with some of the subsidiaries. . . . We were so busy making our quarters and ramping up manufacturing that our development truly did get a back seat."[13] Now, he said, "We want to become a company of solutions' divisions . . . [while remaining] a federation of entrepreneurs."[14]

Although Rodgers is now a "kinder, gentler" CEO, the basic philosophy of Cypress and the systems it uses to implement them have remained largely the same, including how the company attracts, monitors, and compensates its people. Rodgers remains adamant that the only way to succeed in today's competitive environment is to attract the best talent and to motivate and empower these people to do their very best. For this reason, he still believes three systems are important for Cypress's success: people management, performance management, and killer software.

PEOPLE SYSTEMS

Rodgers is clear about what it takes to succeed in any innovation-driven industry—talented people:

> Great people don't guarantee corporate success—but no company can succeed without great people. This may sound like a truism, but few companies are as committed to and scientific about hiring as they are about perfecting the latest market-research techniques or financial maneuvers. Hiring is one of the most bureaucratic, arbitrary, and passive parts of corporate life. In part this is because hiring is such hard work, harder than many other things a manager is asked to do. But it is also because many companies, despite their good intentions, are neither disciplined nor imaginative enough to make it happen right.[15]

Rodgers also believes that money doesn't really motivate people because the amounts involved aren't sufficient to generate the superhuman effort so many people display. Motivation and success result from the career opportunities that are created for the best people. "If you attract the best talent and want to keep them, then you have to offer them these opportunities."[16] He noted that if you don't create these opportunities, you'll simply export this talent to a new wave of start-ups. If the organization remains challenging and exciting, "energy that would otherwise be spent on bureaucratic details and political infighting is redirected into productive negotiations among the subsidiaries."[17] To ensure this discipline, Cypress emphasizes a number of critical aspects in how it manages people. These are the responsibilities of line managers, not human resource professionals, whom Rodgers has referred to as "drones."

Hiring People

According to Rodgers,

> [H]iring is a *process,* not an event. There are only 18 people in the company who are authorized to extend job offers. An offer comes at the end of a demanding evaluation process that takes place only after we pre-screen a huge number of candidates. Speed is also demanded in the recruiting process. The standard is that after the telephone pre-screen interview, there is no reason a hiring manager can't bring in the candidate for two rounds of interviews and make a hire/no hire decision within a week or two. When we make an offer, the offer comes in person, in writing, and ready for the candidate's signature *on the spot.* Before the candidate goes home, we want a signed letter or absolute certainty that we have identified and removed all barriers to signing.[18]

In this way hiring is not just about policies and procedures, interviews, and offers. It is also about mind-set. Getting the person to sign an offer letter is often the beginning of the process, not the end.

To hire outstanding talent, the hiring manager must be responsible for finding and attracting the talent the company needs. All managers have hiring *responsibility* once they've received authorization. The human resources department maintains a database of resumes, but plays no role in evaluating candidates. Prospective employees don't see anyone in human resources until after they've been hired and need to fill out insurance forms. Most companies do just the opposite, with human resources guiding the process and the hiring managers getting desperate and hiring anybody to fill open slots. This ensures that the quality of the workforce will mirror the quality of the labor pool—not a good idea. This more passive approach also means that top managers are likely to lose touch with the job market.

To ensure that Cypress identified and attracted talented people, Rodgers developed the concept of a "raiding party." The idea itself is simple. Rodgers likens it in military terms to a small-unit tactic. "The raiding party's goal was to land in a city, scout out the top few hundred engineers and managers at a particular company, and leave with the ten best people—the absolute cream of the crop. Hit Mostek in Dallas, TI in Houston, Motorola in Austin, Inmos in Colorado Springs, Intel in Phoenix."[19] The process includes keeping detailed records on how many people Cypress was able to recruit from which companies and regularly reporting these statistics to the board of directors.

Raiding parties are well planned. Experience showed that a "distillation factor" of 3 percent is to be expected; that is, it takes a pool of 300 to get 10 people. Cypress hires a headhunter to pass the word about Cypress being in town on a particular date. "We never—*never*—used newspaper advertising, and to this day we don't allow it. . . . If someone was not 'in the loop' enough to know we were coming to town, he or she was, by definition, not our kind of person."[20]

Headhunters then screen the 300 or so resumes for "fatal flaws." These include the following: expecting big housing allowances to move to Silicon Valley (Cypress doesn't offer them), not being willing to move without a big raise (Cypress won't pay it), or expecting Cypress to find jobs for their spouses (something the company refuses to do). Cypress people then filter these resumes down to between 60 and 70 real prospects. A team (usually consisting of Rodgers, three vice presidents, a couple of technical people, and a secretary) flies to the city and conducts five to nine interviews with each of the 60 to 70 candidates, extends offers to 11, and comes home with 10. This process requires SWAT-team precision and can result in unintended consequences, such as the time in Dallas when the hotel called the police because so many of the candidates going upstairs were women.

As an important part of the recruiting process, all hiring managers must submit a "hiring book" that documents the entire process. The first page includes a checklist of thirty-five specific steps and procedures to follow. Detailed results of interviews, reference checks, and career prospects are entered into the book, which is used to help refine the recruiting process in the future. For instance, if a person leaves for poor performance, the hiring book is reviewed to see how the company might have spotted the problem before hiring. This has helped Cypress discover that a few in-depth reference checks are better than many superficial ones.

Although there are sometimes complaints about the rigidity of this process, Rodgers's adamant response is, "Our system, and the hiring book, is a vaccine *against* bureaucracy. It is an enabling tool that energizes and disciplines the process—a tool that documents to everyone who needs to know that the evaluation has been thorough, crisp, and smart. . . . The power of our system is that it doesn't allow middle managers to defeat themselves. Managers understand that not filling slots is one of the quickest ways to fail as a manager in our company."[21]

Although the key to scouting is to keep things loose and informal, the key to interviewing is to be rigorous and thorough. Based on their experience, Cypress has developed seven principles for interviewing:

1. Use big guns.

2. Make interviews demanding (the "pack of wolves").

3. Probe for technical skills and work ethic.

4. Require detailed written assessments from all interviewers.

5. Probe carefully for a cultural misfit (via the career path questionnaire).

6. Take references very seriously.

7. Be speedy.

This process is stressful enough for interviewees that it is often seen as a watershed event by the applicants.

No one, including the direct labor force, gets a job at Cypress without a minimum of four interviews. Exempt employees have a minimum of six, including one with a vice president. Rodgers explains the

rationale for making these interviews tough and technically demanding:

> The quickest way to lose a top-flight prospect is the no-substance
> backslap interview. Who wants to be part of an organization that
> grovels to have you as a member? The best way to sell your candidate
> is to make it tough as hell to get in. When a candidate, no matter how
> outstanding, walks into Cypress, the first message he or she hears is
> "We're Cypress, we work hard, and you're not going to get a raise to
> join up. Should we continue?"[22]

Each interview begins with a clear agenda that communicates several important messages, including the detailed technical skills required by the job, the managers with whom the person will interview,
and basic questions for each session. After several technical interviews, the "pack of wolves" session occurs. Here the tone is aggressive
but not abusive. The candidate is peppered with difficult questions
while standing at a blackboard. Mistakes are pointed out immediately.
The candidate is grilled for forty-five minutes while the interviewers
look for any weaknesses.

All interviews conclude with detailed written assessments of
strengths and weaknesses by the interviewers, not vague oral recollec-
tions. These assessments include numerical ratings. To avoid leniency
biases, all interviewers are encouraged to be fair but tough. This process is referred to as the "Cal Tech effect," where grading is very tough
and new students, who were used to being at the top of their class,
find themselves being seen as average or worse.

For senior-level appointments, the hiring vice president must also
write an interview strategy before the hiring process begins. This
highlights the candidate's strengths and weaknesses, concerns, and
other critical issues. When the candidate talks to Rodgers at the end
of the interview process, Rodgers always shares the numerical ratings
from the earlier interviews, especially when there is weakness in an
area.

During the interview process, an explicit attempt is made to probe
for cultural mismatches by using a career path questionnaire that ex-
plores the candidate's motivation, character, and aspirations. The
questionnaire forces the applicant to be specific about hard-to-
quantify issues. For instance, Rodgers described how the process

helped uncover one candidate who enjoyed political infighting—a value inconsistent with the Cypress culture.

Reference checks are also used to signal to candidates the seriousness of the application process. These are not the usual perfunctory checks but are done in great detail, with Cypress interviewers knowing that the extensive probing will be reported back to the candidate. This is done to get the candidate's "mind share" and make him or her aware of Cypress's seriousness. It is intended to keep candidates anxious and interested.

One of the inviolate principles of hiring at Cypress is that "We don't buy employees." The company is explicit in trying to avoid hiring people who want to join for a raise or a better dental plan. Instead, it wants joining to be seen as a career move. One early expression of this principle was that if any new employee had received a raise at their previous place of employment within the past four months, they came to Cypress without a raise. Cypress now offers only a nonnegotiable 8 percent prorated increase. This policy is made clear to all candidates right from the beginning of the recruitment process.

Once the interviews are completed, the executive with hiring authority always has a completed offer letter ready for a signature when he or she meets the candidate for the final session. This small ceremony has two functions. First, it creates some emotion in the candidate, often relief that he or she has made the grade. Second, it creates an important psychological break from the old company. To accentuate this, Cypress recruiters explicitly prepare the candidate for three emotions that can undermine their acceptance: fear, uncertainty, and doubt. They know that when a valued employee decides to leave, there can be an intense campaign to win a reversal.

Cypress wants to inoculate against these pressures. It does this by alerting the candidate to what will happen and coaching the recruit on how to quit. Recruits are told not to take the easy way out in how they quit, such as dropping a note in the boss's mailbox at 5:00 P.M. on a Friday. They are told, "You quit at 8:00 A.M. on a Monday. You give them the whole week to talk you out of it. You listen politely to what they have to say. We know you've made the right decision, and that you'll end up here. But you can't screw a great company, and you've got to respect your boss. You've got to play by the rules." The idea is to fight tough but fair. This process is designed to persuade the individual to act properly and to Cypress's advantage—since a firm will fight harder if it feels wronged—and to put Cypress's actions above the fray in that the candidate then sees the pressure as coming from his or her old employer, not Cypress.

"We treat these match-ups like judo: We know our opponents, we know how they are going to react, and we turn their reaction to our advantage."[23] As an example, candidates are told that their company may respond in one of two ways: throwing the individual out immediately or giving him or her a big raise. They are told in advance, "If you are worth 20 percent more than what you get, why didn't the company do right by you *before* you quit?" Or, even more subtly, Cypress recruiters inform the candidate that they know he or she will cave in because the employer will give him or her a raise and lots of stock options (which they often know a particular company won't give). Then, when the pressure is on and the employer doesn't offer the stock options, the candidate feels undervalued.

Part of the recruiting effort includes daily phone calls during the week after the candidate gives notice. In some cases where there's wavering, this effort can also include a home visit by senior Cypress executives to reiterate the case and to talk to the spouse. Cypress measures and tracks the hit rate on job offers by location and vice president. These records are reviewed for all interviewees—successes and failures—to determine how applicants were treated (e.g., waiting time in the lobby) and what might be done to improve the process.

Retaining People

Even with all the effort to treat people fairly and reward them well, Cypress still worries about headhunters poaching its best people. After all, the company recruited many of these people by raiding other firms. To protect themselves against headhunters, Cypress uses two systems: one to seal off the company from headhunters, and the other to win reversals when a valued employee decides to leave.

First, to erect barriers to entry, Cypress keeps confidential the names of all employees other than those listed in public documents. It attempts to protect these listings by making it as difficult as possible for outsiders to get names or to contact employees. Like a military unit, the company tests its systems by having "friendly" headhunters try to penetrate its defenses. Employees are taught the various ploys used by headhunters and how to thwart them. Secretaries and other gatekeepers learn that phone requests from "students" for information about the company, or requests for individuals without a last name, are to be routinely rejected. Inquirers may be asked for their names and phone numbers, which are then checked. If the inquiry is identified as coming from a headhunter, the human resources and legal departments are notified.

The system to win reversals from valued employees who have resigned includes making an immediate response (within five minutes) and keeping the resignation secret in order to reduce the barrier for the employee to change his or her mind. Instructions on how to listen carefully to the employee and on ways to address the issues raised in these talks are provided. The guidelines conclude with an instruction to "Wipe out the competitor" by cutting off all subsequent contact between the employee and the other firm.

Controlling Headcount

In addition to attracting and retaining the best people, Rodgers believes that controlling headcount is one of the most important processes at Cypress. "Why? Because directly and indirectly, people drive all costs in a company." Estimates are that hiring one additional person, even at the lowest level, adds almost $100,000 to a company's cost structure. He says "Being a 'tough' boss is not about unflinchingly sending people to the unemployment line during hard times. It's about maintaining discipline during good times so the organization can weather the inevitable storms." He goes on to note that during prosperity, danger lurks everywhere. "Growth masks waste, extravagance, and inefficiency."[24] A slowdown reveals the sins of the past on the bottom line. For this reason, Cypress demands ever-increasing productivity. To help achieve this, every quarter the company benchmarks itself on critical measures against its competitors. This exercise reinforces the shared mind-set about the importance of productivity growth.

All managers make a quarterly presentation to their peers at which they make the case for added headcount. This includes not only their requests and justifications, but also a micro performance index that reports the zero-based operating efficiency of their unit over time. This index shows the productivity improvements of the current workforce. Unless there are significant improvements, the manager can't request additional people. The logic underpinning this process is to run as lean as possible so that layoffs will not be required during a downturn.

Compensation

The systems to motivate and evaluate employees and ensure equitable pay are as detailed as those designed to attract the best people. There are four principles at the core of the Cypress philosophy about rewards:

1. **Every group of peers in the company, no matter the organizational level, receives the same average percentage raise.** All groups (e.g., research and development, corporate vice presidents, technicians) must use the same weighted-average company increase.

2. **Outstanding performers deserve outstanding raises.** Great people know the value of their contribution and expect to be rewarded for it. Along with the corporate average raise, there is also a minimum top-to-bottom spread that will be allowed. A further rule is that 3 percent of the people must receive *no* raise.

3. **Merit and equity must remain distinct.** Equity means that salaries should be distributed so that the top-ranked performer in any group of peers is paid 50 percent more than the lowest-ranked performer, and people with more or less comparable performances receive more or less comparable salaries. For example, in a ten-person design unit where the best designer makes $75,000, the lowest-ranked designer should make $50,000 and the remaining eight should be distributed evenly between the extremes.

4. **Precision matters.** Raises are as much about messages as they are about money. A spread between the top and bottom raise of just 3 percent, as found in many firms, conveys an important

message about how important performance really is. Cypress doesn't use fuzzy categories like "acceptable" or "above average." All employees are allocated into comparison groups of peers and ranked from top to bottom. These rankings are used for both equity and merit raises. At the end of the process, each employee is given three numbers: his or her merit raise, the equity adjustment, and the total raise.

Although sometimes misportrayed in the business press as reminiscent of Big Brother, the basic performance assessment process is very simple. The numbers are generated in three phases in a tightly monitored process described in the following sections. The final results are entered into a program that processes performance information, organizes it, and displays it to help the manager make an accurate decision about compensation. The system is quite simple and efficient to use after an hour of training. It is designed to alert the reviewer to big, obvious mistakes and to create a paper trail for explaining decisions to those evaluated. It compels managers to think about their judgments. Rodgers says that it is important to realize that the system as constituted is based on the Cypress philosophy but could be easily changed to reflect other assumptions. Doing this would simply give the evaluator different answers based on the new assumptions.

Phase I: Performance Ranking. The process of awarding raises begins with the selection of focal groups (between five and twenty-five people with comparable skills and responsibilities, for example, all weekend shift operators). Before the ranking, the placement of individuals into focal groups is posted so people can challenge their placement. Each focal group has a ranking committee composed of at least three members, each with a different role. The chairman of the committee, or focal leader, is the lowest-level supervisor with direct responsibility for members of the focal group (i.e., the person who writes quarterly reviews). The second member represents internal customers. The third person is chosen as one who can judge the quality of each person's contribution. The whole committee is charged with a single question: How much did each person contribute to the company last year? They are explicitly instructed to not rate potential—

that is done with stock options. The only criterion considered in this phase is merit.

Human resources provides the focal leader with a diskette containing evaluations of the members of the comparison group. The leader then convenes the ranking committee and shares the written evaluations for each member of the group. Ranking is done via a forced-choice process with pairwise comparisons so that all candidates are compared on a head-to-head basis. Rodgers offers the following rationale:

> We *must* rank people in order to keep them. Our business, like so many fast-changing, highly competitive businesses, is filled with tough, aggressive, sharp-elbowed people. Silicon Valley's "culture of meritocracy" is not all that unlike the culture at high-powered law firms or investment banks. People . . . are eager to know where they stand, how they stack up against their peers, whether they are meeting the company's expectations for them, whether it's time to move on. . . . Indeed, any company in Silicon Valley that used a pass/fail system would likely get its bones picked clean within a year.[25]

He goes on to argue that "Great people expect to be rewarded. You can't reward great people unless you identify them fairly and accurately. . . . Ranking *is* a contentious process. There is potentially a dangerous contradiction in the psychology of ranking: all people want to know where they stand, but most everyone thinks he or she is above average. . . . So ranking, if done mechanically, can make lots of people feel like 'losers.' We want as many people as possible to feel like winners. Our ideal outcome is for two-thirds of the people to hear good news, that is, to receive above-average raises. So we build a budget reserve into the focal review software to make that outcome possible. We also don't punish good people who rank below average. . . . The solid-citizen raise (which goes to about 10% of work force annually)— the minimum increase we allow each year—is designed to reassure people even as it motivates them to do better. The message is that you know the quality of people we have here. Not everyone can be above average. We value your contribution. We want you to stay."[26]

Phase II: Merit Raises. Forced rankings are also used in giving merit raises. Merit means a good raise for good performance and a low raise for low performance. This decision, however, is not made by the com-

mittee but by the focal leader. In this part of the process, actual salaries of the group members are not disclosed; thus, the emphasis is explicitly on the merit raise. This decision is solely in percentages. The
initial calculation is done by the software. The program reviews the
ranking and recommends raises based on ranking. This method ap-
portions raises and maintains the budget. The results are used as a
rough starting point for any ultimate judgments, and the program reviews the manager's decisions for compliance with company policies.
There are fourteen quality checks designed to ensure, among other
things, that people higher in the ranking get higher percentage raises,
that there is a minimum spread between the lowest and highest raise,
and that any attempt by a rater to cluster raises around the mean is
flagged. Further, no one at Cypress is allowed to receive the precise
corporate average raise, and the weighted-average raise for the group
cannot exceed the corporate average. Managers can't exceed the budget or leave money on the table.

Phase III: Equity. The goal of the equity phase is to adjust merit
raises so as to move salaries closer to the ideal distribution. This is the
first time decision makers can see individual salaries. For each focal
group, the program generates a graph that compares salaries of each
member (the vertical axis) with merit rankings (the horizontal axis). It
also displays a trend line based on the 50 percent top-to-bottom
spread (described earlier) and how that compares with the actual. The
decision here is to simply adjust merit raises up or down to move people closer to the ideal trend line. The same basic quality checks are
used again, plus one for equity. This makes sure that the decision
maker does not try to soften the tough choices made in the second
phase. Equity adjustments can be made gradually over time or done
in larger increments. The choice is up to the manager. What the program will not approve is inconsistency; that is, it will not approve big
adjustments for some people and gradual ones for others.

    Although the focal review system sounds complicated, in reality
the system is quite straightforward for a manager sitting in front of a
personal computer. Overall, it may take a couple of hours to decide
and adjust merit and equity raises. For the entire company, the process lasts about six weeks. Focal groups are selected at the end of the
year, and guidelines for average raises, required ranges, and solid-
citizen raises are made in late January.

When it comes to deciding salaries for executives, Rodgers is equally firm in his opinions. He has accused perk-happy CEOs as being the "Jimmy Swaggarts of industry."[27] For his own salary, Rodgers uses a standard that he can be paid no more than the highest-paid vice president, and no more than twenty-five times an entry-level worker. His salary is set at the end of the corporate process when the highest-paid vice president is identified. He indicates that this decision takes no more than ten seconds of the board's time.

Stock Option Grants. Rodgers believes that all employees deserve stock options, and the company allocates them using the same focal review process. Whereas raises reward past performance, stock options are used to reward future potential. This is particularly important in a place like Silicon Valley, where a person can change jobs without changing car pools. At Cypress, the board usually allots about one million stock options annually. Since options vest over four years, they can create a strong incentive to stay with the firm. Using a system similar to the merit and equity allocations, each focal group is allotted a certain portion of shares. The ranking committees again do pairwise comparisons, only the merit question now is: Who can we least afford to lose over the next four years? The equity question becomes: Is the number of a person's unvested stock options fair relative to his or her ranking on long-term potential?

KILLER SOFTWARE

The Cypress management approach that caught the attention of most people who knew about the company was the use of killer software. This was a system of computer applications to help track and improve performance without the development of a large bureaucracy. It was the Cypress philosophy manifest in a set of computer programs: a behind-the-scenes application that sorted through various databases to detect whether units had violated previously agreed-upon performance targets. The system warned the offending individual or group and, if the slippage reached unacceptable levels and the group had not reacted, the software shut down the group's computers that ran the manufacturing system. This meant material couldn't be moved or inventory shipped, and the group could not continue with daily activities until the problem was eliminated. The severity of these consequences meant that people rarely let performance slip to a point at which this occurred. The paradox was that management's credible threat to shut down operations meant that it was seldom needed.

From Rodgers's perspective this system helped managers think about priorities, make trade-offs, and create realistic agreements about what needed to be done. It was, he believes, equivalent to the red lever, or *andon,* system on the Japanese assembly line that workers can use to halt the line when quality deteriorates. In explaining the system, he says, "Some people misunderstand. . . . Killer software [was] not designed to pressure people or speed up operations. It [was] not, in that sense, a productivity tool. It [was] a quality tool that improved execution without imposing bureaucracy."[28]

Killer software had its origins in 1988 when the vice presidents were late submitting quarterly performance reviews. Outraged and concerned that Cypress was replicating the management failures of the "bloated rhinos" of his nightmares, Rodgers responded by threatening to cut off their paychecks. He called the human resources director and instructed him to make a list of all late reviews for managers reporting to the vice presidents. The vice presidents were notified that if the reviews weren't completed in two weeks, the human resources manager would stop their checks. When this happened and a vice president complained, Rodgers, with his best impression of a psychopath, vowed that "You won't get another paycheck until your manager does his reviews. I'm prepared to watch your kid drop out of school and your house auctioned off on the courthouse steps."[29] This did the trick. However, Rodgers himself has fallen afoul of the same system when he failed to complete his reviews and had his own paycheck stopped on more than a few occasions.

Not surprisingly, the killer software system had some unintended consequences. Some employees developed their own software to override the killer software and trick the system. For example, one person described a program that he developed that automatically changed the dates of his goals—but not the goals themselves—so that he was never behind. For other employees, the process of entering goals into a central system became so cumbersome and time-consuming that goals were recorded only sporadically. Of greatest significance was Rodgers's acknowledgment that rigid adherence to the system had led some people to behave in ways that were counterproductive to company goals. Chief among these counterproductive results was the creation of a risk averse, political environment within the organization. A tendency developed among some individuals to hide potential problems rather than acknowledge that a specific goal had not been met. Others became "checklist robots" who would follow a list rather than use their own judgment.

Faced with these undesirable side effects, Rodgers wrote a companywide memo in 1994 noting that "The 'no mistakes' culture and the 'do what is best for Cypress' culture are irrevocably at odds." He encouraged people to make choices that were best for the company. His suggestion was, "Think about your mom, the investor. Suppose she had just called you up and told you she was about to invest her entire retirement fund in Cypress stock. Would you give her minimal 'no mistakes' data, or would you tell her exactly what's going on?" In his view, employees should provide a full and fair disclosure of all the facts in a way she could understand. She should not have to hire Perry Mason to ferret out the true situation. "Treat your boss and me like your mom, the investor . . . and do what's right for Cypress as if it were your own money, because it is—you are all shareholders." Finally, in 1997, Rodgers made a decision to eliminate the killer software system.

THE GOALS SYSTEM: PLANNING AND ACCOUNTABILITY

Rodgers is a strong believer in the importance of goals and commitments: "To win, people need clear and quantifiable goals, the resources to achieve these goals, and confidence that their goals matter to the larger corporate purpose."[30] To implement this philosophy, Cypress uses a goal system that tracks important goals, called "critical success factors." The idea behind the system is straightforward: People, in consultation with their bosses, mutually identify execution problems that can cause real long-term harm to the company. These are converted into quantifiable targets, and agreements are made about completion dates. These goals are entered into a common data system to which all employees have access. This transparency ensures that all Cypress employees are able to track the progress of critical deadlines.

The system has not required major investments in computer hardware and software. It runs on the corporate network using basic database and spreadsheet technology. Its philosophy harkens back to the old management-by-objectives techniques from the 1970s. The basic premise is that most people want to achieve, and that most people are also capable of extraordinary levels of commitment and performance—much more than their bosses give them credit for. Achieving this potential requires clear goals and agreements to deliver as promised. People set their own goals, review them with their managers, and commit to achieving them by a specific date.

The system was designed to monitor the progress of all employees in their accomplishment of their agreed-upon goals. A "goal" includes a description of the task, the person who has agreed to complete it, the manager or project leader to whom the person reports, the vice president to whom the manager reports, when the goal was set, what project the goal supports, when it is due for completion, what priority it is, what generic type of goal it is (quality, new product, strategic, or other), and its on-time status. A typical foreman might have 20 to 30 goals in the system, most of which take only a week or two to complete and two or three of which are strategic or longer-term goals. All goals are ranked in priority of importance. A vice president might be ultimately responsible for 1,000 to 2,000 goals depending on the type of work and number of people in the organization.

For example, on a typical day, the system might have over 10,000 active goals, of which 1,300 are due within the week and another 9,000 due within the month. Over 800 of these are related to improving quality and roughly 300 to new product development. At any given time, about 650 goals may be behind schedule (not necessarily a problem), but over 300 may be behind schedule by five weeks (a problem). There are usually about 100 people with more than two delinquent goals and almost 30 managers with more than 20 percent of their goals behind schedule. As a rule of thumb, Rodgers believes managers shouldn't have delinquency rates above 20 percent, but this number represents only a warning flag, not a death knell.

Delinquency rates are more often a signal of the need for help and additional resources than for control and punishment. However, the one area where there is more scrutiny and less tolerance is in new product development. The milestones in this process are tracked and monitored carefully. For instance, the company's most important new product developments are tracked by the "Top 10 Program," with each of these products having a "godfather," typically a vice president or Rodgers himself, who can cut through any red tape to ensure that the project stays on time. To further drive home the negative impact of delays in the development of new products, an estimate is made of the "cost of quality" (in terms of lost shipment and revenues) from any delay, and everyone is made aware of this number.

At its loosest, the goals system functions as an electronic bulletin board. At its extreme, it can be used as an authoritarian tool. Rodgers claims:

> We don't embrace either extreme. . . . We want people to decide what they are going to do, why it makes sense, how important it is, and when they will complete it. We give people plenty of freedom to use the system in ways they find helpful. There is no "right" number of goals . . . so long as the critical activities on which they will be spending most of their time, and that will have an impact on other people in the organization, get recorded.[31]

In talking about the monitoring systems, Rodgers says, "Think of it [the goals system] as an instrument panel that not only indicates how fast the organization is traveling, and in what direction, but also helps explain what's holding us back."[32] He goes on to acknowledge that "some people envision me, or other top Cypress managers, huddled in our offices like Captain Kirk on the bridge of the *Enterprise,* scrolling through reports, wandering through databases, and running the company from a computer screen. Instead of barking 'Scotty, we need more power!' the instructions are 'Marketing. We need more goals!' or 'Manufacturing. We need a lower delinquency rate!' This is ridiculous and represents a fundamental misunderstanding of the philosophy behind the system."[33] Rodgers says, "In a semiconductor company, problems and opportunities come at you at one hundred miles an hour from every direction. Without some way to make sense of all these demands, many (if not most) of our people would be overwhelmed. Think about how many high technology companies skyrocket to glory and then crash and burn overnight. Failure isn't the problem; *success* is the problem. With success comes growth, with growth comes more work, with more work comes more people, and with more people come more opportunities for the organization to spiral out of control."[34]

In describing the function of the goals system, Rodgers also calls attention to the inherent tension between a functional organizational structure and the need for a project or product organization:

> A company the size of Cypress needs the best of both worlds. We want to be project-driven, which helps emphasize speed and agility, as well as functionally accurate, which guarantees good execution. And we want to avoid cumbersome experiments like matrix management. That's where the goals system helps out. . . . The goals system is organized by product and function.[35]

There are more than 200 ongoing projects at Cypress that involve members from different parts of the organization. Some projects relate to safety, others to cost, and still others to new products. Every week project leaders sit down with their teams and review the goals and priorities. Functional managers do a similar review with their units, including the goals their members have taken on in project teams. This check helps managers to sort out priorities and avoid overcommitment. Their job is to solve problems and sort out conflicts, not push people to work harder. Typically, people spend two hours a week in meetings about goals and priorities.

Rodgers is sensitive to the fact that the feedback provided by the goals system is inherently negative—highlighting failures more than successes. He understands the importance of positive feedback and tries to emphasize the value provided by the completed goals. He argues that one positive effect of the goals system is that it attenuates the recency bias that affects all performance judgments, that is, the tendency of people to only recall recent performance—whether good or bad—when doing an annual review.

Since 1997, the goals system has been optional for managers to use, not mandatory. The only thing that is required is to enter the list of critical success factors into the system. In 1998 Rodgers reported that a new system was under development that would make it easier to record and access goals. All managers would be given Palm Pilot computers with software that would interface with the goals system software. Managers will be able to record goals while they are in meetings and then automatically load these goals into the system.

LESSONS FROM CYPRESS SEMICONDUCTOR

Rodgers has built a remarkable company that has grown from an idea in 1982 to a major player in one of the most competitive high-technology industries. Cypress does many of the things that the other firms we have described do. But the company has not achieved its growth goals and has been a less than stellar performer. What's missing?

In some ways, Cypress is similar to the firms we have described in earlier chapters. Cypress, like AES, NUMMI, PSS World Medical, and Cisco, has an emphasis on a set of core values: frugality, cost control, productivity, and continuous improvement. As is true at Southwest, AES, and PSS, Cypress provides employees with extensive financial and operational data so that everyone understands the direction and performance of the firm. Cypress, like Southwest, AES, NUMMI, and PSS, has a carefully targeted selection process designed to screen for cultural compatibility. Like NUMMI and The Men's Wearhouse, Cypress goes to great lengths to ensure that compensation is performance related and equitable. As a CEO, Rodgers, like Bakke at AES, Kelly at PSS, Kelleher at Southwest, Zimmer at The Men's Wearhouse, and Goodnight at SAS, lives the culture and is a visible example of the underlying values.

But in some other important ways, Cypress is very different from the other companies we have described. In assessing any company, perhaps the first question to ask is, Do the core competencies produced by its management approach permit it to effectively execute its intended business strategy? In each of the other companies we have described, there are close links among values, management practices, the capabilities those practices produce, and a strategy for competing successfully using those capabilities. Unless the alignment between values and core capabilities exists, it is unlikely that a firm can leverage the talent of its people.

As we have described, Cypress has two separate strategies. The first is to compete in high-volume, low-cost integrated circuits, such as computer memory chips. To succeed in that marketplace, Cypress needs to be fast and extremely cost efficient, and needs to maintain competitive levels of quality and yield. The Cypress values and culture, emphasizing control, discipline, and an obsession with accountability, have enabled it to compete successfully in this market segment against much larger companies. But Rodgers has acknowledged that this is an uphill battle. The company only has to miss one generation of product to drive its profits to zero. Two misses and it is dead.

Recognizing this fact, Cypress has also pursued a second strategy: to compete via technical innovation in low-volume, high-margin businesses. What are the capabilities needed to succeed at this game? Besides having talented people, competing in technical innovation requires risk taking and a tolerance for failure; teamwork, both within and across functions; and speed. Does the Cypress approach produce these capabilities? Although Rodgers would argue the point with great vigor, we think not. There is little in the set of Cypress management practices that would encourage teamwork—the company is founded on an individualistic, competitive philosophy and its practices reflect that philosophy well. Although there is talk about encouraging risk taking, even the title of Rodgers's book, *No Excuses Management,* would seem not to foster a risk-taking attitude. Many of the practices, such as the goals system, the performance management process, the highly individualistic reward system, and the killer software, emphasize accountability and assessment—which is fine for the short-term incremental improvements needed for improving quality and yield, but is not aligned with the discontinuous innovation required for major technological change.

Put another way, the Cypress management approach emphasizes short-term individual achievement, not the long-term risk taking associated with discontinuous change. Technical innovation invariably involves some degree of uncertainty. The Cypress management approach is designed to reduce or eliminate uncertainty through elaborate controls, monitoring, and information gathering and sharing. This emphasis has been a critical part of Cypress's ability to compete against much larger competitors in the high-volume, low-cost SRAM business. However, to the extent that this approach, and the supporting systems, incentives, and culture, is applied to the parts of Cypress charged with breakthrough innovation, it seems counterproductive and misaligned.[36] It is in the area of revolutionary innovation for new products that Cypress seems to be less successful than some of its competitors. Why? Because the very capabilities that its culture and values produce offer the company little leverage in pursuing this strategy.

An important lesson from Cypress is that as fundamental as values and capabilities are, to produce long-term success they must also be aligned with the business strategy and produce capabilities that are useful in the marketplace. Values and philosophy are the foundations for building capabilities, but to be valuable, capabilities need to offer a competitive advantage for the execution of a business strategy. Cypress's capabilities do not seem to lend themselves to at least one important part of their business.

Second, there is some degree of inconsistency between the stated values of individual autonomy and empowerment—encouraging individual risk taking and entrepreneurship—and the actual operating style and management practices of the company. Cypress is not the only company we have ever seen that says one thing and does another, or even the worst example of this, but there is nevertheless a clear misalignment between what the company claims and what it actually does. The talk is of delegation, but Rodgers himself gets involved in minute details, even to the point of taking over meetings. The rhetoric is of empowerment, but there are elaborate controls and monitoring systems that essentially signal a lack of trust. Although Rodgers may claim not to be looking at people's goal performance closely, those subjected to the various assessments and computer-based monitoring and control may not agree.

But perhaps the most important inconsistency is this: Although Cypress Semiconductor claims to want talented, creative people and to value innovation and change, it has created a culture and environment that these people may not find particularly attractive. Think back to AES, The Men's Wearhouse, Southwest Airlines, SAS Institute, and the other companies we have studied. In each instance, these organizations have created systems that support people and help make them "better than they ever thought they could be," in the words of The Men's Wearhouse. The organizations do this not because they are soft headed, but because they understand competitive labor market realities. If you offer an attractive work environment in which people can learn, develop, try new things, and support each other, in the process you will create a big recruiting and retention advantage. Cypress says it wants the best, but the company has created an environment that is, in many ways, unlikely to attract some of the talented, creative, entrepreneurial people it claims to be seeking. Cypress has built a culture that does attract people who work hard, like to compete, and want to win—all potentially important ingredients for its primary strategy of short-term incremental innovation. But the values that promote this capability may also run counter to those needed for its secondary strategy of breakthrough technical innovation.

It is also important to reiterate a lesson from the AES and Cisco cases. There is a difference between trying to avoid bad decisions and poor performance to the extent possible and imposing a set of controls and constraints that limit creativity and inhibit the ability to attract and retain entrepreneurs. Contrast Cypress's killer software and goals systems with Cisco's planning matrix and business development process. Both could be considered formal control systems that are designed to minimize undesirable variability in performance and reduce the incidence of poor decisions. But notice that Cisco's management practices are *not* designed to eliminate individual discretion—in fact they are designed to encourage individual creativity—and do not produce attempts to beat the system. Or, contrast Cypress's controls with those at AES. Just because AES doesn't have a computer system that monitors people and a CEO who is ubiquitous in everything doesn't mean the company is out of control. Peer advice and help is offered, and people ask for assistance and advice when they need it. People watch out for each other—which is different than watching each other—and for the company. Or consider NUMMI. Again, the team-oriented social control system leads to actual controls that are probably more effective than Cypress's without the negative side effects. Don't make the Cypress mistake and confuse systems that ostensibly hold people accountable with actual effective control.[37]

The Cypress story says that good intentions are not enough. Actions must be consistent and aligned. The Cypress story also suggests that effective leaders need to get beyond ideology and sound bites to consider the substantive connections between management practices and the actual consequences of those practices. The good news is that Cypress is filled with smart people who learn from their mistakes. Recently, the company has begun an effort to realign its values, culture, and practices in ways that foster more innovation. Rodgers, like the other managers we have profiled, understands the importance of continual adaptation to the competitive environment.

Chapter 10

Unlocking the Hidden Value in *All* of Your People

IN THE FIRST chapter we posed two management mysteries for you to solve. First, we asked why it was that some companies were able to succeed, often over long periods of time, in highly competitive industries without having any of the usual sources of sustainable competitive advantage, such as barriers to entry or sources of market power. Second, we asked why it was that the competitors of these remarkable companies seemed to be unable to copy what they did.

We've now given you enough details about a set of these companies and how they have succeeded—not by winning the war for talent but by fully using the talent and unlocking the motivation of the people they already have in their organizations—for you to have formed your own opinions about the keys to their success. Although the firms we have described are interesting examples, they are not the only ones that have succeeded in this way. The companies described in this book are unusual, to be sure, but they are not unique.

In this concluding chapter, we offer you our perspective on what these companies, and the others that also succeed in the same way, have in common. Then we address the two most common objections we hear when we teach this material: (1) there are other organizations that appear to do exactly the same things but haven't always done so well, so maybe these companies are lucky or the lessons from them aren't really transferable; and (2) even if there are lessons here, I can't implement them in my company for a lot of reasons. We hope that by addressing these two frequently stated concerns, we can help you and your organization get beyond knowing to also acting on that knowledge and building a really high-performing work environment.

In offering our own conclusions, we do not claim to have found the only correct answer and solved the mysteries once and for all. We have spent too many years studying organizations and been surprised too often to make such a claim. Different leaders will come to other conclusions that are likely to be as good as ours. What we offer is a more modest proposal. We believe that underlying the oft-stated cliche that "people are our most important asset" is a deeper truth: To the extent that any organization can truly unleash the hidden value in its people, it will increase its chance of success. This is particularly true in a world in which intellectual capital and knowledge are increasingly important. Most organizations do not capture this value. The firms we have described have solved this puzzle better than their competitors. Here is how we believe they have done it.

WHAT PEOPLE-CENTERED COMPANIES DO

What explains the success of the companies we have described? A complete listing of the many separate factors and management practices could easily fill up a blackboard. But underlying the many discrete things these companies do to develop and tap the potential of their people are three common themes. First, each of these companies has a clear, well-articulated set of values that are widely shared and act as the foundation for the management practices that build the core capabilities that in turn provide a basis for the company's competitive success. Second, each of these organizations has a remarkable degree of alignment and consistency in the people-centered practices that express its core values. Finally, the senior managers in these firms, not just the founders or the CEO, are leaders whose primary role is to ensure that the values are maintained and constantly made real to all of the people who work in the organization.

Values and Culture First

The most visible characteristics that differentiate the companies we have described from others are their values and the fact that the values come first, even before stock price. But why should values be a source of sustained advantage? Most organizations purport to have values—often listed on a handy three-by-five-inch laminated card to be carried in a wallet, or expressed in a widely circulated corporate mission or vision statement. Given the prevalence of these statements, how can "values" offer any advantage? And besides, a cynic might ask, what business does management have in emphasizing values (other than shareholder value, of course)? These are important questions that need to be examined carefully, not dismissed as they often are. Superficially at least, the notion of corporate values seems like just another management fad. But look a little deeper and you'll see why the values in the companies we've described do offer them a competitive advantage.

First, let's be clear what a company value is. A value is typically defined as "a belief about what is worthwhile or important . . . principles or standards that are seen as important by a person or group."[1] In this sense, all organizations define what is important for people to pay attention to (e.g., cost control, profit, customers). Organizations have values, whether formally articulated or not. For a person to succeed in any organization, he or she has to understand what is really important to that firm—its values. People do this by looking carefully at what's actually rewarded, observing how people get ahead and who gets promoted, and watching and listening to what senior managers do and where they spend their time. The policies and practices of the company signal clearly what is valued and important.

Unfortunately, too often what senior managers say and what they do are ambiguous at best and contradictory at worst.

Anyone who has spent any time at all in an organization understands this. The underlying values of the company will invariably become clear, even if senior managers aren't explicit about them or deny that "values" are important. Too often these implicit values take the form of "follow orders," "please your boss," "don't take risks," "don't fail," "results count, people don't," and "act in your own best interest because the organization won't." Of course, these aren't the values that are printed on the three-by-five-inch laminated cards, but they are often the unspoken but widely shared values that people understand. Thus, regardless of what the mission statement or senior management says, employees will inevitably come to understand how the company operates and what the real values are.

Lest you think this view is too cynical, consider the implicit values conveyed in the modern management practices adopted by many companies. Most firms today emphasize, among other things, the employee's responsibility for being career resilient, employment at will and no-fault dismissal, pay for performance, downsizing to cut costs, and maximizing shareholder value above all else. What is the message any sentient employee takes from these practices? Pursue what is best for you, not the firm or the customer, adopt a free-agent mentality, and do not invest any more in the firm than it is willing to invest in you. The underlying values are crystal clear, even if they are never expressed in a formal way. In this sense, arguments by managers that value statements are irrelevant or inappropriate miss the point: All organizations have values; the only question is how explicit they are about them.

And what happens when employees behave in accordance with these values? First, a rational employee is not likely to exert much effort in activities beyond what he or she is explicitly rewarded for. A "show me the money" mood prevails. Second, a smart employee will be constantly alert for new and better job opportunities in other organizations—loyalty is for fools. Third, unless cooperation is explicitly monitored and rewarded, teamwork is viewed as optional. Of course, this does not mean that people won't help their fellow group members. Reciprocity is too strongly ingrained for people not to help those with whom they work directly. However, teamwork across groups or divisions with others whom a person sees infrequently is not likely to be highly valued. In this world, status comes from getting more money and more promotions, not helping customers or fellow employees. The culture, or shared norms about what's important, emphasizes individual achievement and short-term success, not mutual obligation, trust, and loyalty. To resolve some of these problems, management's job is to design ever more sophisticated control and incentive systems to ensure that the necessary teamwork occurs and that the loss of intellectual capital is minimized. But this is difficult, since those charged with this responsibility are also playing according to the same rules and may themselves leave.

Compare these values and the cultures they imply with those of Southwest, Cisco, AES, The Men's Wearhouse, NUMMI, and SAS Institute. What is not different is the importance placed on performance. Each of these companies is notable for how fiercely it competes. Each has a culture in which there are clear performance norms and in which people who don't live up to those norms soon find themselves working elsewhere. What is different in these firms, however, is the emphasis they place on two dimensions frequently absent from their competitors: a sense of purpose—*why* what they are doing is important—and the importance and dignity of people. Whether it is the singular importance that NUMMI places on the team member on the line, AES's emphasis on using a person's gifts to the fullest, or The Men's Wearhouse's willingness to invest in people and give them second chances, each of these firms conveys the importance of people and the larger purpose of the organization through both management actions and practices.

Why are values so important? Although none of us would work for very long if we believed we were not fairly compensated, money by itself isn't sufficient for motivating really long-term high performance. As David Russo has noted, a raise is only a raise for thirty days; after that, it's just your salary. Most of us would like to believe that what we are doing makes a difference to others and that our work is important. No one can be very motivated if they genuinely believe that what they are doing is worthless or violates their fundamental values. Moreover, most of us also want to feel that we are valued as people, not simply as economic agents. We want to be respected for who we are, not simply what we do. And most of us also respond positively to being around others who share similar beliefs and with whom we can build relationships.

If you accept this characterization of people as being generally true, ask yourself how a leader or an organization can create an environment in which these motivations are unleashed. Possible examples are by setting high performance standards and expectations for people (recall The Men's Wearhouse's goal of helping people to be better than they ever thought possible), offering a sense of purpose for the organization with which people can identify (AES's goal of bringing energy to the world, even when there are financial risks involved), and creating a sense of belonging and trust among the employees.

These values also act as a gyroscope for the organization, keeping it focused on its core capabilities. Confronted with difficult questions about strategy or policies, such as whether to enter a particular business or institute a specific practice, the values provide a test that people in the organization can use to decide what is appropriate. The crucial question is, Is this consistent with our values? For instance, when Dave Russo at SAS is asked to consider new policies, he asks himself whether the proposed practice is consistent with the values and culture of the organization and whether it will have a positive effect on a significant number of employees and their families. If the answer is "yes," the practice is adopted.

Each of the organizations we have profiled uses their values as a litmus test for solving the inevitable perplexing problems that arise. In this sense, the values help keep the organization pointed in the right direction. Contrast this with organizations without such values, or with "values" that aren't deeply ingrained. Confronted with similar thorny issues, leaders may either vacillate or adopt contradictory policies that undermine their credibility. For example, in one large organization senior management talked incessantly about trusting their employees and then adopted a measurement system that signaled the opposite. In another firm, management encouraged teamwork and then, unwittingly, approved a powerful performance management system focused on individual performance metrics. How likely would it be that AES or Southwest would make the same mistakes? To us, it seems highly unlikely precisely because managers in those organizations would think first about the company's values and whether the proposed systems were inconsistent with those values.

Finally, these values provide a cornerstone for the design of a selection process that helps attract the right types of people. The management practices then convey to them that these values are real and important. The result is that these organizations are able to capture more of the skills and talents of their employees than their competitors. Their people are more in sync with the overarching goals of the organization, more energized, and more loyal; because of this, these firms are better able to invest in their employees and recapture their investment. Meanwhile, their competitors often end up paying more to attract people and to design elaborate control and coordination systems, and are more likely to lose those employees who don't fit or have better opportunities elsewhere.

Why can't competitors easily imitate the strategy of the successful firms we have described? The answer is almost too obvious to spend much time on. Can anyone be very successful for very long at imitating another person all the way down to his or her values? Even Robert DeNiro would have a hard time staying in role for as long as needed to convince thousands of employees of his sincerity—and most CEOs can't act with the skill of a DeNiro. People are good at ferreting out deception and insincerity, and managers aren't good at pretending to be something they are not. In the organizations we have described, the values and cultures reflect the strong beliefs of their leaders and the people in them. The only way a competitor could replicate these would be to truly believe in them and to consistently behave in accordance with them—not an easy task.

Unlike companies that follow the conventional strategic management model, the companies we have described do not begin with an intellectually driven exercise to define their strategy and then align the organization to reflect this choice, with management policies decided as an afterthought. Instead, they begin with a set of clearly articulated values that are reflected in how employees are to be treated. These values and philosophy drive the management practices of the firm and help define its strategy—almost the exact opposite of what conventional wisdom teaches.

Making the Values Real: Alignment and Consistency

Although values are the crucial ingredient in the success of these companies, by themselves values are insufficient—only words. How are they made real in these organizations? First, senior managers must believe in them and act consistently. Employees are smart. They're good observers and listeners. If management says one thing and does another, smart people will quickly become skeptical and reluctant to act on the espoused values, no matter how attractive they sound. Second, there must be absolute consistency between the organization's values and the practices, or levers, that express these values. As different as the firms we have described are, each relies on the same six management practices to ensure that the values are reinforced. When aligned, each of these levers communicates the importance of the values and is consistent with the others. When misaligned, they signal that the values are not to be taken seriously. Worse, they undermine the credibility of those espousing the values.

Table 10-1 illustrates how the alignment and consistency of these levers reinforce the values of the companies we have profiled. In our view, this alignment is a critical source of the success of these companies. It is important to note that it is the overall alignment and consistency among these levers, not the presence or absence of one or two practices, that unleashes the talent in these firms. As you think about each of the companies, consider how these six levers enable each firm to express its values.

Strong Culture. A value that is the basis for a set of norms or expectations about what are the appropriate attitudes and behaviors can act as a powerful social control system. This is what organizational culture really is: a social control system in which shared expectations guide people's behavior. In each of the people-centered firms we have described, there is a clear and consistent alignment among the values, the norms that express these values (the culture), and specific attitudes and behaviors that are based on these values and that build core capabilities. For instance, at AES the core value of "fun" has a very specific meaning: Fun means establishing an environment in which people can use their gifts and skills to make a difference in society without fear of being squelched. It does not mean watching TV or kidding around. At Cisco, success is defined by delivering technology solutions that the customer wants and staying in front of the technology curve. The company's values of eschewing a technology religion, really listening to the customer, and being frugal help ensure this by guiding people's behavior. Frugality at Cisco means watching costs carefully, from the price of soft drinks to the price for new facilities. At Cypress, the values of winning, working hard, and hiring the best people are well aligned with the competitive nature of the semiconductor industry. However, the emphasis on individualism appears to undercut the teamwork needed to compete in the innovative segment of the market. In this sense, the Cypress values and the systems that express them may not be aligned with an important part of the Cypress strategy. Each of the firms we described has a strong culture that

Table 10-1 Alignment of HR Levers

HR Levers	Southwest Airlines	Cisco Systems	The Men's Wearhouse	SAS Institute	PSS World Medical	AES	NUMMI	Cypress Semiconductor
Values, culture, and strategy alignment	✓✓	✓✓	✓✓	✓✓	✓✓	✓✓	✓✓	X
Hiring for fit	✓✓	✓	✓	✓✓	✓✓	✓✓	✓✓	✓✓
Investing in people	✓✓✓	✓	✓✓	✓✓	✓✓	✓✓✓	✓✓✓	0
Widespread information sharing	✓✓✓	✓	✓	✓	✓✓✓	✓✓✓	✓✓✓	✓✓✓
Team-based systems	✓	✓	✓	✓	✓	✓✓	✓✓	X
Rewards and recognition	✓✓	✓	✓	✓	✓✓	✓	✓	✓

provides explicit norms and helps people understand exactly what attitudes and behaviors are expected in order to fit in, and what attitudes and behaviors will not be tolerated.

Hiring for Fit. Once the values and culture are made clear, these companies then design screening processes that help them identify people who will fit in and screen out those who do not share these values. Most companies focus on hiring based on the skills needed for a specific job. People-centered firms hire for how well the person will fit the company. This doesn't mean that they ignore a candidate's abilities. Instead they recognize that to really contribute over a long period, a person must feel comfortable in the organization; the abilities that are important are thus those that help someone grow, change, and develop to meet changing business challenges. These abilities include a willingness to learn and try new things, to be part of a team, and to accept responsibility. Southwest, for example, hires people not for the first job that they will hold, but for their potential to move up in the organization over a career. At NUMMI, the screening process focuses on attitudes, team skills, and a willingness to fit in. Hiring based solely on job skills can be short sighted and expensive. If someone doesn't fit the culture, either the culture will change or the person will leave.

To hire for cultural fit, these companies are clear about what "fit" means (e.g., what specific attitudes they are looking for).[2] Also, the recruiting process is largely driven by employees who know the job best and can accurately convey the expectations required to succeed. The process itself invariably involves multiple steps and enough time so that the applicant gets a good sense for what the culture is and is given plenty of opportunity to bow out. As Cisco's Chambers puts it when describing why the company puts so much effort into the screening process, "If you are selecting a partner for life, your ability to select the partner after one date isn't very good."[3] By beginning with an explicit set of values and screening people against these, each of the companies we have described increases the chance that people who join will share the values and maintain the culture.

Investing in People. Having screened for people who fit the culture and values of the organization, people-centered companies then signal clearly to their employees how important each of them is to the future of the company. At Southwest, for example, the new orientation process begins with a celebration to welcome the new employees as members of the team. The company's long-term commitment to employees is signaled by the practice of hiring people not for a particular job but with a sequence of jobs in mind. It is further demonstrated through the eighty hours of annual training required for all Southwest employees. At The Men's Wearhouse, all new associates are treated to a trip to northern California for skills training and socialization. Should an employee have a problem with substance abuse, free treatment is provided. At Cisco, the importance of assimilation is shown in the immediacy with which new employees are given training in the Cisco way, followed by continuous opportunities to update skills. At NUMMI, rather than laying people off during slowdowns, assembly line workers are trained in statistical quality control techniques. At SAS Institute, all employees are encouraged to think about having two or three separate careers, all within the company. At PSS World Medical, employees attending PSS University may stay in the homes of the senior executives.

Each of these firms makes continued investments in people by providing opportunities for development and career growth. Often, this training is explicitly oriented toward socialization to the culture, not simply skills training. What is different between these firms and some of their competitors is that the message conveyed to all levels of employees through this investment is that each employee matters as a person and that the company is committed to him or her over the long term.

Widespread Information Sharing. Many firms offer training. What differentiates the firms we have described is what happens after the employee is trained. In most companies, operational and financial data are not shared with employees. Doing this is seen as somehow risking the security of the firm or compromising important information. In people-centered firms the opposite is true. The assumption is that if employees' intellectual capital is really to be used, they must understand in detail how the firm is doing and what it is trying to do. For this reason, there is extensive sharing of information throughout the organization.

At AES, all employees are considered "insiders" by the Securities and Exchange Commission. At PSS, employees are given all the relevant financial and accounting data so they can make informed choices about how to run their business. At Southwest, all employees have access to the critical numbers assessing turnaround times, on-time performance, lost bags, and customer complaints. The signal from senior management is clear: Employees are smart, trustworthy people who have the ability and desire to do the right thing for the company.

Whether intentional or not, most firms with need-to-know information policies send the opposite message: Either employees aren't smart enough to need the information (they lack the ability) or they aren't reliable enough to be trusted with it (they might disclose it). No wonder even extraordinary employees sometimes cannot contribute to the full extent of their capabilities and that employees in people-centered firms make a real contribution.

Team-Based Systems. The people-centered companies we have described rely heavily on team-based systems once a person is part of the organization. Examples include the total team-based approach of AES, the formal teams at NUMMI and Southwest, and the informal teams at Cisco Systems, SAS, and The Men's Wearhouse. Even in those organizations where the work might lend itself to significant specialization (e.g., SAS, NUMMI, and The Men's Wearhouse), there is an emphasis on collective responsibility. This emphasis on teams as an organizing principle derives not from a current fad but from a belief in the fundamental importance of teams as a way of both getting the work done and of promoting autonomy and responsibility—of tapping the ideas and energy of everyone. Teams, in spite of their difficulties, can promote a sense of purpose and give people a sense of belonging. At NUMMI and AES teams take responsibility for the production process. Supervisors aren't in control. Teams are. Instead of relying on formal monitoring and control systems, teams rely on the social control of others to ensure that people behave consistently with the norms and values.

Rewards and Recognition. A final lever used to express the values in these companies is the careful alignment of reward systems—but not in ways that many organizations do. These people-centered companies do not emphasize money as a primary motivator. Go to work at SAS, Cisco, AES, or Southwest and you'll be fairly compensated, but you won't make as much as you could at some of their competitors. Certainly people-centered firms understand that money is important to people and can be a powerful driver of behavior. For this reason, however, they are careful in how they use monetary incentives. These companies emphasize the intrinsic rewards of fun, growth, teamwork, challenge, and accomplishment. They do this by providing continual opportunities for employees to feel good about their accomplishments and to hear this expressed from others who matter to them— like their colleagues and bosses. Whether it is the social budget and "frequent flyer" points for suggestions at NUMMI, the on-the-spot cross-functional teamwork awards and birthday breakfasts at Cisco, the M&Ms at SAS, the celebrations at The Men's Wearhouse, PSS, and Southwest, or any number of other ways, these organizations constantly reinforce the self-esteem of their people and emphasize the family nature of the organization. People aren't "workers" or "headcount" or "truck drivers" but "wardrobe consultants," "team members," and "CEOs." Trivial stuff, but when added up, the sum total of these signals is a powerful reminder to people that they matter, both in what they do and who they are.

The overall alignment and consistency among these levers is what makes the values come alive in these organizations. Partial alignment doesn't result in partial credit. The payoff function is not linear but exponential. Firms that invest in people but don't have systems that encourage long-term employment and career development are unlikely to reap the rewards from their investment. Long-term employment isn't likely to be productive unless people have the information necessary to be productive and the autonomy necessary to act on the information. Having an "enlightened" management without clear values, norms, and strategy only results in confusion. Aligning rewards and recognition systems with unskilled or unmotivated employees offers only a small increment in long-term performance. The point that most imitators simply do not get is that there must be alignment and consistency among *all* of these levers if the values are to be real and effective. And this is difficult, detail-oriented work. As

Pat Kelly says, "Making work fun for employees is hard work."[4] The evidence suggests that it is too hard for most companies.

Leading, Not Managing

The senior managers in each of these companies see their roles not as managing the day-to-day business or even as making decisions about grand strategy but as setting and reinforcing the vision, values, and culture of the organization. Dennis Bakke at AES claims that he made only two decisions in 1998, one of which was not to write a book on the company. His job, he believes, is to continually ensure that the AES values of fun, fairness, integrity, and social responsibility are faithfully transmitted throughout the organization. Cisco's Chambers spends his time emphasizing customers, frugality, teamwork, and the need for avoiding a technology religion. Pat Kelly at PSS acknowledges that most business people are uncomfortable talking about values, but argues that without them, the enterprise is reduced to simply making money, which is not a very sustainable proposition. Jim Goodnight at SAS, George Zimmer at The Men's Wearhouse, Gary Convis at NUMMI, and Herb Kelleher and Colleen Barrett at Southwest are living examples of the values of their organizations. They appreciate that their primary mission is to create a vision and reinforce the values of the firm.

In this sense, each of these people is a leader, not a manager. Rather than spending time making operational decisions, their role, and that of their executive teams, is to help people in the organization understand *why* what they are doing is important and makes a difference. They pay careful attention to ensuring that there is alignment between the values, strategy, systems, culture, and core capabilities of the company. Doing this means giving up power, not accumulating it. Kan Higashi at NUMMI talks about managing as though you had "no power." Dennis Bakke and George Zimmer are explicit in talking about servant leadership and the importance of leaders in serving customers and employees.

This is a far cry from the imperial tradition adopted by many American CEOs or the trappings of power often seen in companies. There are no fleets of private aircraft, private dining rooms, or large entourages for the leaders we have described. Instead, we see the opposite: comparatively low CEO salaries, modest offices, and a relentless effort to live the company's values. It is these actions, and the consistent re-inforcement provided by the actions of other leaders in the company, that more than any words or company documents form the foundation of the organizational cultures of these firms.

As a result of their emphasis on values and culture, each of these organizations has built a reciprocal trust between management and employees. Employees believe that the company is being managed in a way that considers their interests as well as that of the shareholders. Consequently, each of the firms we have described has a long-term view of employment—which is not the same as guaranteeing jobs. Indeed, one of the notable commonalities across these companies is their intolerance for those who do not live the values, including that of high performance. As a result, there is an emphasis on the mutual obligation between workers and the company: The firm works hard at providing long-term employment in return for flexibility and perfor-mance by the workforce.

The CEOs of the companies you have read about in this book are, in the words of Jack Welch, "relentless and boring" in their efforts to convey the importance of the organization's values and culture.[5] It is this consistency of signaling from the top that keeps the values of these firms alive. Anything less than this and the values would cease to be lived throughout the organization. No wonder that we seldom see competitors successfully imitate these companies. It's too hard and too boring for most CEOs to accomplish. After all, they have big-ger, more important strategic decisions to occupy their time—like hir-ing extraordinary people.

BUT WHAT ABOUT . . . ?

When we present this material about how companies achieve excep-tional returns in competitive environments by tapping the knowl-edge and energy of their people, skeptical listeners often respond with the following: X (some company such as People Express or Levi Strauss) did what you have talked about, and look at the troubles they have had anyway. It is worth considering at least some of these pre-sumed counterexamples in some detail to help us better understand in what ways they actually differed from the companies we have de-scribed.

We certainly don't want to oversimplify what are complex stories. And we don't want to suggest that *all* organizational performance can be explained by the ideas and models we have proposed. Nonetheless, it seems clear that in each of these counterexamples, there are some important, easily discerned, and fundamental differences from the companies we have described in this book that help to explain the divergence in performance. Many of these differences concern the degree of decentralization and delegation of decision-making authority. The companies we have described all succeed not only by attracting and developing talent and intellectual capital and building relationships of mutual commitment with their people, but by doing something even more difficult—organizing so that the intellectual capital and energy can actually be used to affect business decisions and operations.

As we will see, many organizations have done a reasonably good job on the first part—attracting and training people. Fewer have succeeded in implementing organizational structures that permit the knowledge, skills, and insights of all of their people to be recognized and implemented. And very few indeed have developed a set of practices that are at once internally consistent and also aligned with a business model that makes economic sense. It is in this alignment, consistency, and actual delegation of discretion that the companies described in this book excel.

People Express

When people read or hear about Southwest Airlines, they often think of People Express—a company that seemingly had a very similar philosophy, business model, and approach to its people but that failed miserably, at the end running out of cash and, on the verge of bankruptcy, being purchased by Frank Lorenzo and Texas Air Corporation. Indeed, there are a number of similarities between the two organizations. Like Southwest, the original strategy of People Express (PE) focused on providing frequent low-cost flights using underutilized airports (Newark, in the case of PE). Costs were to be kept low by the extremely productive use of assets, including both people and equipment.[6] The airline offered a simple, no-frills service and charged extra for things such as meals. Just like Southwest, PE offered no interline connections to other airlines. The company sought to differentiate itself on the basis of positive, upbeat service, with the goal being "to make flying with People the most pleasant and memorable travel experience possible."[7] Like Kelleher at Southwest, Donald Burr, the founder and CEO of People Express, emphasized the company's employees and managing them in a better, more humane fashion. In fact, the very name, People Express, reflected this emphasis on people. For instance, Burr stated:

> I guess the single predominant reason that I cared about starting a new company was to try and develop a better way for people to work together. . . . Most organizations believe that humans are generally bad and you have to control them and watch them and make sure they work. At People Express, people are trusted to do a good job until they prove they definitely won't.[8]

PE's initial fleet, seventeen Boeing 737 airliners, consisted of the same equipment used by Southwest. Recruiting was carefully done, at least initially, to ensure that those hired fit the culture that was being built. Prospective employees had to come back for several rounds of interviews to demonstrate their interest in and commitment to the company. Employees owned stock in the company—in fact they were forced to buy stock at a discounted price when they were hired (although the company provided loans to help). Senior executive salaries were low compared with the industry norm and were compressed across levels, just like at Southwest, and profit-sharing bonuses and stock options were important additional elements of compensation for all employees. The emphasis on collective rewards parallels Southwest's emphasis on stock ownership and profit-sharing bonuses. Corporate headquarters were spartan, in keeping with the egalitarian culture. Even senior executives did not have assistants or fancy perquisites. People Express promised job security to its people as well as "opportunities for personal and professional growth through continuing education, cross-utilization, promotion from within the company, and compensation higher than other companies paid for similar skills and experience."[9] It is little wonder that people often see the airlines as quite similar in their approaches.

There are, however, some important differences between the two companies. First, there are differences in the companies' willingness and ability to stick with their strategy. Southwest has been extremely disciplined in its growth, entering markets only when it can reasonably expect to succeed. In some years more than thirty cities will approach the airline and request it to come to their airports, but it will add routes to only one or two. This selectivity in entering new markets is one of the reasons the company has never had to lay off or furlough its employees during its entire history. The slow growth has permitted Southwest to maintain its focus on getting the right people and being selective in its recruiting while still being adequately staffed. Also, Southwest remained committed to using only Boeing 737s, making maintenance and flight training easier because of less variation in equipment.

By contrast, People Express actively sought rapid growth, even though this growth strained its systems and its culture. The airline reached almost $1 billion in revenues after just three years of operation, whereas it took Southwest about sixteen years to get that big. The company "began buying much larger planes, jumbo Boeing 747s and 185 seat 727s."[10] People Express began by flying underserved routes such as Newark to Buffalo, but soon added routes to major cities such as Chicago and Dallas, thereby directly challenging larger competitors.[11] Although he had promised to grow the company organically in order to permit promotion from within and the development of a consistent culture and philosophy, Burr didn't stick to that plan either. "People also went on a buying spree, acquiring Britt Airways and Provincetown-Boston Airline, both commuter carriers, and Frontier, a major regional carrier based in Denver."[12] This rapid growth strained the company. People Express was continuously understaffed, putting more pressure on those people who had to carry the load and putting pressure on the company to compromise in its hiring process. Buying other airlines when he said he wouldn't made Burr look like any other executive and created the difficulties of combining People's unique culture with those of the acquired airlines.

This difference in strategy between the two airlines came from a fundamental difference in philosophy and approach to people. Don Burr's management style was completely different from Kelleher's. Although both claimed to value their people and the contributions they were making to the organization, Burr was much more authoritarian and controlling, and didn't listen to his people. When People Express employees complained about the stresses of rapid growth, his answer was to note that there was a perfection imperative and that health problems and marital problems were just natural. His answer to the problems of growth was to grow faster: "[W]ith no growth horizon, people have been disempowered. We've started getting sleepy. So, we've decided to set a new growth objective."[13] That objective was to grow even *faster* than planned. When people argued with this strategy, Burr stated that people could either agree with the approach or leave. Four of People's seven original managing officers quit or were dismissed.[14] Belying its presumed emphasis on people and their welfare and on involving employees in the governance of the airline, People Express soon came to be characterized by fear, turnover, and dissatisfaction:

> His hard-driving style has sent several key subordinates packing—including . . . a managing officer who helped devise People's unique personnel policies. And he has created a new climate at headquarters far removed from the family-like culture he preaches. Says one former top executive: "Employees aren't allowed to ask questions anymore. Fear pervades the place. . . . It's become a one-man show."[15]

The two companies also could not have been more different in their customer service realizations. People Express used temporary help, and not enough at that, to staff its phones. Because neither PE nor Southwest sells proportionately as much through travel agents as other airlines do, phones are the first and most important point of contact for most of their customers. Southwest uses its own people, not temps or contractors, in its telephone reservation centers. Moreover, Southwest leaders know this is a difficult and demanding job, and drop by occasionally to express their appreciation to their people. Whereas a caller to PE got busy signals, callers to Southwest are almost invariably answered on the first ring. Southwest has won the annual Triple Crown award for service (best on-time performance, fewest lost bags, and fewest customer complaints) almost every year it has been given. Service is so important that the word "Customer" is always capitalized. People Express, by contrast, came to be known as People Distress. Its record of lost bags, late flights, and customer complaints was soon so well known that the only people who would fly the airline chose it solely for price and were willing to put up with anything for its low fares. When the company finally had to raise its fares because of its huge operating losses and rapidly diminishing cash reserves, customers deserted in droves.

What the difference between the two airlines comes down to, in the end, is that People Express *talked* about a particular philosophy and approach to management, whereas Southwest Airlines actually *lives* by its values and its espoused management principles. Talk cannot substitute for action, and words do not substitute for deeds. In thinking about differences among companies, be careful to look at how the firms operate, not just what they say. It is the reality that matters in affecting performance.

Levi Strauss

Levi Strauss is another company that would seem to fit most of the characteristics of the successful organizations we have described in this book. It is a values-driven company, committed to social responsibility. "When the firm went public in 1971, its offering prospectus made corporate history by warning that profits might be affected by a commitment to social programs."[16] In 1987, Robert Haas, the CEO, developed the Levi Strauss Mission and Aspirations Statement, and he has consistently emphasized the importance of the company's values and its culture, noting that "that's the glue that unites us, the beacon that guides our actions."[17] Levi's gave money to the University of California at Berkeley for research on business ethics, pulled manufacturing out of China to protest human rights abuses, and implemented gain sharing and teamwork in its U.S. manufacturing facilities in an effort to make them more cost competitive so they could stay open. Part of the initiative to change plant operations involved training and sharing more information and decision-making power with line employees. Levi's was one of the early apparel manufacturers to move from a command-and-control system to a more participative management approach.

However, Levi's has definitely been having some business reversals recently. It has lost a lot of market share, particularly in the trend-setting teen and young adult market. Sales fell 13 percent between 1997 and 1998, and the company has been forced to close numerous manufacturing plants in the United States and Europe. There is some internal dissension in the family (which owns essentially all of the stock of this private company), with some shareholders feeling unhappy with the governance structure and the company's performance. Delivery of its product to retailers has been late. Since a second leveraged buyout in 1996, the company's market value has shrunk substantially.[18]

In considering what went wrong at the company, we need to note at the outset that even with its problems, Levi's is in no way a disaster. Between 1985, when the company went private in a leveraged buyout, and 1996, the company's stock price climbed from $2.53 to $265 a share, an increase of more than 10,000 percent.[19] Even at its reduced sales level of $6 billion in 1998, the company generated about $1.1 billion in cash flow, more than Tommy Hilfiger, Polo, Ralph Lauren, and Liz Claiborne combined, and even more than the Gap.[20]

What caused Levi's problems? A *Fortune* article trashing Bob Haas for his emphasis on values and the softer side of management actually provides some hints as to what went wrong—which has little or nothing to do with what the magazine blames for the company's troubles, namely, attention to work-family balance, values, and concern for its people. First, there was no consensus in the company concerning its values and operating principles, in contrast to what we saw at SAS Institute, AES, and Southwest Airlines, for instance. Levi's president, Peter Jacobi, said, "The value-based people look at the commercial folks as heathens; the commercial people look at the values people as wusses getting in the way."[21] The ongoing conflict over basic operating principles and philosophy made decision making time-consuming and difficult.

Second, there is little evidence that Levi's listened to the market and was customer focused, unlike SAS Institute, Cisco, PSS World Medical, or The Men's Wearhouse. Howard Gross, CEO of Miller's Outpost, a western wear retailer with 220 stores that sells a lot of Levi's, maintained that he and other retailers told Levi's about changes in the market, but the company either didn't hear or didn't listen. "We told Levi's about extreme fits. . . . We showed them our numbers. We told them what kids were asking for. They even attended some of our focus groups. But they didn't want to believe."[22]

Third, unlike PSS World Medical, SAS Institute, AES, The Men's Wearhouse, and Southwest Airlines, Levi's was enamored with outside consultants, not only for its training and development—something that these other companies do almost entirely internally—but also for operating initiatives. One of the innovations in apparel manufacturing has been to change both production operations and other logistical arrangements in order to reduce in-process inventory and to compete in serving retailers not just on price but on product availability, so those retailers don't have to keep as much stock on hand. When in 1993 Levi Strauss embarked on a supply chain initiative, the company brought in "at least 100 Andersen consultants" for a project that grew to consume $850 million and that wound up making delivery times worse.[23] We are reminded of the comments of George Zimmer of The Men's Wearhouse, who noted that it was fear of failure that drove people into the arms of consultants.

Fourth, there is little evidence that Levi's actually practices delegation of authority, as opposed to some variant of participative decision making. The distinction is important. Recall the comments of Dennis Bakke of AES. In typical participative decision making, people are asked their opinions, but in the end the leader makes the decisions. In real delegation and empowerment, people consult others from throughout the organization, including senior leadership, but in the end they make the decisions and are held accountable for their results. At Levi Strauss, the evidence is that there was a stifling bureaucracy of meetings and, more to the point, that senior leaders were involved in minute details. Robert Haas is "known for extraordinary (some say obsessive) attention to detail. Poring over press releases and in-house memos, he corrects split infinitives and misplaced modifiers. . . . Everything had to go into a corporate process, so nothing ever got resolved."[24]

Fifth, driving out fear and making people feel secure is something that all of the organizations described in this book practice. NUMMI and Southwest Airlines have never had a layoff or furlough. PSS World Medical affords people a "soft landing," and AES and The Men's Wearhouse talk about forgiving honest mistakes and learning by doing. At Levi's, the Customer Service Supply Chain Initiative redesigned jobs, after which people were made to reapply for their positions. "Levi's employees freaked out. Some who didn't get the jobs they had applied for, or reapplied for, broke down. Others simply quit."[25]

These differences in management approach are neither small nor unimportant. They illustrate the importance of consistency in culture and values across the organization, and of alignment across the entire range of management practices. The contrast between Levi's and some of the other companies we have examined illustrates the importance of driving out fear and of truly letting people make decisions. These practices are important components of building organizations that succeed through their people.

The example of Levi Strauss illustrates another critical point. Values are important. But values about social responsibility and similar things, worthwhile though they are, are not enough. Recall the model in chapter 1. The companies in this book begin with values linked to a metatheory of organizational performance—for example, people are our most important asset in an intellectual capital business (SAS Institute), service is important and that requires creating a positive relationship with our people (Southwest Airlines, The Men's Wearhouse), success depends on tapping the motivation and knowledge of all of our people (NUMMI, The Men's Wearhouse). These values are linked to a business environment that permits these organizations to change the competitive dynamics. Levi Strauss's values for the most part did not have such a link. And, in fact, the values were not even strongly shared within the company. Good intentions are not enough. The philosophy must produce some capability on the part of the employees that differentiates the organization from the competition and provides value in the marketplace.

Learn the Right Lessons

We're sure you could provide other examples of organizations in which, with possibly good intentions and high-sounding words, executives talked about the importance of people as being key to their competitive advantage. But, all too often, these easily spoken words aren't consistently put into practice. For example, although both IBM and Xerox were founded on strong values, and although both have done many things for their people (such as investing in training and promoting from within), both firms have also been characterized by excessive bureaucracy and too much centralization of decision making. Recall that when IBM wanted to get into the personal computer business in the early 1980s, the company opened its PC division headquarters in Florida, far away from the corporate processes that slowed things down. Xerox, too, suffered from inertia. The company invented, but then did not successfully develop and market, the first personal computer, word processing software, and many other technologies.[26]

To say that companies are similar to those discussed in this book just because they invest in training and emphasize promoting people from within misses the more subtle points of alignment and consistency of values and practice. NUMMI relies on the insights of its frontline people. PSS World Medical puts "CEO" on its drivers' business cards. AES practices radical decentralization. Southwest gives all of its employees the home phone numbers of its officers, who listen to what they say about the culture and the operation. Cisco has no particular love of any specific technology, but is ready to go where the market dictates. The critical factor is not just selecting good people and training them, but also organizing the company so that they are motivated and can put their ideas into action.

So we have uncovered the critical lesson and possibly the biggest pitfall in implementing the models we have seen in this book. In thinking about what needs to be aligned, the answer is "everything." Many companies implement a mission and values statement, or try more collective compensation such as gain sharing, or open their books and share some information, or try selective recruiting for cultural fit. But these things work only in concert. Moreover, talented, motivated people must have the opportunity to make real decisions. And as we saw when we considered AES, giving up real decision-making power is the most difficult, but possibly the most crucial, thing of all. What good does it do to have smart, trained, informed, committed people who can't take action (which is precisely what happened at IBM and Xerox in the 1980s)? The answer, of course, is that it only increases frustration.

GETTING BEYOND EXCUSES FOR WHY IT CAN'T BE DONE

After we hear about why these ideas don't work, with people citing counterexamples that, on close inspection, turn out to be quite different from the companies we have described, the next thing we often hear is why the person's particular organization can't be changed and why he or she can't do what has just been learned. The barriers cited are usually quite real, at least at first glance. But providing reasons why nothing can be changed does little to make a company more effective. You may recall one definition of insanity: doing the same thing over and over again and expecting different results. If nothing changes, then it is unlikely that the company's results or competitive position will change either.

David Russo tells some wonderful stories about excuses for not doing anything different. After SAS Institute was listed two years in a row as number three on the *Fortune* list of best places to work in America, people came to visit SAS or invited Russo to come speak to their firms about attracting and retaining talent. And in many instances an interesting thing happened. He would describe, at the audience's specific behest, what SAS Institute did—its management practices and the philosophy and values that provide the foundation for those practices. But people would immediately begin to interrupt to explain why they couldn't do what he was describing. Russo commented on the case of on-site child care:

> For years, companies would come to me and say, you're doing on site child care. Tell me how you do it. I'd say, "Well, we did it." They said, "What about the liability?" And I would say, "Why don't you just go away now?" When people start trying to look for reasons they can't do something, they're dead. They don't want to do it, and they're looking for reasons not to do it.[27]

The wonderful irony is that companies would expend effort to learn what SAS Institute was doing and, as soon as they began to learn—as soon as they began to understand what was involved—they would come up with reasons why they couldn't do the same thing. Why spend the effort to learn if you aren't going to do anything with that knowledge?

There are always reasons why something can't be done. In many companies, human resources is the function that says no. Concerned about treating everyone the same, about avoiding any chance of legal liability, and about maintaining stability and predictability, the HR function is all too frequently the keeper of the rules. But if these rules get in the way of solving real problems that decrease the effectiveness of people in the company, what HR has essentially done is get in the way of management. That is why at Southwest Airlines, people in human resources who say no three times to line managers are fired. The job is not to tell people what they can't do but to find ways to help managers attract, retain, and motivate the talent that provides the competitive edge.

At SAS Institute, David Russo led an effort to reinvigorate HR and refocus the function on helping managers manage rather than getting in the way:

> I stuck a stick of dynamite down the stovepipe of HR about four years ago and said, "We're supposed to be a customer friendly company and we have allowed ourselves to become what every HR department is, and that is the people who say no." . . . If a manager, an employee, anybody, comes to you with a request, the rules are this. Find out not what the request is but what the end result is that they desire, and then seek to satisfy that need, provided that, number one, you don't break any law, number two, you don't harm any employee, and number three, you don't get us on the front page of *The Wall Street Journal*.[28]

This attitude of not taking "no" for an answer, of responding to questions of "why" with "why not," is something that characterizes the companies whose stories we have detailed. It is an attitude essential in making the changes necessary to enhance performance and to avoid becoming hopelessly mired in the past.

WHY THESE COMPANIES SUCCEED

In terms of using the talents of all their people, we believe that the companies we have profiled here are big successes. As you have seen, these organizations are characterized by employee involvement, loyalty, a sense of fun, lower than average turnover, and higher than average financial performance. But we don't want to oversimplify what are complex and dynamic stories. Dennis Bakke at AES decided not to let a book about the company be written precisely because he understands that his organization, and all others, are works in progress. Just because a firm is successful today does not imply that it will be successful tomorrow. The cliché that change is inevitable is, sadly, true. Senior managers sometimes make mistakes in strategies, as may be the case with PSS; new technologies could easily undermine the current advantage of Cypress, SAS, or NUMMI; Wall Street's current love affair with e-commerce could change, much to Cisco's detriment; a dramatic change in regulations or economic conditions could undermine AES's ability to compete; and competitors may find new ways to compete with Southwest or The Men's Wearhouse.

But even if bad things happen to these good organizations, we believe that they are still great examples for us to learn from—for they have developed management systems that show how the hidden value in a workforce can be unleashed. Regardless of the future performance of these individual companies, the reasons *why* these systems are so powerful will not change. They work for some good reasons that are broadly applicable to almost all organizations. In a world in which all work is knowledge work and intellectual capital is crucial for economic success, it is logical that the ability to attract, retain, and use the talents of people provides a competitive edge. Research corroborates this common sense.

First, the evidence shows that commitment and motivation come from involvement and from how people are treated. Although many companies currently emphasize financial rewards such as stock options, bonuses, and salary as ways to attract and motivate their people, the data are conclusive that money is not a high-leverage way to solve organizational problems. For instance, McKinsey's "War for Talent" study surveyed the top 200 executives in a number of companies, asking them why they joined, stayed, or left a company. Of 5,679 respondents, 58 percent cited values and culture as being absolutely essential, 50 percent cited good management, 38 percent mentioned the company having exciting challenges, and 56 percent mentioned freedom and autonomy. Only 23 percent mentioned high total compensation, and 29 percent cited differentiated compensation.[29]

Giving people a stake and say in what they do is essential for building commitment. How committed would you be to something that is not yours and in which you have no say, no voice, and make no decisions, perhaps because you aren't even given relevant data? Probably not very committed. Ironically, that is why it is so hard to delegate decision making—people think that those things in which they have been more involved are better than those in which they have had less involvement and control. Permitting people to learn more about the business through open book management, and permitting them to use that knowledge to make real decisions, produces much more commitment and acceptance of responsibility.

We read books that talk about "Internet time" and the faster pace of competition and technological change today. Although some of this is clearly hyperbole, there is no question that the pace of information creation and diffusion has increased, and there is no question that with increasing deregulation and globalization, competition is fiercer and appears from more directions. How does a company cope? One way, and perhaps the best way, is by distributing information across the organization and permitting people to make rapid local adjustments and adaptations without always going up a chain of command. AES succeeds because it is fast—in an industry in which speed never mattered. Southwest Airlines and The Men's Wearhouse empower their people to take care of customer complaints and respond to customer needs without relying on a long chain of command. Cisco has created small, entrepreneurial subunits that track, develop, and implement new technologies without worrying about whether the new technologies are the established religion.

There are many advantages to distributed intelligence. Think of ants. Ants quickly find food and respond to local threats. For them it is more instinctual than conscious, but the point is the same. Local adaptations are quicker. Dennis Bakke has commented that he may not be as smart as some other CEOs, but that collectively, AES's people, all 10,000 of them, are very smart and he would bet them against any single CEO. The ability to mobilize and use the ideas, information, and creativity of everyone in the organization provides real advantages in a world undergoing constant change. This requires having people who are recruited for their willingness to accept responsibility, who are trained and developed so they can do so effectively, who are given information so they can make good decisions, and who are placed in a structure that encourages them to use what they know and ask questions of others. It is not surprising that companies organized in this fashion outperform those mired down in hierarchy, rules, and buck passing.

Many people have commented that prices are falling—not just

commodity prices, but prices for computers, semiconductors, electronic appliances, software, and even automobiles when you control for inflation and quality changes. Success depends, therefore, on being able to reduce costs faster than prices are declining, in order to maintain or even expand margins. How do you reduce costs? We suppose one way is to hire some consulting firm to do a cost study. When they are finished, you will have (1) paid a big fee, (2) instilled lots of fear in the organization, as people wonder who will be cut, and (3) if you are lucky, not choked on the paperwork like Levi Strauss did. A second way is to cut people willy-nilly, another technique that seldom works. Often the wrong people leave, and there is little evidence that simply cutting people cuts costs.

How about a third, and better, way? Use the ideas, insights, and wisdom of the people who do the work every day to help you become more productive and efficient. That's what NUMMI has done. That's what Southwest Airlines has done. That's what AES has done. And, by getting rid of layers of management, your company does something to really save on costs—eliminates people who aren't directly adding value. It is not surprising that in industries ranging from automobiles to steel, from retailing to finance, companies that follow the high-commitment models we have described outperform their peers. They possess trained, motivated people making decisions every day that enhance operations and product quality. They don't need binders full of procedures and lots of meetings. Speed cuts costs, and the things companies do to build speed, commitment, and intelligence therefore provide them with substantial cost advantages.

BEYOND ORGANIZATIONAL MODELS TO ORGANIZATIONAL ACTION

Overcoming objections and excuses and providing the rationale for why the models we have described work so well can get you only so far. As David Russo so nicely put it when asked about on-site child care, "we just did it." The organizational stories and accompanying details help one see what companies have done to achieve extraordinary results from their people and how they have done it. You should have a better sense of the what, the how, and the why. But understanding by itself is not enough. You and your company must be willing to act on that understanding, to turn your insights and knowledge into action.

In doing so, some suggestions. First, this is a process and a journey, not a set of pat answers. AES has refused to have a book written about it because it believes it is on a journey and that the journey is not complete, that all the answers aren't in. In each of the companies we have described, you can see trial-and-error learning and efforts at continuous improvement. SAS Institute has a small working group that looks at what other companies are doing and considers ideas that will make SAS an even better place to work. George Zimmer and his colleagues at The Men's Wearhouse are continually trying new things to renew and develop their spirit and to work toward helping people be better than they ever thought they could be. Continuous improvement and learning are part and parcel of the Toyota production system implemented at NUMMI. Learning by doing, and continually learning and trying new things, is something that characterizes all of the companies we have described. It is an important component of any implementation effort in any company.

Second, involve as many people as possible in the process. This doesn't mean endless committee meetings, planning sessions, and documents. It does mean that if your company is going to tap the intellectual capital of all of its people, it is useful to tell all of them what you are trying to do and why. Let people sign on to work on aspects of the implementation. Southwest Airlines, with its multitude of culture committees, has a system that not only helps spread the culture as the company grows and expands geographically but also permits it to tap ideas from all levels and parts of the organization and to involve more people in its continuing evolution. Involvement doesn't mean just discussions. Involvement means giving people real responsibility to do things that implement elements of the models we have described in this book.

Third, emphasize real events. The monthly Challenge meetings at PSS World Medical, the values survey at AES, and the celebrations at Southwest Airlines provide tangible reminders of what each company is about, how it operates, and what it stands for. Don't let talk substitute for action. It is what companies do, not just what they say, that is important.

We seldom see companies that can't improve significantly by unleashing the energy and skill of all of their people. Achieving exceptional results by engaging the hearts and minds of all of your people is not something that just a few companies can or should do, and not something that requires some special magic formula to work. Although it requires a consistent philosophy and set of practices, the tremendous rewards and advantages are potentially available to any company and any leader with the courage and wisdom to take the necessary steps.

Notes

CHAPTER 1

1. Elizabeth G. Chambers, Mark Foulon, Helen Handfield-Jones, Steven M. Hankin, and Edward G. Michaels III, "The War for Talent," *McKinsey Quarterly* 3 (1998): 6.
2. Charles Fishman, "The War for Talent," *Fast Company,* August 1998.
3. See, for instance, Pierre Mornell, *Hiring Smart: How to Predict Winners and Losers in the Incredibly Expensive People-Reading Game* (Berkeley, Calif.: Ten Speed Press, 1998); and Bill Birchard, "Hire Great People Fast," *Fast Company,* August–September, 1997.
4. John Huey and Geoffrey Colvin, "The Jack and Herb Show," *Fortune,* 11 January 1999.
5. Eric Nee, "Interview with John Chambers," *Upside,* July 1996.
6. E. Randsell, "They Sell Suits with Soul," *Fast Company,* October 1999, 66.
7. Charles Fishman, "Sanity Inc." *Fast Company,* January 1999, 85–96.
8. Ibid., 89.
9. Ibid.
10. Patrick Kelly, *Faster Company* (New York: Wiley, 1998), 106.
11. Dennis Bakke, "An Alternative View of Corporate Governance," *Director's Monthly,* September 1998, 2.
12. Charles O'Reilly, "New United Motors Manufacturing, Inc. (NUMMI)," Case HR-11 (Stanford, Calif.: Graduate School of Business, Stanford University, 1998), 3.
13. Edward L. Gubman, *The Talent Solution* (New York: McGraw-Hill, 1998), 61.
14. Fishman, "The War for Talent."
15. See, for instance, Dwight L. Gertz and Joao P. A. Baptista, *Grow to be Great: Breaking the Downsizing Cycle* (New York: Free Press, 1995). On page 33, they note that "the greater variation is between companies within industries, rather than among the industries themselves. Within a given industry, the range of performance between the fastest-growing and the slowest-growing companies is greater than the range of performance between the fastest- and slowest-growing industries."
16. Victor H. Vroom, *Work and Motivation* (New York: Wiley, 1964).
17. See, for instance, Michael L. Tushman and Charles A. O'Reilly III, "The Tyranny of Success," chap. 1 in *Winning through Innovation* (Boston: Harvard Business School Press, 1997).
18. For a discussion of this point, see Jeffrey Pfeffer and Robert I. Sutton, *The Knowing-Doing Gap: How Smart Companies Turn Knowledge into Action* (Boston: Harvard Business School Press, 2000).
19. Gubman, *Talent Solution,* 15.
20. Ibid.
21. Dana Weschler Linden and Bruce Upbin, "Boy Scouts on a Rampage," *Forbes,* 1 January 1996.

22. Thomas Stewart, "Allied Signal's Turnaround Blitz," *Fortune*, 30 November 1992.
23. See, for example, the literature on oversufficient justification described in chapter 3 of Philip Zimbardo and Michael Leippe, *The Psychology of Attitude Change and Social Influence* (New York: McGraw-Hill, 1991).
24. Brian E. Becker and Mark A. Huselid, "High Performance Work Systems and Firm Performance: A Synthesis of Research and Managerial Implications," in *Research in Personnel and Human Resources Management*, ed. G. R. Ferris, no. 16 (Greenwich, Conn.: JAI Press, 1998), 53–101.
25. Mark Huselid, "The Impact of Human Resource Management Practices on Turnover, Productivity, and Corporate Financial Performance," A*cademy of Management Journal* 38 (1995): 645.
26. Theresa Welbourne and Alice Andrews, "Predicting Performance of Initial Public Offering Firms: Should HRM Be in the Equation?," *Academy of Management Journal* 38 (1996): 891–919.
27. James Womack, Daniel Jones, and Daniel Ross, *The Machine That Changed the World: The Story of Lean Production* (New York: Harper Perennial, 1990).
28. Casey Ichniowski, "Human Resource Practices and Productive Labor-Management Relations," in *Research Frontiers in Industrial Relations and Human Resources*, eds. David Lewin, Olivia Mitchell, and Peter Sherer (Madison, Wisc.: Industrial Relations Research Association, 1992), 239–271.
29. See Pfeffer and Sutton, chapter 2, *The Knowing-Doing Gap*.
30. Marcus Buckingham and Curt Coffman, *First, Break All the Rules* (New York: Simon & Schuster, 1999), 32.
31. Linda Bilmes, Konrad Wetzker, and Pascal Xhonneux, "Value in Human Resources," *Financial Times*, 10 February 1997, 10.
32. Jangwood Lee and Danny Miller, "People Matter: Commitment to Employees, Strategy and Performance in Korean Firms," *Strategic Management Journal* 20 (1999): 579.
33. See, for instance, Jeffrey Pfeffer, *The Human Equation: Building Profits by Putting People First* (Boston: Harvard Business School Press, 1998).

CHAPTER 2

1. *Condé Nast Traveler*, December 1995.
2. Suzanne Wooton, "Off the Wall Airline," *Baltimore Sun*, 14 September 1997.
3. Kevin Freiberg and Jackie Freiberg, *Nuts: Southwest Airlines' Crazy Recipe for Business and Personal Success* (Austin, Tex.: Bard Press, 1996).
4. Allen R. Myerson, "Air Herb," *New York Times Magazine*, 9 November 1997, 38.
5. Stewart Toy, *Business Week*, 15 June 1987, 76.
6. Adam Byrne, "Continental Is Dropping 'Lite' Service," *New York Times*, 14 April 1995, C1.
7. Scott McCartney and Michael J. McCarthy, "Southwest Flies Circles around United's Shuttle," *Wall Street Journal*, 20 February 1996, B1.
8. Myerson, "Air Herb," 38.
9. Michael Tushman and Charles O'Reilly, *Winning through Innovation: A Practical Guide to Leading Organizational Change and Renewal* (Boston: Harvard Business School Press, 1997).
10. Kristin Dunlap Godsey, "Slow Climb to New Heights," *Success*, October 1996, 21.

11. Myerson, "Air Herb," 38.
12. Edward Welles, "Captain Marvel," *Inc.,* January 1992.
13. Kenneth Labich, "Is Herb Kelleher America's Best CEO?," *Fortune,* 2 May 1994.
14. Freiberg and Freiberg, *Nuts,* 49.
15. Scott McCartney, "Southwest Airlines Lands Plenty of Florida Passengers," *Wall Street Journal,* 11 November 1997, B4.
16. "Investment Winners and Losers," *Money,* October 1992, 133.
17. Wendy Zellner, "Southwest's New Direction," *Business Week,* 8 February 1999, 58.
18. E. Scott Reckard, "Shuttle Dogfight Good News for Air Travelers," *San Francisco Chronicle,* 2 October 1994.
19. Jeff Pelline, "Southwest Air's Driving Force," *San Francisco Chronicle,* 10 June 1993.
20. James Campbell Quick, "Crafting an Organizational Culture: Herb's Hand at Southwest Airlines," *Organizational Dynamics,* Autumn 1992, 51.
21. Godsey, "Slow Climb," 26.
22. Labich, "America's Best CEO?," 50.
23. Charles A. O'Reilly III and Jeffrey Pfeffer, "Southwest Airlines," Case F-HR-1 (Stanford, Calif.: Graduate School of Business, Stanford University, 1994), 15.
24. Quick, "Crafting an Organizational Culture," 51.
25. Bredna Paik Sunoo, "How Fun Flies at Southwest Airlines," *Personnel Journal,* June 1995, 62.
26. Molly Ivins, "From Texas, with Love and Peanuts," *New York Times,* 14 March 1999, BU11.
27. Ann Rhoades, interview by authors, Dallas, Tex., 1994.
28. Wendy Zellner, "Go-Go Goliaths," *Business Week,* 13 February 1995.
29. Wooton, "Off the Wall," 1D.
30. Libby Sartain, interview by authors, Dallas, Tex., 1994.
31. Sunoo, "How Fun Flies," 68.
32. Subrata Chakravaty, "Hit 'em Hardest with the Mostest," *Forbes,* 16 September 1991.
33. Rita Bailey, interview by authors, Dallas, Tex., 1994.
34. Delise Zachry, interview by authors, Dallas, TX, 1994.
35. Labich, "America's Best CEO?"
36. Charles Boisseau, "Southwest's Pilot," *Houston Chronicle,* 10 March 1996, D-1.
37. Charles Boisseau, "Barrett Ensures Culture, Courtesy Fly in Formation," Houston Chronicle, 10 March 1996, 10.
38. Sunoo, "How Fun Flies," 62.
39. Libby Sartain, interview.
40. Kenneth Hein, "Rewarding Relationships," *Incentive,* January 1999.
41. Labich, "America's Best CEO?," 47.
42. Scott McCartney, "America West Contract War Is Over More Than Money," *Wall Street Journal,* 8 March 1999.
43. Scott McCartney, "Salary for Chief of Southwest Air Rises after 4 Years," *Wall Street Journal,* 29 April 1996, C16.
44. Personal communication.
45. Labich, "America's Best CEO?," 45–52.
46. Ivins, "From Texas."
47. Charles Boisseau, "Barrett Ensures Culture," 10.

48. Boisseau, "Southwest's Pilot," D-3.
49. Godsey, "Slow Climb," 26.

CHAPTER 3

1. "The Brand Called You," *Fast Company,* August/September 1997.
2. See James Baron, M. Diane Burton, and Michael Hannan, "The Road Taken: Origins and Evolution of Employment Systems in Emerging Companies," *Industrial and Corporate Change* 5 (1996): 239–276, for a description of how founders of high-technology start-up companies think about designing the employment practices in their companies.
3. Lee Gomes, "Cisco Tops $100 Billion in Market Capital," *Wall Street Journal,* 20 July 1998.
4. Peter Henig, "Cisco Rocks the House–Again," *Redherring.com,* 17 February 1999, <http://www.herring.com>.
5. Andrew Kupfer, "Lucent Has a Brand-New Battle," *Fortune,* 25 May 1998.
6. Mark L. Sirower, "What Acquiring Minds Need to Know," *Wall Street Journal,* 22 February 1999, A18.
7. Kathleen Doler, "Wellfleet, SynOptics to Merge; Shares of Both End Day Lower," *Investor's Business Daily,* 7 July 1994, A2.
8. Ken Presti, "Company's Ideas to Preserve Industry Status Should Emerge at Networld-Interop–Bay Master Plan in the Works," *Computer Reseller News,* 14 April 1997.
9. Geoffrey Colvin, "America's Most Admired Companies," *Fortune,* 21 February 2000; and Shelly Branch, "The 100 Best Companies to Work for in America," *Fortune,* 11 January 1999.
10. Charles O'Reilly, "Cisco Systems: The Acquisition of Technology Is the Acquisition of People," Case HR-10 (Palo Alto, Calif.: Graduate School of Business, Stanford University, 1998).
11. Ann Lawrence, "Cisco Systems and Its Insanely Clever Products," *Computergram International,* 11 June 1997.
12. John Gallant, "Cisco Opens Up on New Challengers," *Network World,* 6 October 1997.
13. Joe Nocera, "Cooking with Cisco," *Fortune,* 25 December 1995.
14. Glenn Rifkin, "Growth by Acquisition: The Case of Cisco Systems," *Strategy & Business* (Booz, Allen & Hamilton, 1997).
15. Patricia Nakache, "Cisco's Recruiting Edge," *Fortune,* 29 September 1997.
16. James Daly, "The Art of the Seal," *Business 2.0,* October 1999.
17. Andrew Osterland, "No Kidding. Cisco Isn't Done Yet," *Financial World,* 21 January 1997.
18. Pat Dillon, "Is Selling Out 'Selling Out'?," *Fast Company,* February–March 1998.
19. Hal Plotkin, "Cisco's Secret: Entrepreneurs Sell Out, Stay Put," *Inc. Online,* March 1997, <http://www.inc.com>.
20. Osterland, "No Kidding."
21. Luc Hatlestad, "Routing the Competition," *Red Herring,* March 1997.
22. Rifkin, "Growth by Acquisition."
23. Ibid.
24. Jonathan Marshall, "Cisco Stepping Out," *San Francisco Chronicle,* 11 November 1997.

25. Henig, "Cisco Rocks."
26. Beau Parnell, interview by Charles O'Reilly, San Jose, Calif., 1998.
27. Rifkin, "Growth by Acquisition."
28. Ibid.
29. Brent Schlender, "Computing's Next Superpower," *Fortune,* 12 May 1997.
30. Mike Volpi, interview by Charles O'Reilly, 1998.
31. Rifkin, "Growth by Acquisition."
32. Schlender, "Computing's Next Superpower."
33. Rifkin, "Growth by Acquisition."
34. Hatlestad, "Routing."
35. Alice LaPlante, "The Man Behind Cisco," *Electronic Business,* December 1997.
36. Schlender, "Computing's Next Superpower."
37. Hatlestad, "Routing."
38. Joe Flower,"The Cisco Mantra," *Wired,* March 1997.
39. Hatlestad, "Routing."
40. LaPlante, "The Man Behind Cisco."
41. Rifkin, "Growth by Acquisition."
42. Michele Hostetler, "Cisco Systems' John Chambers," *Investor's Daily,* 28 August 1996.
43. Rifkin, "Growth by Acquisition."
44. Flower, "Cisco Mantra."
45. Barbara Beck, interview by author, San Jose, Calif., 1998.
46. Nakache, "Cisco's Recruiting Edge."
47. Fredrik Broden, "Hire Great People Fast," *Fast Company,* August–September 1997.
48. Beau Parnell, personal communication.
49. Cecily Barnes, "Why Go Home?," *MetroActive Central,* 27 August 1997.
50. Gallant, "Cisco Opens Up."
51. Mimi Gigoux, personal communication.
52. "Take It from the Top: An Interview with John Chambers," *NetworkWorld,* 6 October 1997.
53. Hatlestad, "Routing."
54. Eric Nee, "John Chambers," *Upside,* July 1996.

CHAPTER 4

1. The business strategy literature has maintained that these factors are important, if not essential, for earning high economic returns. See, for instance, Michael Porter, *Competitive Strategy* (New York: Free Press, 1980).
2. Needham & Company, "The Men's Wearhouse, Inc. (SUIT)," June 1995, 21.
3. Robertson Stephens, "The Men's Wearhouse, Inc.," 30 April 1996, 1.
4. Charlie Bresler, transcript from a talk at Stanford Business School, 14 May 1998.
5. U.S. Bureau of the Census, *Statistical Abstract of the United States: 1996* (Washington, DC: U.S. Government Printing Office), 405.
6. Thomas Bailey and Annette Bernhardt, "The Reorganization of the Workplace in Service Industries: Effect on Job Quality and Organizational Performance," working paper 7, National Center for the Workplace, Berkeley, Calif., 1996, 12.
7. Standard and Poor's Stock Reports, "The Men's Wearhouse," 13 March 1999, 2.
8. George Zimmer, transcript from a talk at Stanford Business School, 14 May 1998.

9. Jeffrey Pfeffer, "The Men's Wearhouse: Success in a Declining Industry," Case HR-5 (Stanford, Calif.: Graduate School of Business, Stanford University, 1997), 6.
10. Ibid., 5.
11. Zimmer, transcript.
12. Pfeffer, "The Men's Wearhouse," 1.
13. Ibid., 4.
14. Ibid., 26.
15. Ibid., 5.
16. Frederick Reichheld, *The Loyalty Effect* (Boston: Harvard Business School Press, 1996), 91.
17. Ibid., 33.
18. Bresler, transcript.
19. Pfeffer, "The Men's Wearhouse," 15.
20. Ibid., 10.
21. Zimmer, transcript.
22. Ibid.
23. Ibid.
24. Ibid.
25. Charlie Bresler, interview with author, 5 May 1997.
26. Pfeffer, "The Men's Wearhouse," 12.
27. Ibid., 12–13.
28. Zimmer, transcript.
29. Bresler, interview.
30. Pfeffer, "The Men's Wearhouse," 12.
31. Ibid., 4.
32. Ibid., 6

CHAPTER 5

1. Charles Fishman, "Sanity, Inc.," *Fast Company,* January 1999, 87.
2. The idea that the business corporation, rather than unions or the government, would be the source of stability and security for employees and the practices associated with making this happen, was called "welfare capitalism." A good description of this system of employment, which did not completely disappear even under the pressures of the Depression, can be found in Sanford M. Jacoby, *Modern Manors: Welfare Capitalism Since the New Deal* (Princeton, N.J.: Princeton University Press, 1997).
3. Randall Lane, "Pampering the Customers, Pampering the Employees," *Forbes,* 14 October 1996, 74.
4. Fishman, "Sanity," 94.
5. There is little doubt that relations between people and their employers have become, in general, more marketlike over time. See, for instance, Peter Cappelli, *The New Deal at Work* (Boston: Harvard Business School Press, 1999).
6. Fishman, "Sanity," 87.
7. Jeffrey Pfeffer, "SAS Institute: A Different Approach to Incentives and People Management Practices in the Software Industry," Case HR-6 (Stanford, Calif.: Graduate School of Business, Stanford University, 1998), 1.
8. Lane, "Pampering the Customers," 74.
9. Ibid.

10. Pfeffer, "SAS Institute," 2.
11. Fishman, "Sanity," 94.
12. Lane,"Pampering the Customers," 74
13. SAS Institute, Inc., *Annual Report* (Cary, N.C., 1966), 1.
14. Fishman, "Sanity," 87.
15. Angela Walker, "A Walk in the Park," *Human Resource Executive,* April 1997, 64.
16. Lane, "Pampering the Customers," 74.
17. Ibid.
18. Pfeffer, "SAS Institute," 3.
19. Lane, "Pampering the Customers," 74.
20. Pfeffer, "SAS Institute," 3.
21. David F. Russo, transcript from a talk given at Stanford University Graduate School of Business, 15 May 1998.
22. Pfeffer, "SAS Institute," 4.
23. Ibid.
24. Walker, "Walk in the Park," 64.
25. Pfeffer, "SAS Institute," 5.
26. Sharon Overton, "And to All a Goodnight," *Sky* (Delta Airlines Flight Magazine), October 1996.
27. Pfeffer, "SAS Institute," 5.
28. Russo, transcript.
29. Walker, "Walk in the Park," 64.
30. Fishman, "Sanity," 89.
31. Pfeffer, "SAS Institute," 5.
32. Fishman, "Sanity," 89.
33. Pfeffer, "SAS Institute," 9.
34. Russo, transcript.
35. Pfeffer, "SAS Institute," 9.
36. Fishman, "Sanity," 89.
37. Ibid.
38. Walker, "Walk in the Park," 65.
39. Fishman, "Sanity," 87.
40. Ibid., 93.
41. Russo, transcript.
42. Pfeffer, "SAS Institute," 11.
43. Ibid., 10.
44. Russo, transcript.
45. Pfeffer, "SAS Institute," 7.
46. Ibid.
47. Ibid., 8.
48. Ibid.
49. Ibid.
50. Russo, transcript.
51. Pfeffer, "SAS Institute," 12.
52. Ibid., 13.
53. Ibid., 11.
54. Peter Cappelli, *The New Deal at Work* (Boston: Harvard Business School Press, 1999), 1.
55. Fishman, "Sanity," 93.

CHAPTER 6

1. Charles A. O'Reilly III and Jeffrey Pfeffer, "PSS World Medical: The Challenges of Growth and the Financial Markets," Case HR-12 (Palo Alto, Calif.: Graduate School of Business, Stanford University, 1999), 10.

2. Wall Street Research Net (WSRN.com), *QuickSource Report,* 13 December 1999, <http://www.wsrn.com/home/dataset/quicksource.html?symbol=PSSI&page=1>.

3. Wall Street Research Net (WSRN.com), *QuickSource Report,* 13 December 1999, <http://www.wsrn.com/home/dataset/quicksource.html?symbol=PSSI&page=1>.

4. Mark L. Sirower, *The Synergy Trap: How Companies Lose the Acquisition Game* (New York: Free Press, 1997).

5. Steven Safier and Jeff Shiraki, "A Study of Mergers and Acquisitions: Lessons Learned," The Hay Group, 10 September 1999.

6. Patrick Kelly, *Faster Company* (New York: John Wiley, 1998), 178.

7. Ibid., 33–35.

8. Standard and Poor's Stock Reports, "PSS World Medical," 6 February 1999, 2.

9. Jerre Stead, conversation with author, 1997.

10. Kelly, *Faster Company,* 58.

11. Ibid., 178.

12. "Top of the Charts," *Sales and Marketing Management,* July 1998.

13. O'Reilly and Pfeffer, "PSS World Medical," 5.

14. Ibid., 95.

15. Ibid., 5.

16. Ibid., 222.

17. Ibid., 24.

18. Ibid., 9–10.

19. Ibid., 7.

20. Ibid., 8.

21. Ibid., 11.

22. Kelly, *Faster Company,* 122.

23. "Top of the Charts," *Sales and Marketing Management,* July 1998.

24. Charlie Alvarez, interview by authors, 1998.

25. O'Reilly and Pfeffer, "PSS World Medical," 14.

26. Ibid., 13.

27. Ibid., 17.

28. Alvarez, interview.

29. O'Reilly and Pfeffer, "PSS World Medical," 17.

30. Ibid., 18.

31. Ibid., 19–20.

32. Ibid., 20.

33. Kelly, *Faster Company,* 189.

34. O'Reilly and Pfeffer, "PSS World Medical," 21.

35. Ibid., 22.

36. Ibid., 23–24.

37. Kelly, *Faster Company,* 106.

38. Michael Weise, interview by authors, 1998.

39. Pat Kelly, interview by authors, 1998.

CHAPTER 7

1. Wall Street Research Net (WSRN.com), *QuickSource Report,* 14 December 1999, <http://www.wsrn.com/home/dataset/quicksource.html?symbol=AES&page>.
2. Ibid.
3. Phyllis Berman, "Throwing Away the Book," *Forbes,* 2 November 1998, 174.
4. Ibid.
5. AES Corporation, *Annual Report* (Arlington, Va., 1998), 56.
6. AES Corporation, *Annual Report* (Arlington, Va., 1997), 5.
7. Jeffrey Pfeffer, "Human Resources at the AES Corporation: The Case of the Missing Department," Case SHR-3 (Stanford, Calif.: Graduate School of Business, Stanford University, 1997).
8. AES, *Annual Report* (1998), 15.
9. Dennis Bakke and Robert Waterman, transcript from a presentation at Stanford Business School, 24 April 1998.
10. Berman, "Throwing Away," 177.
11. Laura Rittenhouse, "Roger W. Sant–Visionary Internationalist: An Interview with the Chairman, AES Corporation," *Electricity Journal,* January–February 1998, 40.
12. Ibid., 41.
13. Dennis Bakke, transcript from a talk to a Stanford Business School class, 24 April 1998.
14. Robert Waterman, transcript from a talk to a Stanford Business School class, 24 April 1998.
15. Berman, "Throwing Away," 176.
16. Pfeffer, "Human Resources," 3.
17. Ibid., 4.
18. Laura Rittenhouse, "Dennis W. Bakke–Empowering a Workforce with Principles," *Electricity Journal,* January–February 1998, 52.
19. Dennis W. Bakke, "Erecting a Grid for Ethical Power," *The Marketplace,* May–June 1996, 5.
20. Dennis W. Bakke, "An Alternative View of Corporate Governance," *Director's Monthly* 22 (September 1998), 2; emphasis in original.
21. Bakke, transcript.
22. Ibid.
23. AES, *Annual Report* (1997), 6.
24. Bakke, transcript.
25. Suzy Wetlaufer, "Organizing for Empowerment: An Interview with AES's Roger Sant and Dennis Bakke," *Harvard Business Review,* January–February 1999, 123.
26. Pfeffer, "Human Resources," 22–23.
27. Ibid., 8.
28. Ibid.
29. Alex Markels, "Power to the People," *Fast Company,* February–March 1998, 156.
30. Ibid., 160.
31. Pfeffer, "Human Resources," 5.
32. Bill Birchard, "Power to the People," *CFO, March 1995, 41.*
33. Wetlaufer, "Organizing for Empowerment," 114.
34. Ibid., 112.

35. Ibid., 112.
36. Pfeffer, "Human Resources," 10.
37. Berman, "Throwing Away," 177.
38. AES, *Annual Report* (1997), 9.
39. Ibid.
40. Berman, "Throwing Away," 180.
41. Wetlaufer,"Organizing for Empowerment," 112–113.
42. AES, *Annual Report* (1998), 13.
43. Alex Markels, "Blank Check," *Wall Street Journal,* 9 April 1998, R11.
44. Pfeffer, "Human Resources," 3–4.
45. AES, *Annual Report* (1998), 15.
46. Rittenhouse, "Roger W. Sant," 43.
47. Ibid., 52.
48. AES Corporation, Proxy statement, 30 March 1999, 10.
49. Bakke, transcript.
50. Ibid.
51. Pfeffer, "Human Resources," 8.
52. Ibid., 9.
53. AES, *Annual Report* (1998), 9.
54. Bakke, transcript.
55. Ibid.
56. Wetlaufer, "Organizing for Empowerment," 112.
57. AES, *Annual Report* (1997), 6.
58. Rittenhouse, "Dennis W. Bakke," 51.

CHAPTER 8

1. Daniel Howes, "GM, UAW Deal Buys Temporary Peace," *Detroit News,* 29 July 1998.
2. Katherine Yung and Dave Phillips, "GM Ponders Its Future in Changing Marketplace," *Detroit News,* 30 July 1998.
3. Jane Gardiner, "Japanese and South Korean Plants Dominate World Car Productivity," *The Economist Intelligence Unit,* 1998, <http://www.eiu.com>.
4. National Association of Manufacturers, 28 April 1999.
5. Productivity Consulting Group, 28 April 1999, <http://www.productivityconsulting.com>.
6. "When GM's Robots Ran Amok," *Economist,* 10 August 1991.
7. For a complete description of the Toyota production system, see Steven Spear and H. Kent Bowen, "Decoding the DNA of the Toyota Production System," *Harvard Business Review,* September–October 1999.
8. "If Ford Can Do It, Why Can't GM?" Business Week, 29 June 1998.
9. "New United Motor Manufacturing, Inc. (NUMMI)," Case HR-11 (Palo Alto, Calif.: Graduate School of Business, Stanford University, 1998).
10. Ibid.
11. Ibid.
12. Ibid.
13. George Nano, interview by author, Fremont, Calif., 21 January 1987.

14. There are numerous news accounts of NUMMI's history and operations. Perhaps the best is Paul Adler, "The Learning Bureaucracy: New United Motor Manufacturing, Inc.," *Research in Organizational Behavior* 15 (1993): 111–194. For broader coverage of lean manufacturing, see also James Womack, Daniel Jones, and Daniel Roos, *The Machine That Changed the World* (New York: Harper, 1991) or Steve Babson, ed., *Lean Work: Empowerment and Exploitation in the Global Auto Industry* (Detroit: Wayne State University Press, 1995). For a more historical account see Paul Ingrassia and Joseph B. White, *Comeback: The Fall and Rise of the American Automobile Industry* (New York: Simon and Schuster, 1994).

15. NUMMI internal document, 1983.

16. W. Wilms, D. Zell, O. Kimura, and D. Cuneo, "Reinventing Organizational Culture across International Boundaries," working paper 94–3, Carnegie-Mellon University, 1994.

17. Kan Higashi, interview by author, 21 January 1987.

18. C. Brown and M. Reich, "When Does Cooperation Work? A Look at NUMMI and GM-Van Nuys," *California Management Review* 31 (1989): 26–37.

19. N. Chetnik, "Inside NUMMI," *San Jose Mercury News,* 9 February 1987.

20. John Holusha, "A Blending of Cultures Produces a Car," *New York Times,* 5 April 1985.

21. Interviews by author, 21 January 1987.

22. Chetnik, "Inside NUMMI."

23. Personal communication, 2 October 1998.

24. Gary Convis, personal communication.

25. Wilms, "Reinventing Organizational Culture."

26. Ibid.

27. Jamie Hresko, interview by authors, October 1998.

28. U.S. Department of Commerce, "Report of the Conference on the Future of the American Workplace," 26 July 1993.

29. Ibid.

30. Ibid.

31. Ibid.

32. Neil Chetnik, "Japanese Auto Ideal Is Hard Taskmaster," *San Jose Mercury News,* 9 February 1987.

33. Michelle Levander, "Union Adapts to Partnership," *San Jose Mercury News,* 1 May 1990.

34. U.S. Department of Commerce, "Report of the Conference on the Future of the American Workplace."

35. Wilms, Zell, Kimura, and Cuneo, "Reinventing Organizational Culture."

CHAPTER 9

1. See "Cyprus Overview," <http://www.cypress.com>.

2. Standard and Poor's Stock Reports, "Cypress Semiconductor," 19 June 1999, 1.

3. Charles O'Reilly and David Caldwell, "Cypress Semiconductor (A): Vision, Values, and Killer Software," Case HR-8A (Palo Alto, Calif.: Graduate School of Business, Stanford University, 1998), 2.

4. For a complete description of the origins and practices of Cypress, see T. J.

Rodgers, W. Taylor, and R. Foreman, *No Excuses Management* (New York: Currency Doubleday, 1992). Much of the material in the following section was drawn from this book.

5. Rodgers, *No Excuses,* 19.
6. Kate Button, "America's Toughest Boss," *Computer Weekly,* 10 March 1994.
7. D. Bottoms, "Roaring Back," *Industry Week,* 4 November 1996.
8. T. J. Rodgers, "Response to Sister Doris Gormley," 23 May 1996. More information on the letter from T. J. Rodgers to Sister Doris Gormley, dated 23 May 1996, is available on the Cypress Web site at <http://www.cypress.com:80/cypress/cyp_news/gormley.htm>.
9. Bottoms, "Roaring Back," 20.
10. David Altany, "Bull in a Chip Shop," *Industry Week,* 6 July 1992, 18.
11. Rodgers, *No Excuses.*
12. Paul Plansky, "Changes in Mr. Rodgers' Neighborhood," *Semiconductor Industry & Business Survey,* 26 June 1995.
13. Robert Ristelhueber, "The Humbling of T.J. Rodgers," *Electronic Business,* February 1993.
14. Rodgers, *No Excuses.*
15. Ibid., 27.
16. Ibid.
17. Ibid.
18. Ibid., 28.
19. Ibid., 29.
20. Ibid.
21. Ibid., 34.
22. Ibid., 39.
23. Ibid.
24. T. J. Rodgers, transcript of class discussion, Graduate School of Business, Stanford University, 1998.
25. Rodgers, *No Excuses,* 58.
26. Ibid., 27.
27. Altany, "Bull," 16.
28. T. J. Rogers, "Letter from T. J. about the Goals System," letter to all Cypress employees, 8 April 1997.
29. Rodgers, *No Excuses,* 237.
30. Ibid., 104.
31. Ibid., 106
32. Ibid.,125.
33. Ibid., 125.
34. Ibid.,107.
35. Ibid., 114.
36. Michael Tushman and Charles O'Reilly, *Winning through Innovation* (Boston: Harvard Business School Press, 1997).
37. Charles O'Reilly and Jennifer Chatman, "Culture as Social Control: Corporations, Cults, and Commitment," *Research in Organizational Behavior* 18 (1996): 157–200.

CHAPTER 10

1. Charles O'Reilly and Jennifer Chatman, "Culture as Social Control: Corporations, Cults, and Commitment," *Research in Organizational Behavior* 18 (1996): 157–200.
2. J. Chatman, "Matching People and Organizations: Selection and Socialization in Public Accounting Firms," *Administrative Science Quarterly* 36 (1991): 459–484.
3. Glenn Rifkin, "Growth by Acquisition: The Case of Cisco Systems," *Strategy & Business* (Booz, Allen & Hamilton, 1997).
4. Patrick Kelly, interview with authors, 1998.
5. Jack Welch, transcript from an address to the management of The Southern Company, Atlanta, Georgia, 1995.
6. Leonard A. Schlesinger and Debra Whitestone, "People Express (A)," Case 9-483-103 (Boston: Harvard Business School, 1983), 2.
7. Ibid., 8.
8. Ibid., 4.
9. Ibid., 12.
10. William M. Carley, "New Flight Plan: Struggling to Survive, People Express Alters Operations and Image," *Wall Street Journal*, 31 July 1986, A1.
11. Ibid.
12. Ibid.
13. Schlesinger and Whitestone, "People Express (A)," 1.
14. Steven Prokesch, "Behind the Fall at People Express," *New York Times*, 23 September 1986.
15. John Byrne, "Up, Up and Away?" *Business Week*, 25 November 1985, 81.
16. Nina Munk, "How Levi's Trashed a Great American Brand," *Fortune*, 12 April 1999, 86.
17. Ibid.
18. Ibid., 83–90.
19. Ibid., 83.
20. Ibid., 85.
21. Ibid., 86.
22. Ibid., 86–88.
23. Ibid., 88.
24. Ibid., 85.
25. Ibid., 88.
26. Douglas K. Smith and Robert C. Alexander, *Fumbling the Future* (New York: William Morrow, 1988).
27. David F. Russo, transcript from a talk given at Stanford University Graduate School of Business, 15 May 1998.
28. Ibid.
29. Elizabeth G. Chambers, Mark Foulon, Helen Handfield-Jones, Steven M. Hankin, and Edward G. Michaels III, "The War for Talent," *McKinsey Quarterly* 3 (1998).

Index

About the Authors

Charles A. O'Reilly III is the Frank Buck Professor of Human Resources and Organizational Behavior at the Graduate School of Business at Stanford University and the Henry Ford Carroll Visiting Professor at the Harvard Business School. He received his B.S. from the University of Texas at El Paso and his M.B.A. and Ph.D. in organizational behavior from the University of California at Berkeley. He previously taught at the Haas School of Business and the Institute of Personality Research at the University of California at Berkeley and the Anderson Graduate School of Management at UCLA. He consults to a variety of public and private firms in the United States, Europe, and Japan and has published more than eighty papers on topics such as corporate culture, employee commitment, executive compensation, organizational demography, and human resources management. He is also the coauthor (with Michael Tushman) of *Winning through Innovation: A Practical Guide to Leading Organizational Change and Renewal* and is currently working on his next book, *Ambidextrous Organizations: Resolving the Innovator's Dilemma.*

Jeffrey Pfeffer is the Thomas D. Dee II Professor of Organizational Behavior at the Graduate School of Business at Stanford University, where he has taught since 1979. He received his B.S. and M.S. from Carnegie-Mellon University and his Ph.D. in business from Stanford. Dr. Pfeffer has served on the faculties at the University of Illinois, the University of California at Berkeley, and as a visiting professor at the Harvard Business School. He has taught executive seminars in twenty-four countries throughout the world and was Director of Executive Education at Stanford from 1994 to 1996. He serves on the board of directors of Audible Magic, Portola Packaging, Resumix, and SonoSite, as well as on numerous editorial boards of scholarly journals. He is the author of *The Human Equation, New Directions for Organization Theory, Competitive Advantage through People, Managing with Power, Organizations and Organization Theory, Power in Organizations,* and *Organizational Design,* and coauthor of *The Knowing-Doing Gap* and *The External Control of Organizations,* as well as more than 100 articles and book chapters.